P9-BAT-504

Where's Your Light?

DOUGLAS F. GRADY

WestBow
PRESS
A DIVISION OF THOMAS NELSON

Copyright © 2011 Douglas F. Grady

All rights reserved. No part of this book may be used or reproduced by any means, graphic, electronic, or mechanical, including photocopying, recording, taping or by any information storage retrieval system without the written permission of the publisher except in the case of brief quotations embodied in critical articles and reviews.

Biblical verses were obtained from The 1599 Geneva Bible (ISBN 0-9754846-1-3)

WestBow Press books may be ordered through booksellers or by contacting:

WestBow Press
A Division of Thomas Nelson
1663 Liberty Drive
Bloomington, IN 47403
www.westbowpress.com
1-(866) 928-1240

Because of the dynamic nature of the Internet, any web addresses or links contained in this book may have changed since publication and may no longer be valid. The views expressed in this work are solely those of the author and do not necessarily reflect the views of the publisher, and the publisher hereby disclaims any responsibility for them.

Any people depicted in stock imagery provided by Thinkstock are models, and such images are being used for illustrative purposes only.

Certain stock imagery © Thinkstock.

ISBN: 978-1-4497-2745-1 (sc)

Library of Congress Control Number: 2011917013

Printed in the United States of America

WestBow Press rev. date: 11/17/2011

Contents

Introduction

Romans 8:5-9, 12-13

Corinthians 2:10-13

John 8:32

John 10:34

Ephesians 2:22

Micah 6:8

Matt 10:42

Isaiah 1:17

Zechariah 9:10

Revelation 3:12

Ephesians 6:10-12

Luke 10:27-28

1 John 4:7-8

Section 1.1.1

I am with you always

John 8:32

1 Timothy 2:4

Ephesians 1:13, 17, 18

Romans 1:1, 3, 4, 7-10

Matthew 6:22

Revelation 3:12

Colossians 2:8

Ephesians 4:14

Section 1.1.3

New Law

Hebrews 10:14-26

Micah 6:6-8

John 1:15-18

Hebrews 10:4-6

Section 1.1.4

The Way

Revelation 7:13-17

2 Corinthians 1:12, 19

Matthew 6:22

Section 1.2.1

Word

Colossians 1:25

1 Peter 1:23-25

Section 1.2.2

Walk

2 Corinthians 6:16

Ephesians 2:4-14

John 12:35-36

Matthew 11:1-5

Rev 3:4-5

Deuteronomy 8:6

Deuteronomy 6:5-6

Ezekiel 8:3

2 Kings 23:3

Daniel 7:13

2 Corinthians 12:2

Colossians 2:5

Colossians 2:6

2 Thessalonians 3:11

Micah 6:8

Section 1.2.3

Ye are gods

Psalm 82:6

John 10:34-35

Isaiah 42:17

1 Corinthians 3:16

1 Corinthians 3:17

Isaiah 41:23

1 John 3:9

1 John 3:2

1 John 4:4

Section 1.2.4

Holy of Holies

Hebrews 9:11

Rev 21:3

John 3:19-22

1 Corinthians 2:9

Hebrews 13:10

2 Corinthians 5:6

Section 1.2.5

Epinoia

Genesis 3:20

Genesis 5:24

Section 1.2.6

Meditation

Job 7:13-14

Matthew 7:7-8

2 Corinthians 4:16

Philippians 4:5-7

Galatians 1:16

Psalms 119:148

Acts 9:17-18

2 Corinthians 11:28

1 Thessalonians 1:8

2 Corinthians 5:8-9

1 Corinthians 6:19

1 Thessalonians 1:3

Romans 8:25

Galatians 4:9

Ephesians 6:15-20

Romans 8:24

Hebrews 9:28

Matthew 16:24

John 14:7-8

John 14:1-4, 13-20

Ephesians 5:8-14

Section 1.2.7

Fullness

Ephesians 3:19

2 Timothy 1:14

Galatians 6:18

Philippians 3:3

John 14:26-28

1 John 3:24

Ephesians 3:18

Section 1.3

Kingdom of God

Romans 14:17

Isaiah 66:1-2

Luke 12:29-32

Revelation 21:1

John 3:5

Luke 13:24

John 3:13-14

John 10:9

Luke 17:21

Matthew 19:13-15

Mark 10:14-15

Mark 9:47

Daniel 10:11-12

Section 1.4

Christian Life and Faith

Matthew 7:20

Isaiah 64:4-6

Colossians 2:8

Jeremiah 31:33-34

Section 1.5.1

Creation of Human soul (spirit)

Ephesians 3:16

1 Corinthians 2:9-11

Revelation 2:4

Section 1.5.2

Creation of Human Flesh

Ephesians 4:18

Romans 8:5-16

Acts 26:18

Galatians 2:16

Revelation 3:12

1 Corinthians 15:42-50

Section 1.5.3

1.5.3 Christ Consciousness

Section 1.5.4

1.5.4 Anti-Christ

Acts 8:37-40

2 Samuel 5:9

1 Kings 6:1-7

Isaiah 57:15

Hebrews 11:1-3

Section 1.5.5

1.5.5 Fruit of the Holy Spirit

Galatians 5:22-26

1 Thessalonians 1:4

Section 1.5.6

1.5.6 Holy Land

Ezekiel 37:14

Revelation 21:1

Psalms 24:4-6

Section 2.1

Grace of God

2 Thessalonians 2:13

Acts 2:38-39

Titus 3:4-7

Romans 10:9

Ephesians 2:8

John 3:3-7

Galatians 3:11-27

2 Peter 3:9

1 Thessalonians 4:15

Ezekiel 37:12-14

Section 2.2

Contemptible Spirit vs. Holy Spirit

Genesis 6:5-9

Section 2.3

Baptism

Matthew 27:51

Hebrews 9:3

Hebrews 10:19-20

Section 2.4

Salvation

Romans 10:10

John 6:53-61, 64-66

Hebrews 6:19-20

Section 2.5

Gabriel's Trumpet

Revelation 3:12

1 Corinthians 15:52

John 6:62, 63

Job 8:19-22

Job 14:12-14

Revelation 20:14-15

1 Timothy 6:9-11

Matthew 18:8-9

Section 2.6

Saved

John 1:12

Romans 5:1

Romans 5:9

Romans 10:13

John 3:15-21

John 5:22-24

John 6:36-40

John 20:29-31

John 6:45-47

John 11:25

John 12:44-50

Section 2.7

Statements from Jesus

Section 2.8

First Death, Second Death

Numbers 16:29-30

Psalms 36:5

Section 2.9

Afterlife / Paradise / Purification

1 Samuel 28:7

Psalms 104:1-2

Zechariah 13:9

Ezekiel 1:28

Hebrews 12:23

Isaiah 6:5-7

1 Peter 1:7

Section 3.1

Gospel of the Nazirenes

Section 3.2

The Secret Book of John

Nehemiah 1:5

Section 3.3

The Secret Book of James

Section 3.4

Apocalypse of Peter

Section 4.2

Body Prison

Section 4.3

Fiery Trial

Ephesians 6:10-12

2 Corinthians 12:7

Luke 21:33-36

Romans 8:38-39

Colossians 2:15

2 Timothy 2:26

Section 4.4

End of Time

Matthew 24:29-33

1 Corinthians 15:20-26

Revelation 20:14-15

Revelation 20:5

Revelation 20:6-13

Section 4.5

Angels: Messengers of God

Hebrews 1:1-7

Mark 12:25

Revelation 4:5

Introduction

This book begins with an exchange between Jesus and Peter by spiritual meditation. It took place on Good Friday when Jesus was arrested and crucified. This is how Peter learned the visions that Jesus had been teaching him. The visions were seen by Peter from his body temple. The following is an event that enabled Peter to learn the transcendental world of the Savior. There was a torment Jesus (flesh), and the invincible Christ (spirit).

From the APOCALYPSE OF PETER, Chapter XII, section 4 on page 192,

"Peter, come! Let us go and fulfill the will of the incorruptible Father. Behold, those who will bring judgment upon themselves is coming. They will put themselves to shame. But me they cannot touch. And you, Peter, will stand in their midst. Do not be afraid because of your cowardice. Their minds shall be closed for the Invisible One has opposed them."

In the last sentence of this quotation, the attention is shifted from arrest to the crucifixion scene. Curiously enough, even during the crucifixion Christ remained Peter's *angelus interpres* and answered the questions posed by the apostle:

And I said, "What am I seeing O Lord?

Is yourself whom they take? And are you holding on to me?

Who is the one who is glad and laughing above the cross?

Do they hit one another one on his feet and on his hands?"

The Saviour said to me,

"The one you see above the cross, glad and laughing, is the living Jesus,

But the one into whose hands and feet they are driving the nails is his fleshly part (sarkikon), which is the substitute.

They put to shame that which came into existence after his likeness, the son of their glory, instead of my servant, they have put to shame."

An essential feature of this vision account is the distinction made between the suffering Jesus and the impassable Saviour. What is more, the two figures are related to conflicting powers. The Saviour is an agent of the incorruptible Father, whereas the human body of Jesus is supposedly being a product (the son) of the cosmic powers. Such an interpretation implies that the wrongdoers who arrested and crucified Jesus, did not torture the Saviour but a human body. Above the cross, "the living Jesus" laughs at their blindness. Thereupon, Peter reports, he perceived another figure:

And I saw someone about to approach us who looked like him and like the one who was laughing above the cross. He was woven in Holy Spirit. He was the Saviour. And there was a great ineffable light, surrounding them, and the multitude of ineffable and invisible angels, blessing them. And I saw that the one who glorifies was revealed.

After the vision of what seems to be a higher dimension of the Saviour, Christ resumed his explanations to Peter:

And he said to me, "Be strong! For you are the one to whom these mysteries have been given through revelation in order that you will know that the one they crucified is the first-born, the home of the demons, the clay vessel in which they dwell; it belongs to Elohim and to the cross that is under the law."

Romans 8:5-9, 12-13

5 For they that are after the flesh, savor the things of the flesh: but they that are after the Spirit, the things of the Spirit.

6 For the wisdom of the flesh is death: but the wisdom of the Spirit is life and peace,

7 Because the wisdom of the flesh is enmity against God: for it is not subject to the Law of God, neither indeed can be.

8 So then they that are in the flesh, cannot please God.

9 Now ye are not in the flesh, but in the Spirit, because the spirit of God dwelleth in you: but if any man hath not the Spirit of Christ, the same is not his.

12 Therefore brethren, we are debtors not to the flesh, to live after the flesh:

13 For if ye live after the flesh, ye shall die: but if ye mortify the deeds of the body by the Spirit, ye shall live.

Author's note:

You are considered a first born when you are born into this world. You will need to be born again in order to attain salvation. Baptism will save you, but Chrism is better. See section 2.3 for explanation of Chrism.

—But he who stands near him, is the living Saviour, he who was him before, in the one who was seized. And he was released. He stands joyfully, looking at those who treated him violently. They are divided among themselves. Therefore, he laughs at their inability to see. He knows that they are born blind.

- So, the one who suffers will stay behind, because the body is the substitute.

- But the one who was released is my incorporeal body.

- I am the intellectual spirit filled with radiant light.

- The one you saw coming to me is our intellectual Pleroma, who unites the perfect light with my holy spirit.

Peter's visions are characterized as "mysteries" given exclusively to him. In his explanations, Christ paid special attention to the temporal dwelling of the Saviour in the physical Jesus: until the arrest of Jesus, the Saviour was in him (he was in him before); after his "release" from Jesus, he witnessed how "the one staying behind" was seized and treated violently.

Douglas F. Grady

Author's note:

As a member of the Self Realization Fellowship back in 1998, I became more proactive about Christianity. I practiced meditation and studied the Bible for 6 years before moving to Tulsa, Oklahoma where I became a member of the First Baptist Church, studying for four more years. I have studied numerous books on Christianity; however, I was able to obtain the fruit of spirit through meditation. One morning back in 1999, I felt a bounce in my body while I was asleep. I just knew it was coming from the Lord. Ever since then, I have not looked back. My quest for finding the truth had begun.

Before I begin, I want to share you my situation. I am a Baptist. I agree wholeheartedly with the following, "The Baptist Faith and Message":

The Baptist Faith and Message

Christianity is supernatural in its origin history. We reject every theory of religion which denies the supernatural elements in our faith.

Baptists are a people who profess a living faith. This belief is established and grounded in Jesus Christ.

Baptists emphasize the soul's competency before God, freedom in religion, and the priesthood of the believer.

The Baptist Faith and Message of Southern Baptists is based on upon the competency of the soul in religion. Those who drew up the original statement in 1924-25 were careful to preserve the individual conscience. The committee, which revised it in 1962-63, retained this provision. The introduction clearly states "that the sole authority for faith and practice among Baptists is the Scriptures of the Old and New Testaments".

Baptists must continue to apply to their primary and clear concept of the competency of the soul in religion. This is the rock whence they are hewn.

Baptists believe that a person has the right to be a Baptist, Methodist, Presbyterian, Roman Catholic, Jew, Infidel, or Atheist.

Baptists believe the power of the Holy Spirit helps men understand the Scriptures.

Baptists are the most broad minded of all people in religion. They grant to every person the truth that he shall be free to believe as he wants.

The competency of the soul in religion entails the establishment of the Scriptures and the Lordship of Jesus Christ. The priesthood of believers grants to every Christian the right to read and interpret the Scriptures as led by the Holy Spirit.

In 1924, the evolution debate was in, especially teaching of evolution in public schools. This is what established by the convention in 1925 "The Baptist Faith and Message". For many years, many people had been saying that the Southern Baptists were becoming more liberal in their religious views.

1963 Statement—"The New Testament speaks also of the church as the body of Christ which includes all of the redeemed of all of the ages". This statement is not an official statement of faith and message among Southern Baptists. But it serves as counsel to the churches and guidelines to various agencies of the Southern Baptist Convention.

The Conventions in 1969 and 1970 refused to do this necessary for its institutions and agencies. Thus, this proves this issue in its belief in the competency of the soul in religion.

Baptists emphasize the soul's competency before God, freedom in religion, and the priesthood of the believer.

The benchmark by which the Bible is to be interpreted is Jesus Christ.

Baptists have been called a people of the Book. The Book is the Bible.

The Bible is composed of 66 books—39 in Old Testament and 27 in New Testament.

The New Testament was written in the language of the everyday communication of the people.

The Holy Bible was written by men divinely inspired. It is the form of God's revelation of himself to man.

Revelation—God unveils Himself and His Will to human messengers.

Illumination—Holy Spirit's work as He enlightens the human mind with spiritual knowledge in order that persons might perceive the revealed truth.

Inspiration—Divine guidance of chosen human messengers through the Holy Spirit to deliver or log God's revealed message.

God reveals himself in the most powerful way through Jesus Christ.

Holy Spirit illumined the minds of the gospel writers, Paul and other New Testament writers. The apostles did not fully understand Jesus words to them. But Jesus promised that Holy Spirit would help them understand all things that he had said to them. The Spirit still illumines the mind and heart of serious students of God's word so that they discover truths unknown to them.

In Corinthians 2:10-13, Paul insisted that his message came to him through the inspiration of the Holy Spirit.

Is the Bible a holy book or a human book? Both, it is holy that it is inspired word of God. It is human in that God chose to show his revelations through men inspired.

The Bible speaks of God's Judgment against sin. God hates sin, but he loves sinners. It shows what God has done to deliver man from judgment (John 3:16-18). But it points to God's final judgment upon unrepentant sinners (Rev. 20:11-15). It also speaks of the judgment of all men (Roman 14:10)-the saved as to their level of reward in heaven and the fallen as to their level of punishment in hell (Luke 12:47-48; Rev. 20:12-15).

The Bible is the standard by which God regulates human behavior. The Sermon on the Mount is the constitution of the kingdom of God. It is designed not to disclose lost men how to be saved, but to teach Christians how to live the redeemed life (John 15; Rom 6; 12; 1 Cor. 12-14).

Author's note:

I could remember my pastor saying in one of his sermons that he wanted to feel closer to God. He would pray and pray, but it seemed as he was missing something. The only way to feel closer to God is to contact the Father through meditation and "walk" with him. The experience of love from God is beyond comprehension.

Most of the contents in this book are guided by the verses of the Bible. I'm assuming the majority of the people who read this book has an innate knowledge of the Bible. I have discovered new revelations from texts of the Nag Hammadi and Dead Sea caves:

The Secret Book of John

Apocalypse of Peter

Books of Enoch

The Secret Book of James

The Treatise on Resurrection

The Revelation of Peter

The Letter of Peter to Philip

The Gospel of Philip

The Tripartite Tractate

The Teachings of Silvanius

The Nature of the Rulers

The Revelation of Paul

The Gospel of Truth

Gospel of Thomas

The Gospel of the Nazirenes

These texts provided details about the angelic realms in heaven and the nature of Cosmic Rulers (fallen angels) that opposed God's Kingdom. Some of this was captured in the Book of Genesis.

However, there are challenges for us as we seek to understand The Way of Jesus Christ for redemption of our souls. Our enemy is not man, but the unseen evil forces. These evil forces began in the book of Genesis where the angels of God fell from grace. They were led by Lucifer who was a high ranking Archangel in God's kingdom. He wanted to break away from God's Kingdom to pursue his own power. It is their desire to stop us from returning to God's Kingdom.

However, God, through Jesus, has grand plans for us, so we are never alone in our search for God.

This book also intends to know the truth as Saint John alluded;

John 8:32

8 And shall know the truth, and the truth shall make you free.

Beyond Belief, Page 165:

"People grow old without joy . . . and die . . . without knowing God."

Secret Book of James, Nag Hammadi Scriptures, page 29

"Do not let heaven's kingdom become a desert within you"

John 10:34

34 Jesus answered them, Is it not written in your Law, I said, Ye are gods?

Ephesians 2:22

22 In whom ye also built together to be habitation of God by the Spirit.

Micah 6:8

8 He hath shewed thee, O man, what is good; and what doth the Lord require of thee, but to do justly, and to love mercy, and to walk humbly with thy God?

Matt 10:42

42 A cup of cold water to a little one.

Isaiah 1:17

17 To seek justice and encourage the oppressed. He wants us to defend the cause of the fatherless, and plead the case of the widow.

Zechariah 9:10

10 And I will cut off the Chariots from Ephraim, and the horse from Jerusalem: the bow of the battle shall be broken, and he shall speak peace unto the heathen, and his dominion shall be from sea unto sea, and from the River to the end of the land.

Revelation 3:12

12 Him that overcometh will I make a pillar in the temple of my God, and he shall go no more out; and I will write upon him the name of my God, and the name of the city of my God, which is new Jerusalem, which cometh down out of heaven from my God; and I will write upon him my new name.

Beyond Belief, page 94

The path of kabbalah is seeking to know God, not through dogmatic theology, but through living experience and intuition. Among the mystically inclined group, Paul is considered a teacher. He taught "secret" wisdom teaching.

Gospel of Truth, page 42 of Nag Hammadi Scriptures

"Good for one who comes to himself and awakens. And blessed is one who has opened the eyes of the blind."

Gospel of Nazirenes, page 22, Chapter 7, verse 10

10 And to all he spoke, saying, "Keep yourselves from blood and things strangled and from dead bodies of birds and beasts, and from all deeds of cruelty, and from all that is gotten of wrong; Do you think that the blood of beasts and birds will wash away sin? I tell you, no! Speak the Truth, be

just, and merciful to one another and to all creatures, and walk humbly with your Creator."

Ephesians 6:10-12

10 Finally, my brethren, be strong in the Lord, and in the power of his might.

11 Put on the whole armor of God, that ye may be able to stand against the assaults of the devil.

12 For we wrestle not against flesh and blood, but against principalities, against powers, and against the worldly governors, the princes of the darkness of this world, against spiritual wickedness, which are in the high places.

Author's note:

Our real enemy isn't mankind, but with cosmic rulers (Satan). Their goal is to prevent us from returning to God. Jesus gave us two commandments to help humanity love one another.

And Jesus answered him, "The first of all the commandments is, 'Hear, O Israel; the Lord our God is one Lord: And thou shalt love the Lord thy God with all thy heart, and with all thy soul, and with all thy mind, and with all thy strength': this is the first commandment. And the second is like, namely this, 'Thou shalt love thy neighbour as thyself.' There is none other commandment greater than these."

Luke 10:27-28

27 And he answered and said, Thou shalt love thy Lord God with all thine heart, and with all thy soul, and with all thy strength, and with all thy thought, and thy neighbor as thyself.

28 Then he said unto him, Thou hast answered right: this do, and thou shalt live.

Author's note:

The key here is we shall love our neighbor as "thyself". We are God's sheep, and Jesus is our shepherd. He showed us how to make our way back to the Kingdom of God.

1 John 4:7-8

7 Beloved, let us love one another: for love cometh of God, and every one that loveth is born of God, and knoweth God.

8 He that loveth, not knoweth not God, for God is love.

Gospel of the Nazirenes, Chapter 44, verse 12, page 107

Chapter 44

12 Woe is the time when the spirit of the world shall enter into the Congregation, and my doctrines and precepts are made void through the corruptions of men and women. Woe is the world when the Light is hidden. Woe is the world when these things shall be.

Chapter 1

Light

This Chapter contains verses and information that are associated with the Light. Section 1.1.1 describes the timeline for consideration to be saved and returned back to Kingdom of God. There is a narrative before the time of Adam and Eve. As a matter of fact, this was going on for 200,000 years. We were once angels and characters of God's Kingdom. Angels were all connected with the Creator as evidenced by verse 4 from Chapter 2 of the Book of Revelation;

4 Nevertheless, I have somewhat against thee, because thou hast left thy first love.

However, when certain angels fell from grace, led by Lucifer, they broke away from God's Kingdom to pursue their own power.

Section 1.1.2 contains details and quotes regarding "truth". Sections 1.1.3 and 1.1.4 talk about the "New Law" and "The Way" based on the teaching of Jesus.

In Section 1.2 "Light", there are seven sub-sections for better understanding of the terms that are often mentioned in the Bible such as "word", "walk", "ye are gods", "holy of holies", "epinoia", and "meditation".

Section 1.3 provides information about the "Kingdom of God".

Section 1.4 contains wisdoms from selected sources to help Christians protect themselves from harm.

Section 1.5 is broken up into three subsections that talk about the development of human flesh and spirit, describing traits of "Anti-Christ", and the seven gifts of the Holy Spirit.

Section 1.6 has details on "Holy Land". This will give you a better understanding about where your soul resides.

Section 1.1.1

I am with you always

Isaiah Effect, page 39:

Following the time when Adam and Eve were driven from the garden, a rare timetable was given to them, describing the duration of their exile, extended to all of their descendants, until a specific in time. In what may be the first of the great prophecies, Adam and Eve are told by their Creator that he has ordained for this earth days and years, and thou and thy seed shall abide and walk in it until the days and years are fulfilled. This time of fulfillment is envisioned following the "great five days and a half," further defined as "five thousand and five hundred years." At the close of a great cycle of time, that "One would then come and save Adam and his descendants."

Ancient Book of Jasher, Appendix A

0001-0930 Adam (930)

0130-1042 Seth (912)

0460-1422 Jared (962)

0622-987 Enoch (365)

0687-1656 Methuselah (969)

1056-2006 Noah (950)

1558-2158 Shem(600)

1656 Flood

The numbers given that are separated by a dash are Birth-Death. The number in parentheses is the age at death.

Author's note:

Using the timescale given in the Book of Jasher, the year 2011 AD is 5771. This is the age where we would experience the "Second Coming of Christ" by the light (meditation).

Edgar Cayce on Angels, page 168:

The Second Coming represents God coming into the spiritual consciousness of the masses. This is an inner as well as an outer experience. In this sense, the so-called Second Coming is happening right now in our time. This is one of the major reasons the angels are active throughout the world at an accelerated rate. "…lo, I am with you always, even unto the end of the world." (Matthew 28:20)

Complete Books of Enoch, page 145:

2 Enoch, Chapter 32

"I said to humankind, 'You are earth, and you will go into the earth from where I took you. I will not destroy you, but send you from where I took you.' Then I can again receive you at my second presence. I blessed all my creatures both visible and invisible. Human was five and half hours in the Garden. I blessed the seventh day (Saturday), which is the Sabbath, on which he rested from all his works."

Author's note:

According to the Book of Enoch, God stated to Enoch that he would not harm human souls. It is tempting to note that animals, reptiles, birds were all created by cosmic rulers. Only God created human souls.

Section 1.1.2

And ye shall know the truth, and the truth shall make you free

Beyond Belief, page 165:

Yet as, Paul says, we now only know only "in a mirror, darkly." Yet, however, incomplete, these glimpses enough to reveal the presence of the divine, for the Secret Book says that, apart from spiritual intuition, "people grow old without joy . . . and die . . . without knowing God."

The Gospel of Truth, page 38 of Nag Hammadi Scriptures:

The Living Book Is Revealed

In their hearts, the living book of living was revealed, the book that was written in the Father's thought and mind and was, since the foundation of the All, in his incomprehensible nature. No one had been able to take up this book, since it was ordained that the one who would take it up would be slain. And nothing could appear among those who believed in salvation unless that book had come out.

For this reason, the merciful, faithful Jesus was patient and accepted his sufferings to the point of taking up that book, since he knew that his death would be life for many.

As in the case of a will that has not been opened, the fortune of the deceased owner of the house is hidden, so also in the case of all that had been hidden while the Father of the All was invisible but that issues from him from whom every realm comes.

Jesus appeared,

put on that book,

was nailed to a tree,

and published the Father's edict on the cross.

Oh, what a great teaching!

He humbled himself even unto death,

though clothed in eternal life.

He stripped off the perishable rags

and clothed himself in incorruptibility,

which no one can take from him.

When he entered the empty ways of fear, he passed by those stripped by forgetfulness. For he encompasses knowledge and perfection, and he proclaims what is in the heart He teaches those who will understand. And those who will learn are the living who are inscribed in the book of the living. They learn about themselves, receiving instruction from the Father, returning to him.

Since the perfection of the All is in the Father, all must go up to him. When all have received knowledge, they discovered what is theirs and rendered it to themselves. For those who are ignorant are in need, and their need is great, because they want what would make them perfect. Since the perfection of the All is in the Father, all must go up to him and discover what is theirs. He inscribed these things first, having prepared them to be given to those who came from him.

Author's note:

When Jesus came back to Earth, he was born into a human body. He had forgotten where he came from; however, he was guided by the invisible forces (angels). When he grew to spirit, his soul remembered its origin.

The Nature of the Rulers, page 190 of Nag Hammadi Scriptures:

The Nature of the Rulers concludes with a few last words of encouragement from Eleleth. "All who know this way of truth," Eleleth assures Norea, "are deathless among dying humanity". In the end, the final liberation will come, "when the true human in human form reveals the spirit of truth that the Father has sent", and then all will be resolved and completed. Eleleth, in the Nature of the Rulers, resorts to poetry to convey the resultant bliss of the children of light, who will say, with a single voice:

The Father's truth is just, the child is over all and with everyone, forever and ever.

Holy, holy, holy!

Amen.

They embrace his head, which is rest for them, and they hold him close so that, in a manner of speaking, they have caressed his face with kisses. But they do not make this obvious. For they, neither exalt themselves nor diminish the Father's glory. And they do not think of him as insignificant or bitter or angry, but as free of evil, unperturbed, sweet, knowing all the heavenly places before they came into being, and having no need of instruction.

Such are those who enjoy something of this immeasurable glory from above, as they anticipate that unique and complete One who is a Mother to them. And they do not go down to the underworld, nor do they have envy or groaning, nor is dying with them. They stay in one who rests, and they are not weary or confused about truth.

John 8:32 "And ye shall know the truth, and the truth shall make you free." (John 8:32)

Edgar Cayce on Angels, page 176:

All the mysteries of heaven and earth, according to the readings, are within us. These mysteries are not unattainable; they are as close to us as our will. And as we begin to search and use the spiritual truths in our lives, then those realms of "heaven within us" will awaken and guide us intuitively, instinctively to a new way of being. The new heaven and new earth are waiting to be born through us. The truth is not "out there" somewhere, but is exactly where we stand in whatever situation we find ourselves.

The Gospel of the Nazirenes, page 224-225:

Chapter 90, verse 7-16

7 But to each, it is the Truth as the one mind sees it, and for that time, till a higher Truth shall be revealed to the same; and to the soul which receives higher light shall be given more light. Wherefore condemn not others, that you be not condemned.

8 As you keep The Holy Law of Love, which I have given to you, so shall the Truth be revealed more and more to you, and the Spirit of Truth which comes from, above shall guide you, albeit through many wanderings, into all Truth, even as the fiery cloud guided the children of Israel through the wilderness.

9 Be faithful to the Light you have, till a higher Light is given to you. Seek more Light, and you shall have it abundantly; for he that seeks will not rest until he finds; and he that has found shall marvel; and he that has marvelled shall reign; and he that has reigned shall rest.

10 The Lord gives you all Truth, as a ladder with many steps, for the salvation and perfection of the soul, and that which seems true today, you will abandon for the higher truth of the morrow. Press unto Perfection

11 Whoso keeps The Holy Law which I have given, the same shall save their souls, however, differently they may perceive these truths.

12 Many shall say to me, "Jesus, we have been zealous for The Truth." But I shall say to them, "No, zealous not for the Truth, but that others may see as you see, and no other truth beside." Faith without charity is dead. Love is the fulfilling of The Law.

13 How shall faith in what they receive profit them that hold it in unrighteousness? They who have Love have all things, and without Love there is nothing of worth. Let each hold what they see to be The Truth in

Love, knowing that where Love is not, Truth is a dead letter and profits nothing.

14 There abide Goodness, and Truth, and Beauty, but the greatest of these is Goodness. If any have hatred to their fellows, and harden their hearts to the creatures of the Earth, how can they see Truth unto salvation, seeing their eyes are blinded and their hearts are hardened to all creation?

15 As I have received the Truth, so have I given it to you. Let each receive it according to their light and ability to understand, and persecute not those who receive it after a different interpretation.

16 For Truth is the Might of the Lord Most High, and it shall prevail in the end over all errors. But the Holy Law which I have given is plain for all, and just and good. Let all observe it for the salvation of their souls.

1 Timothy 2:4

Who will that all men shall be saved, and come unto the acknowledgement of the truth.

The Gospel of Truth, Page 37 of Nag Hammadi Scriptures:

Jesus as Fruit of Knowledge

This is the gospel of him whom they seek, revealed to the perfect through the Father's mercy. Through the hidden mystery, Jesus Christ enlightened those who were in darkness because of forgetfulness. He enlightened them and showed the way, and that way is the truth he taught them. For this reason, Error was angry with him and persecuted him, but she was restrained by him and made powerless. He was nailed to a tree, and he became fruit of the knowledge of the Father. This fruit of the tree, however, did not bring destruction when it was eaten, but rather it caused those who ate of it to come into being. They were joyful in this discovery, and he found them within himself and they found him within themselves.

The Gospel of the Nazirenes page 33, 236, 224-225, 226:

Chapter 95, verse 4

4 But be of good cheer, for the time will also come when The Truth they have hidden shall be manifest, and the Light shall shine, and the darkness shall pass away and the true Kingdom shall be established which shall be in the world, but not of it, and the Word of righteousness and Love shall go forth from the Center, even the Holy City of Mount Zion, and the Mount which is in the land of Egypt shall be known as an altar of witness to the Lord.

The Gospel of the Nazirenes, page xv (Foreword):

It is clear from this Gospel, that Jesus did not want people to worship him, but rather to achieve salvation/enlightenment by following after The Way—a way of grace, self-responsibility and natural living under The Law. (As the Essenes used it, The Law means the earthly laws of nature and the spiritual laws of the cosmos.) The Gospel of the Nazirenes connects us to the eternal I Am that has existed from the beginning of time. It is a reflection of the prophetic teachings of the Elect for thousands of years, reflected and lived by the Essene community at the time of the Dead Sea Scrolls, reintroduced to the world through the enlightened teachings of Jesus. The Gospel of the Nazirenes can be used as an authentic doorway that empowers the reader to live The Way of Jesus the Nazirene.

Ephesians 1:13, 17, 18

13 In whom also ye have trusted, after that ye heard the word of truth, even the Gospel of your salvation, wherein also after that ye believed, ye were sealed with the Holy Spirit of promise,

17 That the God of our Lord Jesus Christ, that Father of glory, might give unto you the Spirit of wisdom, and revelation through the knowledge of him,

18 That the eyes of your understanding may be lightened, that ye may know what the hope is of his calling, and what the riches of his glorious inheritance is in the Saints,

The Gospel of Philip, page 185 of Nag Hammadi Scriptures:

Ignorance is the mother of all evil. Ignorance leads to death, because those who come from ignorance neither were nor are nor will be. But those in the truth will be perfect when all truth is revealed. For truth is like ignorance. While hidden, truth rests in itself, but when revealed and recognized, truth is praised in that it is stronger than ignorance and error. It gives freedom. The word says, "If you know the truth, the truth will make you free."(John 8:32) "Ignorance is a slave, knowledge is freedom." If we know the truth, we shall consider the effect of truth within us. If we connect with it, it will bring us fulfillment.

The Gospel of the Nazirenes

Chapter 17, verses 13, 15

13 Whosever therefore shall confess The Truth before men, them will I confess also before my Parent Who is in the Highest Heavens. But whosoever shall deny The Truth before men, them will I also deny before the Most High.

15 He that finds his life on account of a lie, shall lose it; and he that loses his life for the sake of The Truth, shall find life eternal.

Romans 1:1, 3, 4, 7-10

1 PAUL servant of JESUS Christ called to be an Apostle, put apart to preach the Gospel of God,

3 Concerning his Son Jesus Christ our Lord (which was made of the seed of David according to the flesh,

4 And declared mightily to be the Son of God, touching the Spirit of sanctification by the resurrection from the dead)

7 To all you that be at Rome beloved of God, called to be Saints: Grace be with you, and peace from God our Father, and from the Lord Jesus Christ.

8 First I thank my God through Jesus Christ for you all, because your faith is published throughout the whole world.

9 For God is my witness (whom I serve in my spirit in the Gospel of his Son) that without ceasing I make mention of you.

10 Always in my prayers, beseeching that by some means, one time or other I might have a prosperous journey by the will of God, to come unto you.

Beyond Belief, page 120, 121:

Thus, the Gospel of Truth continues, echoing John's prologue, the "word of the Father, . . . Jesus of the infinite sweetness . . . goes forth into all things, supporting all things," and finally restores all things to God, "bringing them back into the Father, and into the Mother." Acknowledging that believers often see Jesus "nailed to the cross" as an image recalling sacrificial death, this author suggest seeing him as a "fruit on a tree"—none other than the "tree of knowledge" in Paradise. But instead of destroying those who eat the fruit, as Adam was destroyed, this fruit, "Jesus the Christ," conveys guinine knowledge—not intellectual knowledge but the knowing of mutual recognition (a word related to the Greek word gnosis)—to those whom God "discovers . . . in himself, and they discover him in themselves."

This gospel takes its name from the opening line: "The gospel of truth is joy, to those who receive from the Father the grace of knowing him," for it transforms our understanding of God and ourselves. Those who receive this gospel no longer "think of God as petty, nor harsh, nor wrathful"—not, that is, as some biblical stories portray him—"but as a being without evil," loving, full of tranquility, gracious, and all-knowing. The Gospel of Truth pictures the holy spirit as God's breath, and envisions the Father first breathing forth the entire universe of living beings ("his children are his fragrant breath"), then drawing all beings back into the embrace of their divine origin. Meanwhile, he urges those who "discover God in themselves, and themselves in God" to convert gnosis into action. Those who care for others and make good "do the will of the Father."

The Gospel of Truth, page 31 of Nag Hammadi Scriptures:

The Gospel of Truth is a discourse on the gospel, understood as the good news about the appearance of the Savior on earth and the message he brought to humanity. The Gospel of Truth gives an interpretation of that event and explains how everything has been changed as a consequence of it. A peculiar feature of the text, however, is that the story of salvation seems to happen simultaneously on two distinct levels. On one level, we hear about the appearance of the Savior in the world of human beings: he taught them the truth, but he was persecuted by his enemies and was crucified and killed. However, his death brought life to mortal humans, and his instruction woke them up from forgetfulness and made them return to the Father, the source of their being. Parallel with this account, however, a more mythological story is told in the text as a metanarrative. This story tells how the world came into existence as the result of ignorance. Initially, the All, the Entirety of aeons or eternal realms, existed inside the Father, who was so vast and unfathomable that they were unable to perceive him. Because of this, ignorance, anguish, and terror took hold of the aeons; Error was produced instead of truth, and on this illusive basis, the world was created as a solidification of ignorance and fear, a "fog."

The work of the Savior was not only to bring knowledge to earthly humans, but also to rectify the cosmic error. He revealed the unknown Father to the aeons and gave them a proper, harmonious relationship to their originator. Although the Savior, as a historical person, is identical with Jesus, he is also, from a higher and more fundamental perspective, the Son, the Word, and the Name of the Father; he is the first emanation, who manifests the Father to the aeons and causes them to come into being as perfect beings. Thus, the redemption of humans by Jesus in this world is a part of a larger process of the enormous scale and ontological significance, a means by which the aeons are properly brought into being and given knowledge about the Father.

The Testimony of Truth, page 614, 617, 618, 626 of Nag Hammadi Scriptures:

This, therefore, is the true testimony: When a person comes to identify himself and God, who is over the truth, that person will be saved and crowned with the unfading crown.

The Law Versus the Truth

Now, shall speak to those who know how to listen with spiritual ears and not with their physical ones. For many have sought for the truth but have not been able to get it, because the old leaven of the Pharisees and scribes of the law has overcome them due to desire for the error of the angels, demons, and the stars. As for the Pharisees and scribes, they belong to the archons who have authority over them. No one living under the law is able to serve two masters.

For the law's defilement is clear, but undefilement belongs to the light. The law commands one to take a husband or take a wife, and to bear children, to multiply like the "sand of the sea". But passion, which is their pleasure, controls the souls of those who are begotten down here—those who defile and are defiled in return—so that the law might be fulfilled by them. They show that they are helping the world and turning away from the light. For them, it will be difficult to pass by the archon of darkness until they have paid the last cent.

The Son of Humanity came forth from an imperishable realm as one who was a stranger to defilement. He came to the world upon the Jordan River, and the Jordan quickly turned back. John bore witness to Jesus's descent, for it is he who saw the power that came down upon the Jordan River. He realized that the dominion of carnal procreation had come to an end. This is what the Son of Humanity reveals to us: it is proper for you to get the word of truth, assuming one will receive it fully. As for one who is in ignorance, it is scarcely possible for him to diminish the works of darkness that he has done. On the other hand, those who have come to know imperishability have become capable of combating passions I said to you, "Do not build or accumulate things for yourselves where robbers break in, but bring fruit to the Father."

Now, the creator of all creatures is not difficult to know, but it is difficult to comprehend what he is like. For it is not only difficult for human beings to comprehend God, but it is also difficult for every divine nature, the angels and archangels. For it is necessary to know God in the way he is. You cannot know God through any means except through Christ, who bears the image of the Father. For this, image reveals the true likeness of God in a visible way. A king is usually not known apart from an image.

The Gospel of Philip, page 180 of Nag Hammadi Scriptures:

The perfect human can neither be grasped nor seen. What is seen can be grasped. No one can obtain this grace without putting on perfect light and becoming perfect light. Whoever puts on light will enter the place of rest. This is the perfect light, and we must become perfect humans before we leave the world. Whoever obtains everything but does not separate from this world will not be able to attain that realm but will go to the middle place, for that one is not perfect. Only Jesus knows the fate of that person.

Author's note:

Since we are God's sheep, those who don't reach the light during their current life will come back to earth in another body and have another chance to get to the Kingdom of God (light). Typically, you would respond to the same level where you have left from your past life.

Matthew 6:22

"If therefore thine eye be single, thy whole body shall be full of light."

The Gospel of the Nazirenes, page 67:

Chapter 27, verse 4

4 Ask, and it shall be given you; seek, and you shall find; knock and it shall be opened to you; for everyone that asks, receives. And he that seeks, will not rest until he finds, and he that has found shall marvel, and he that has marvelled shall reign, and he that has reigned shall rest.

Revelation 3:12

12 Him that overcometh, will I make a pillar in the Temple of my God, and he shall go no more out: and I will write upon him the Name of my God, and the name of the city of my God, which is the new Jerusalem, which cometh down out of heaven from my God, and I will write upon him my new Name.

Author's note:

After you've attained the light from meditation, you have found the Kingdom of God, and from Revelation 3:12, you shall see "no more out," meaning you won't have to go through renewal again here on Earth.

The Gospel of the Nazirenes, page XIV:

These ancient yet new ways of stating these timeless teachings bring a new understanding to the scriptures on which so many have based their lives. It is significant that these teachings are coming to light now, as Jesus prophesied in this Gospel:

"I have set you as the Light of the world, and as a city that cannot be hid. But the time comes when darkness shall cover the Earth, and gross darkness the people, and the enemies of Truth and righteousness shall rule in my name and set up a kingdom of this world, and oppress the peoples, and cause the enemy to blaspheme, putting for my doctrines the opinions of a man and men, and teaching in my name that which I have not taught, and darkening much that I have taught by their traditions.

Colossians 2:8

8 Beware lest there be any man that spoil you through philosophy, and vain deceit, through the traditions of men, according to the rudiments of the world, and not after Christ.

Ephesians 4:14

14 That we henceforth be no more children, wavering and carried about with every wind of doctrine, by the deceit of men, and with craftiness, whereby they lay in wait to deceive.

Author's note:

Jesus was saying his teaching of "The Way" was not followed by the churches. The Church Fathers even stated to "shun" epinioa during the time they were formulating a strategy for the Church. Epinoia was part of the central teaching of Jesus when he talked about the Kingdom of God. For more details about epinoia, refer to section 1.2.5.

The Gospel of the Nazirenes, Chapter 12, verse 10-12

10 And certain of the Pharisees came and questioned Jesus and said to him, "How can you say that the Lord will condemn the world?" And Jesus answered, saying, "The All-Parent so loves the world, that the First Begotten Son is given, and comes forth into the world, that whosoever lives in The Law may not perish, but have everlasting life." The Son is not sent into the world to condemn it; but that through his example it may be saved.

11 They who believe in The Truth are not condemned; but they that believe not are condemned already, because they have not believed in The Way. And this is the condemnation: that The Light is come into the world, and men love darkness rather than Light, because their deeds are evil.

12 For all evil doers hate The Light, neither do they come to The Light, lest their deeds may be condemned. But they that do righteousness come to "The Light," that their deeds may be made manifest, that they are wrought in The Law.

The Gospel of Nazirenes, Chapter 13, verse 2

2 And when he had opened it, he found the place where it was written, The Spirit of the Lord is upon me, because he has anointed me to preach the gospel to the poor of Spirit; he has sent me to heal the brokenhearted, to preach deliverance to the captives and recovering of sight to the blind, to set at liberty them that are bound.

Section 1.1.3

New Law

The Second Coming of Christ, page 1026-1027:

And, behold, a certain lawyer stood up, and tempted him, saying, "Master, what shall I do to inherit eternal life?"

He said unto him, "What is written in the law?"

And he answering said, "Thou shalt love the Lord thy God with all thy heart, and with all thy soul, and with all thy strength, and with all thy mind; and thy neighbour as thyself."

Then one of them, which was a lawyer, asked him a question, tempting him, and saying, "Master, which is the great commandment in the law?"

Jesus said unto him, "Thou shalt love the Lord thy God with all thy heart, and with all thy soul, and with all thy mind. This is Jesus' declaration of the two greatest commandments is recounted in all three synoptic Gospels, with minor variations. In the Gospels, according to St. Matthew and St. Mark, it occurs during Jesus' last week in Jerusalem, shortly before his crucifixion;

And one of the scribes came, and having heard them reasoning together, and perceiving that he had answered them well, asked him, "Which is the first commandment of them all?"

And Jesus answered him, "The first of all the commandments is, 'Hear, O Israel; the Lord our God is one Lord: And thou shalt love the Lord thy God with all thy heart, and with all thy soul, and with all thy mind, and with all thy strength': this is the first commandment. And the second is like, namely this, 'Thou shalt love thy neighbour as thyself.' There is none other commandment greater than these."

And the scribe said unto him, "Well, Master, thou hast said the truth: for there is one God; and there is none other but He: And to love Him with all the heart, and with all the understanding, and with all the soul, and with all the strength, and to love his neighbour as himself, is more than all whole burnt offerings and sacrifices."

Micah 6:6-8

6 Wherewith shall I come before the Lord, and bow myself before the high God? shall I come before Him with burnt offerings, with calves of a year old?

7 Will the Lord be pleased with thousands of rams, or with ten thousands rivers of oil? shall I give my firstborn for my transgression, even the fruit of my body for the sin of my soul?

8 He hath showed thee, O man, what is good, and what the Lord requireth of thee: surely to do justly, and to love mercy, and to humble thyself, to walk with thy God.

Hebrews 10:4-6

4 For it is impossible that the blood of bulls and goats should take away sins.

5 Wherefore when he cometh into the world, he saith, Sacrifice and offering thou wouldest not: but a body hast thou ordained me.

6 In burnt offerings, and sin offerings thou hast had no pleasure.

But there is an inner meaning to the exhortation to love God with all one's heart, mind, soul, and strength. Jesus used these scriptural terms, but projected his belief that in them is the whole science of yoga, the transcendental nature of divine union through meditation. In India, where spiritual understanding had developed for thousands of years before the time of Jesus, God-knowing sages elaborated these concepts as a comprehensive spiritual philosophy to guide devotees systematically on the path to liberation. When a person makes the effort in meditation to know God, using the sincerity of his heart and deepest feelings, and the intuition of his soul, and all the powers of concentration of his mind, and all his interiorized life energy, or strength, he will surely succeed.

To "love God with all your mind" means with focused concentration. If while offering prayerful devotions the mind is constantly flitting to thoughts of work or food or bodily sensations or other diversions, that is not loving God with all the mind. The Bible teaches: "Pray without ceasing" (1 Thessalonians 5:17) India's yoga science gives the actual methodology to worship God with that fully concentrated mind.

To "love God with all your soul", means to enter the state of superconscious ecstasy, direct perception of the soul and its oneness with God. When no thoughts cross the mind, but there is a conscious all knowingness, when one knows through intuitive realization that he can do anything just by so ordering it, then one is in the expanded state of superconsciousness. It is the realization of the soul as the reflection of God, the soul's connection with the consciousness of God. It is a state of exceeding joy: the soul's crystalline perception of the omnipresent Spirit reflected as the joy of meditation.

Gospel of the Nazirenes, Chapter 6, verse 14

14 So it was that, for several years, he travelled in India and other holy places. And they loved him as he taught the Holy Scriptures. And Jesus went into the desert, meditated and fasted and prayed, and obtained the power of the Holy Name, by which he wrought many miraculous deeds.

Author's note:

Jesus travelled to India and returned to his homeland at a period of 18. This explains unaccounted time of his life in the Bible.

The Gospel of the Nazirenes, page 114-123:

Chapter 47, verse 1, 8, 9

1 And when they came down from the Mount, one of his disciples asked him, "Jesus, if a man keep not all these commandments shall he enter into Life?" And he said, "The Law is good in the letter, but more excellent in the Spirit, for the letter without the Spirit is dead, but the Spirit makes the letter alive.

8 Walk in the Spirit, and thus shall you fulfill The Law and be substance for the Kingdom. Let The Law be within your own hearts rather than on tables of the memorial; which things nevertheless you ought to do, and not to leave the other undone, for The Law which I have given to you is holy, just and good, and blessed are all they who obey and walk therein.

9 The Unbegotten is Spirit, and they who worship the Most High must— worship in Spirit and in Truth, at all times, and in all places.

Chapter 49, verse 3, 4

3 But the true Temple is the body of Man in which The Creator dwells by the Holy Spirit; and when this Temple is destroyed, in three days, the Lord raises up a more glorious Temple, which the eye of the natural man perceives not.

4 Do you not know that you are the Temples of the Holy Spirit? And whoso destroys one of these Temples the same shall be himself destroyed.

Chapter 50, verse 1

1 Then spoke Jesus again to them, saying, "I am the Light of the World; he that follows my example shall not walk in darkness, but shall have the Light of Life."

The Gospel of the Nazirenes, page 148:

Chapter 59, verse 11, 12

11 For they who know the Lord, and have found The Way of Life, the mysteries of Light, and then have fallen into sin, shall be punished with greater chastisement than they who have not known The Law.

12 Such shall return when their cycle is completed and to them will be given time and space to consider, and amend their lives; and learning the mysteries, enter into the Kingdom of Light.

The Gospel of the Nazirenes, page 113:

Chapter 46, verse 22

22 This is the new Law to the true Israel, and The Law is within, for it is The Law of Love, and it is not new but old. Take heed that you add nothing to this Law, neither take anything from it. Verily I say to you, they who believe and obey this Law shall be saved, and they who know and obey it not, shall be lost.

The Gospel of the Nazirenes, page 76:

Chapter 30, verse 5

5 Then Jesus said to them, "Verily, verily, I say to you, that which you believe Moses gave you are not the true bread from the Heavens and the fruit of the Living Vine. For the food of the Lord is that which flows from the Highest Heavens, and gives life to the world."

The Gospel of the Nazirenes, page 87:

Chapter 35, verse 1-3

1 And behold a certain lawyer stood up and tempted him, saying, "Jesus, what shall I do to gain eternal life?" He said to him, "What is written in The Law?"

2 And answering, he said, "Do unto others, as you would that they should do unto you. You shall love the Lord with all your heart, all your soul and all your mind."

3 And Jesus said to him, "You have answered rightly. Do this and you shall live; on these three commandments hang all The Law and the Prophets, for he who loves the Lord, loves his neighbor also."

Hebrews 10:14-26

14 For with one offering hath he consecrated forever them that are sanctified.

15 For the holy Ghost also beareth us record: for after that he had said before,

16 This is the Testament that I will make unto them after those days, saith the Lord, I will put my Laws in their heart, and in their minds I will write them.

17 And their sins and iniquities will I remember no more.

18 Now where remission of these things is, there is no more offering for sin.

19 Seeing therefore, brethren, that by the blood of Jesus we may be bold to enter into the Holy place,

20 By the new and living way, which he hath prepared for us, through the veil, that is, his flesh:

21 And seeing we have a high Priest, which is over the house of God,

Author's note:

Jesus is our new high priest.

22 Let us draw near with a true heart in assurance of faith, our hearts being pure from an evil conscience,

23 And washed in our bodies with pure water, let us keep the profession of our hope, without wavering, (for he is faithful that promised.)

24 And let us consider one another, to provoke unto love, and to good works,

25 Not forsaking the fellowship that we have among ourselves, as the manner of some is: but let us exhort one another, and that so much the more, because ye see that the day draweth near.

26 For if we sin willingly after that we have received and acknowledged that truth, there remaineth no more sacrifice for sins,

Author's note:

The importance of fellowship is to deepen our spiritual growth. Also, this is where we can learn to extend our appreciation for mankind by helping others through actions of the church.

John 1:15-18

15 John bare witness of him, and cried, saying, This was he of whom I said, He that cometh after me, was before me: for he was better than I.

16 And of his fullness have all we received, and grace for grace.

17 For the Law was given by Moses, but grace and truth came by Jesus Christ.

18 No man hath seen God at any time: that only begotten Son, which is in the bosom of the Father, he hath declared him.

Section 1.1.4

The Way

The Gospel of the Nazirenes, page 49, 66:

Chapter 19, verse 1, 3, 4

1 As Jesus was praying in a certain place on a mountain, some of his disciples came to him, and one of them said, "Jesus, teach us how to pray." And Jesus said to them, "When you pray, enter into your secret chamber, and when you have closed the door, pray to Abba Amma, Who is above and within you; and your All-Parent Who sees all that is secret shall answer you openly."

3 "Our Lord Who art in the Highest Heavens: Hallowed be Thy Name. Thy Kingdom come, Thy will be done; on Earth as it is in the Highest Heavens. Give us each day our daily sustenance, and the fruit of the Living Vine. Forgive us our trespasses, as we forgive those who trespass against us. Leave us not in temptation, deliver us from evil."

4 "For Thine are the Kingdom, the Power and the Glory: From Ages of ages, now and forever. Amen."

Chapter 26, verse 13

13 "The lamps of the body are the eyes; if therefore your sight be clear, your whole body shall be full of light. But if your eyes be dim or lacking, your whole body shall be full of darkness. If therefore the light that is in you be darkness, how great is that darkness!"

Matthew 6:22

The light of the body is the eye: if then thine eye be single, thy whole body shall be light.

Revelation 7:13-17

13 And one of the Elders spake, saying unto me, What are these which are arrayed in long white robes? and whence came they?

14 And I said unto him, Lord, thou knowest. And he said unto me, These are they which came out of great tribulation, and have washed their long robes, and have made their long robes white in the blood of the Lamb.

15 Therefore are they in the presence of the throne of God, and serve him day and night in his Temple, and he that sitteth on the throne will dwell among them.

16 They shall hunger no more, neither thirst anymore, neither shall the sun light on them, neither any heat.

17 For the Lamb, which is in the midst of the throne, shall govern them, and shall lead them unto the lively fountains of waters, and God shall wipe away all tears from their eyes.

The Gospel of the Nazirenes, page 123:

Chapter 51, verse 1

1 Then said Jesus to the Jews which believed in him, "If you continue in The Way, then you are true disciples; and you shall know the Truth, and the Truth shall make you free."

The Gospel of the Nazirenes, page 241:

Chapter 96, verse 20-24

20 We shall teach The Way to prepare your children for the indwelling Universal Messiah; and the Kingdom of the Highest Heavens within their hearts, wherein dwells righteousness on the Altar of the Lord. From whence, those in ministry proceed to teach all Truth and offer the pure oblation of praise.

21 As in the inner so in the outer: as in the great so in the small. As above, so below: as in the Highest Heavens, so on Earth. We shall teach the purification of the soul through many births and experiences, the resurrection from the ways of them that sleep to return to Life Everlasting in the Ages of Ages and rest in the Lord forever.—Amen.

22 And as the smoke of the incense arose, there was heard the sound as of many bells, and a multitude of the Heavenly Host praising the Lord and saying;

23 Glory, honor, praise and worship be to the Most High: the Father, Spouse, and Son; One with the Mother, Bride and Maid; from Whom proceeds the Eternal Spirit. By whom are all created things. From the Ages of Ages, Now and to the Ages of Ages—Amen—Alleluia, Alleluia, Alleluia.

24 And if any man take from, or add, to the words of the Gospel, or hide, as under a bushel, the light thereof, which is given by the Spirit through us, the Twelve witnesses chosen of the Lord Most High, for the enlightenment of the world unto salvation, let him be Anathema Maranatha, until the coming of the Messiah with all the Holy Saints. Amen.

2 Corinthians 1:12, 19

12 For our rejoicing is this, the testimony of our conscience, that in simplicity and godly pureness, and not in fleshly wisdom, but by the grace of God, we have had our conversation in the world, and most of all to youwards.

19 For the Son of God Jesus Christ, who was preached among you by us, that is, by me, and Silvanus, and Timothy, was not Yea, and Nay: but in him it was Yea.

Beyond Belief, page 99, 100:

The author of the Prayer of the Apostle Paul, then takes Paul as the paradigm of "those who seek God" and articulates the longing to enter into God's presence, as Paul had:

My redeemer, redeem me, for I am yours, one who has come forth from you. You are my mind; bring me forth. You are my treasure; open to me. You are my fulfillment; join me to you!

The Gospel of the Nazirenes, page 240:

Chapter 96, verse 17

17 Which is incarnate of purity in Jesus and every Messiah of the Most High; is born and teaches The Way of Life, suffers under world rulers, and is crucified and is buried; Who rises again and ascends into glory; from there giving Light and Life to all.

Section 1.2.

Light

Section 1.2.1

Word

The Gospel of Truth, page 45 of Nag Hammadi Scriptures:

He is good. He knows his plants because he planted them in his paradise. And his paradise is his place of rest. Paradise is the perfection within the Father's thought, and the plants are the words of his meditation. Each of his words is the product of his will and the revelation of his speech. Since, they were the depth of his thought, the Word that came forth caused them to appear, along with mind that speaks the Word and silent grace. It was called thought, because they dwelled in silent grace before being revealed. So it happened that the Word came forth when it was pleasing to the will of him who willed it.

The Father is at rest in will. Nothing happens without his pleasure; nothing happens without the Father's will. And his will is incomprehensible. His will is his footprint, but none can understand him, nor does he exist so that they might study him in order to grasp him. Rather, when he wills, what he wills is this, even if the view does not please people before God: it is the Father's will. For he knows the beginning and the end of all, and at their end, he will greet them. The end is the recognition of him who is hidden, and he is the Father, from whom the beginning has come and to whom all will return who have come from him. They have appeared for the glory and joy of his name.

The Gospel of Truth, Page 36 of Nag Hammadi Scriptures:

The gospel of truth is joy for people who have received grace from the Father of truth, that they might know him through the power of the Word. The Word has come from the fullness in the Father's thought and mind. The Word is called "Savior," a term that refers to the work he is to do to redeem those who had not known the Father. And the term "gospel" refers to the revelation of hope, since it is the means of discovery for those who seek him.

The Gospel of Truth, Page 39 of Nag Hammadi Scriptures:

The Word of the Father Appears

As for the Word,

his wisdom meditates on it,

his teaching utters it,

his knowledge has revealed it,

his patience is a crown upon it,

his joy is in harmony with it,

his glory has exalted it,

his character has revealed it,

his rest has received it,

his love has incarnated it,

his faith has embraced it.

Thus, the Father's Word goes out in the All as the fruition of his heart and expression of his will. It supports all and chooses all. It also takes the expression of all and purifies it, bringing it back to the Father, to the Mother, Jesus of infinite sweetness.

27

The Father opens his bosom, and his bosom is the Holy Spirit. He reveals his hidden self, and his hidden self is his Son, so that through the Father's mercy the eternal realms may know him, end their wearying search for the Father, and rest in him, knowing that he is rest. For he has filled what was deficient and has done away with its appearance. The mere appearance of what was deficient is the world, and mere appearance serves in the world.

For where there is envy and strife, there is deficiency, but where there is unity there is completeness. Since deficiency came about because the Father was not known, from the moment when the Father is known, deficiency will cease to be. From then on, the world of appearance will no longer be evident, but rather it will disappear in the harmony of unity.

Now the works of all lie scattered. In time unity will make the heavenly places complete, and in unity, all individually will come to themselves. When they come to knowledge, they will purify themselves from the multiplicity into unity, devouring matter within themselves like fire, darkness by light, death by life.

Since these things have happened to each of us, it is right for us to see to it above all that this house be holy and silent for the sake of unity.

The Gospel of Truth, Page 41 of Nag Hammadi Scriptures:

The Appearance of Truth and the Emanations of the Father

Truth appeared, and all its expressions recognized it. They greeted the Father in truth and power that is complete and joins them with the Father.

Whoever loves truth, whoever touches truth, touches the Father's mouth, because truth is the Father's mouth. His tongue is the Holy Spirit, and from his tongue, one will receive the Holy Spirit. This is the manifestation of the Father and his revelation to his eternal realms. He revealed his hidden self and explained it.

The Gospel of Truth, page 42 of Nag Hammadi Scriptures:

The Beloved Son Reveals What Is New

Knowledge of the Father and the revelation of his Son gave them the means of knowing. For when they saw and heard him, he let them taste him and smell him and touch the beloved Son. He appeared, informing them of the Father, the illimitable, and he inspired them with what is in the thought, doing his will. Many received the light and turned to him. But material people were strangers to him and did not discern his appearance or recognize him. For he came in the likeness of flesh, and nothing blocked his way, for incorruptibility cannot be grasped. Moreover, while saying new things and speaking about what is in the Father's heart, he produced the faultless Word. Light spoke through his mouth, and his voice brought life. He gave them thought and understanding and mercy and salvation and the spirit of strength from the Father's infinity and sweetness. He made punishments and afflictions cease for they caused those in need of mercy to stray from him in error and bondage. He destroyed them with might and confounded them with knowledge.

He became a way for those who strayed,

knowledge for those who were ignorant,

discovery for those who sought,

support for those who tremble,

purity for those who were defiled.

Colossians 1:25

Whereof I am a minister, according to the dispensation of God, which is given me unto youward, to fulfill the word of God.

1 Peter 1:23-25

23 Being born anew, not of mortal seed, but of immortal, by the word of God, who liveth and endureth forever.

24 For all flesh is as grass, and all the glory of man is as the flower of grass. The grass withereth, and the flower falleth away.

25 But the word of the Lord endureth forever: and this is the word which is preached among you.

The Gospel of Truth, Page 32 of Nag Hammadi Scriptures:

The Word, moreover, is the Son, who reveals the Father, replacing ignorance with knowledge and dispersion with unity, in short, deficiency with fullness.

The Testimony of Truth, page 618 of Nag Hammadi Scriptures:

The Son of Humanity clothed himself with their firstfruits and went down to Hades. There, he performed many mighty deeds and raised the dead. And the world rulers of darkness [Ephesians 6:12] became envious of him, for they did not find any sin in him. He also destroyed their works affecting humanity by granting healing to the lame, the blind, the paralyzed, and the demon-possessed. [Luke 7:21-22] And he walked on the waters of the sea. [Matthew 14:25] They are blind guides, like the disciples. They boarded the ship, and at about four miles away they saw Jesus walking on the sea. These people are hollow martyrs who bear witness only to themselves. In fact, they are sick and cannot get themselves up. But when they are full of passion, this is their motivating idea: "If we give ourselves up to death for the sake of the name, [1 Peter 4:14] we will be saved." That is not the way things are. Rather, impelled by planetary forces, they say that they have "completed" their futile "course." [2 Timothy 4:7] And they . . . say . . . . But these . . . they have given themselves up to death his . . . and his . . . . They are like, . . . and are not in possession of the life-giving word.

Author's note:

Hades is here on earth, according to the Scriptures.

Gospel of the Nazirenes, page 21

Chapter 7, verse 1-2

1 It was in the fifteenth year of the reign of Tiberius Caesar, Pontius Pilate being governor of Judaea, and Herod being Tetrarch of Galilee (Caiaphas being the high priest, and Annas chief of the Sanhedrin), that The Word of the Lord came to John the son of Zacharias, in the wilderness.

2 And he came into all the country about Jordan, preaching the baptism of repentance for the remission of sins. As it is written in the Prophets, Behold, I send my messenger before thy face, who shall prepare The Way before thee; the voice of one crying in the wilderness, Prepare ye The Way of the Lord, make straight the paths for the Anointed.

Section 1.2.2

Walk

The Gospel of the Nazirenes, page 22

Chapter 7, verse 10

10 And to all he spoke, saying, "Keep yourselves from blood and things strangled and dead bodies of birds and beasts, and from all deeds of cruelty, and from all that is gotten of wrong; Do you think that the blood of beasts and birds will wash away sin? I tell you, no! Speak the Truth, be just, and merciful to one another and to all creatures, and walk humbly with your Creator."

2 Corinthians 6:16

And what agreement hath the temple of God with idols? For ye are the temple of the living God: as God hath said, I will dwell among them, and walk there: And I will be their God, and they shall be my people.

Ephesians 2:4-14

4 But God which is rich in mercy, through his great love wherewith he loved us,

5 Even when we were dead by sins, hath quickened us together in Christ, by whose grace ye are saved,

6 And hath raised us up together, and made us sit together in the heavenly places in Christ Jesus,

7 That he might show in the ages to come the exceeding riches of his grace through his kindness toward us in Christ Jesus.

8 For by grace are ye saved through faith, and that not of yourselves: it is the gift of God,

9 Not of works, lest any man should boast himself.

10 For we are his workmanship created in Christ Jesus unto good works, which God hath ordained, that we should walk in them.

John 12:35-36

35 Then Jesus said unto them, Yet a little while is the light with you: walk while ye have that light, lest the darkness come upon you: for he that walketh in the dark, knoweth not whither he goeth.

36 While ye have that light, believe in that light, that ye may be the children of the light. These things spake Jesus, and departed, and hid himself from them.

Matthew 11:1-5

1 And it came to pass that when Jesus had made an end of commanding his twelve disciples, he departed thence to teach and to preach in their cities.

2 And when John heard in the prison the works of Christ, he sent two of his disciples, and said unto him,

3 Art thou he that should come, or shall we look for another?

4 And Jesus answering, said unto them, Go, and show John, what things ye hear and see.

5 The blind receive sight, and the halt do walk: the lepers are cleansed, and the deaf hear, the dead are raised up, and the poor receive the Gospel.

Author's Note:

The term "poor" refers to poor in spirit.

Rev 3:4-5

4 Notwithstanding thou hast a few names yet in Sardis, which have not defiled their garments: and they shall walk with me in white: for they are worthy.

5 He that overcometh, shall be clothed in white array, and I will not put out his Name out of the book of life, but I will confess his name before my Father, and before his Angels.

Deuteronomy 8:6

6 Therefore shalt thou keep the commandments of the Lord thy God, that thou mayest walk in his ways, and fear him.

Deuteronomy 6:5-6

5 And thou shalt love the Lord thy God with all thine heart, and with all thy soul, and with all thy might.

6 And these words which I command thee this day, shall be in thine heart.

Ezekiel 8:3

3 And he stretched out the likeness of an hand, and took me by an hairy lock of mine head, and the Spirit lifted me up between the earth and the heaven, and brought me by a Divine vision to Jerusalem, into the entry of the inner gate that lieth toward the North, where remained the idol of indignation, which provoked indignation.

2 Kings 23:3

3 And the king stood by the pillar, and made a covenant before the Lord, that they should walk after the Lord, and keep his commandments, and his testimonies, and his statutes, with all their heart, and with all their soul, that they might accomplish the words of this covenant written in this book. And all the people stood to the covenant.

Daniel 7:13

13 As I beheld in visions by night, behold, one like the son of man came in the clouds of heaven, and approached unto the Ancient of days, and they brought him before him.

Micah 6:8

8 He hath showed thee, O man, what is good, and what the Lord requireth of thee: surely to do justly, and to love mercy, and to humble thyself, to walk with thy God.

2 Corinthians 12:2

2 I know a man in Christ above fourteen years ago, (whether he were in the body, I cannot tell, or out of the body, I cannot tell: God knoweth) which was taken up into the third heaven.

The Gnostic Gospels, page 15:

Paul, referring to himself obliquely in the third person, says that he was "caught up to the third heaven-whether in the body or out of the body I do not know." There, in an ecstatic trance, he heard "things that cannot be told, which many may not utter." Through his spiritual communication with Christ, Paul says he discovered hidden mysteries and secret wisdom, which, he explains, he shares only with those Christians he considers "mature" but not with everyone. Valentinus, the Gnostic poet who traveled from Egypt to teach Rome (c. 140), even claimed that he himself learned Paul's secret teaching from Theudas, one of Paul's own disciples.

Colossians 2:5

5 For though I be absent in the flesh, yet am I with you in the spirit, rejoicing and beholding your order, and your steadfast faith in Christ.

Colossians 2:6

6 As ye have received Christ Jesus the Lord, so walk in Him.

2 Thessalonians 3:11

11 For we hear, that there are some which walk among you inordinately, and work not at all, but are busy bodies.

Section 1.2.3

Ye are Gods

Psalm 82:6

6 I have said, Ye are gods, and ye all are children of the most High.

John 10:34-35

34 Jesus answered them, Is it not written in your Law, I said, 'Ye are gods?

35 If he called them gods, unto whom the word of God was given, and the Scripture cannot be broken,

Second Coming of Christ, page 1020:

Jesus answered them, "Is it not written in your law, I said, Ye are gods?" If he called them gods, unto whom the word of God came, and the scripture cannot be broken; say ye of him, whom the Father hath sanctified, and sent into the world, "Thou blasphemest; because I said, I am the Son of God? If I do not the works of my Father, believe me not. But if I do, though ye believe not me, believe the works: that ye may know, and believe, that the Father is in me, and I in Him" (John 10:31-38).

Is it not written in your holy books exactly what I said—that not only I but all of you are gods? If the scriptures call all people gods because they are born of the Cosmic Vibration emanating from God the Father, that truth cannot be nullified by your disbelief. Then how can you speak of blasphemy to me who have been sanctified and sent by God to the world as a perfect godly example?

Isaiah 42:17

17 They shall be turned back: they shall be greatly ashamed, that trust in graven images, and say to the molten images, ye are gods.

1 Corinthians 3:16

16 Know ye not that ye are the temple of God, and that the spirit of God dwelleth in you ?

1 Corinthians 3:17

17 If any man destroy the temple of God, him shall God shall destroy: For the temple of God is holy, which ye are.

Isaiah 41:23

23 Show the things that are to come hereafter, that we may know that ye are gods: yea, do good or do evil, that we may declare it, and behold it together.

1 John 3:9

9 Whosoever is born of God sinneth not: For his seed remaineth in Him, neither can he sin, because he is born of God.

1 John 3:2

2 Dearly beloved, now are we the Sons of God, but yet it is not made manifest what we shall be: And we know that when he shall be made manifest: We shall be like Him for we shall see Him as he is.

1 John 4:4

4 Little children, ye are God, and have overcome them. For greater is He that is in you, than he that is in this world.

Section 1.2.4

Holy of Holies

The Gospel of Philip, page 186 of Nag Hammadi Scriptures:

Eternal Light

Everyone who enters the bedchamber will kindle the light. This is like marriages that occur in secret and take place at night. The light of the fire shines during the night and then goes out. The mysteries of that marriage, however, are performed in the day and the light, and neither that day nor its light ever sets. If someone becomes an attendant of the bridal chamber, that person will receive the light. If one does not receive it while here in this place, one cannot receive it in the other place.

Those who receive the light cannot be seen or grasped. Nothing can trouble such people even while they are living in this world. And when they leave this world, they have already received truth through images, and the world has become the eternal realm. To these people the eternal realm is Fullness.

This is the way it is. It is revealed to such a person alone, hidden not in darkness and night but hidden in perfect day and holy light.

The Gospel of Philip, page 185 of Nag Hammadi Scriptures:

Temple, Cross, Ark

The mysteries of truth are made known in symbols and images. The bedchamber is hidden, and it is the holy of the holy. At first the curtain concealed how God manages creation, but when the curtain is torn and what is inside appears, this building will be left deserted, or rather will be destroyed. And the whole godhead will flee from here but not into the holy of holies, for it cannot mingle with pure [light] and [perfect] fullness. Instead, it will remain under the wings of the cross [and under] its arms. This ark will be salvation [for people] when floodwaters surge over them.

Whoever belongs to the priestly order can go inside the curtain along with the high priest. For this reason the curtain was not torn only at the top, for then only the upper realm would have been opened. It was not torn only at the bottom, for then it would have revealed only the lower realm. No, it was torn from top to bottom. The upper realm was opened for us in the lower realm, that we might enter the hidden realm of truth. This is what is truly worthy and mighty, and we shall enter through symbols that are weak and insignificant. They are weak compared to perfect glory. There is glory that surpasses glory, there is power that surpasses power. Perfect things have opened to us, and hidden things of truth.

The holy of holies was revealed, and the bedchamber invited us in.

The Apocalypse of Peter, page 73:

Heavenly Temple

In the transfiguration scene based upon Matthew 17, Peter asks the same question as in Matthew 17:4 : 'do you wish that I make three tabernacles here, one for you and one for Moses and one for Elijah?' Matthew 17:5 continues with the voice from the cloud which announces that Jesus is the beloved son, however, Jesus severely rebukes Peter: Satan has veiled his understanding. Peter should not build tabernacles, not made by hands, 'which my Heavenly Father had made for me and my elect'.

Bauckham reads the severe rebuke in the light of Bar Kokhba's presumed intention to rebuild the temple. It would serve as a warning to those Jewish Christians who have been tempted to participate in the attempts to rebuild the temple. Moreover, the following verse would explicitly identify Christ (and therefore not Bar Kokhba) as the true Messiah. It is clear that the text refers to the idea of transcendent temple (such as in Hebrews 9:11 or Revelation 21:3).

Hebrews 9:11

11 But Christ being come an high Priest of good things to come, by a greater and a more perfect Tabernacle, not made with hands, that is, not of this building,

Rev 21:3

3 And I heard a great voice out of heaven, saying, Behold, the Tabernacle of God is with men, and he will dwell with them: and they shall be his people, and God himself shall be their God with them.

John 3:19-22

19 Jesus answered, and said unto them, Destroy this Temple, and in three days I will raise it up again.

20 Then said the Jews, Forty and six years was this Temple a building, and wilt thou rear it up in three days?

21 But he spake of the temple of his body.

22 As soon therefore as he was risen from the dead, his disciples remembered that he thus said unto them: and they believed the Scriptures, and the word which Jesus had said.

1 Corinthians 2:9

9 But as it is written, the things which eye hath not seen, neither ear hath heard, neither came into man's heart, are, which God hath prepared for them that love Him.

Hebrews 13:10

10 We have an altar, whereof they have no authority to eat, which serve in the tabernacle.

2 Corinthians 5:6

6 Therefore, we are always bold, though we know that while we are at home in the body, we are absent from the Lord.

Section 1.2.5

Epinoia

Beyond Belief, page 103-104:

In the Gospel of Mary Magdalene, discovered in Egypt in 1896, the apostles Andrew and Peter raised the same questions that troubled Ireneaus—but this time we hear a response from the visionary's point of view. The Gospel of Mary dramatizes how certain group leaders—here represented by apostles Peter and Andrew, sometimes attacked and denounced those who claimed to see visions. Although the opening is lost, what we have of the Gospel of Mary begins with a vision in which the risen Jesus tells his disciples, "The Son of Man is within you. Follow after him! Those who seek him will find him. Go, then, and preach the gospel of the kingdom." Yet most of the disciples, apparently at a loss to find the divine within themselves, "were grieved, and wept greatly," terrified that they would be killed as Jesus was. Then Mary stood up, spoke, and "turned their hearts to the good":

Do not weep, and do not grieve nor be afraid, for his grace will be with you completely, and will protect you. But rather let us praise his greatness, for he has prepared us, and has turned us into human beings.

Mary asked Jesus after seeing him in vision, how visions occur;

"How does one who sees the vision see it—through the soul, or through the spirit?" The Savior answered and said, "One does not see it through the soul, nor through the spirit, but the mind which is between the two: that is what sees the vision."

Author's note:

The "spiritual eye" is located at the center of your forehead, above your eyebrows.

Beyond Belief, page 164-167:

John's Secret Book intends this story to show that we have a latent capacity within our hearts and minds that links us to the divine—not in our ordinary state of mind but when this hidden capacity awakens. The Secret Book explains that, although God is essentially incomprehensible, the powers that reveal God to humankind include pronoia (anticipatory awareness), ennoia (internal reflection), and prognosis (foreknowledge or intuition), all personified as feminine presences, presumably because of the gender of the Greek words. But according to the Secret Book it is, above all, the "luminous epinoia" that conveys genuine insight. We might translate this as "imagination," but many people take this term as Ireneaus did, to refer to fantasy rather than conscious awareness. Yet as the Secret Book envisions it, epinoia remains an ambiguous, limited—but—indispensable—gift. When John asks whether everyone receives the luminous epinoia, the Savior answers yes—"The power will descend upon every person, for without it, no one can stand"—and adds that epinoia strengthens those who love her by enabling them to discriminate between good and evil.

Douglas F. Grady

Author's note:

Here, Jesus was telling Apostle John that every man was capable of receiving the "Light". Jesus was referring to the soul of human, not the flesh of human. When the soul has matured after experiencing many lives, then that person is ready to receive the Light. This was one key issue dividing Christians with Gnostic belief from the Orthodox Christians where the Orthodox did not believe in reincarnation.

The author of the Secret Book stresses that the insights this spiritual intuition conveys are neither complete nor certain; instead, epinoia conveys hints and glimpses, images and stories, that imperfectly point beyond themselves toward what we cannot now fully understand. Thus, the author knows that these very stories—those told in the Secret Book—are to be taken neither literally nor too seriously; for these, too, are merely glimpses that, as Paul says, we now know only "in a mirror, darkly." Yet, however, incomplete, these glimpses suffice to reveal the presence of the divine, for the Secret Book says that, apart from spiritual intuition, "people grow old without joy . . . and die . . . without knowing God."

How is it, then, that many people remain oblivious to epinoia? To answer this question, the Secret Book tells a story intended to show that although the creator-god pictured in Genesis is himself only an anthropomorphic image of the divine Source that brought forth the universe, many people mistake this deficient image for God. This story tells how the creator-god himself, being unaware of the "blessed one, the Mother-Father, the blessed and compassionate One" above, boasted that he was the only God ("I am a jealous God; there is none other besides me") (Isaiah 45:5-6, 21). Intent on maintaining sole power, he tried to control his human creatures by forbidding them to eat the fruit of the tree of knowledge. But when Adam and Eve disobeyed him, and chose to seek knowledge of the divine Source above, he realized that they had listened to their inner resource, the luminous epinoia. As soon as the creator-god realized what they had done, he retaliated; first he punished them both, and even cursed the earth itself because of them; then he tried to force the woman to subject herself to the man, saying, "Your husband shall rule over you" [Genesis 3:16]; and, finally, "all his angels cast them out of Paradise," burdening them with "bitter fate" and with daily cares to make them oblivious to the "luminous epinoia." But this is a mythical explanation. Can we find a more practical reason for the suppression of the "luminous epinoia"? I suggest that the author of the Secret Book knew how Christians like Irenaeus challenged those who spoke of the "God beyond God," and insisted that everyone worship only the creator. But while Valentinus's followers often met such challenges with silence, But it would take more than theological argument for Irenaeus's viewpoint to prevail in churches throughout the world: it would take, in fact, the revolution initiated by the Roman emperor Constantine.

This part goes on to reveal how Adam acquired his true spiritual nature and was enlightened by Insight (Epinoia) appearing in the form of the spiritual Eve and by eating of the tree of knowledge, was expelled from paradise, and begot Seth.

Gnostics Gospel, page 49-53:

Other texts discovered at Nag Hammadi demonstrate one striking difference between these "heretical" sources and orthodox ones: Gnostic sources continually use sexual symbolism to describe God. One might expect that these texts would show the influence of archaic pagan traditions of the Mother Goddess, but for the most part, their language is specifically Christian, unmistakably related to a Jewish heritage.

One group of Gnostic sources claims to have received a secret tradition from Jesus through James and Mary Magdalene. Members of this group prayed to both the divine Father and Mother.

Following the gender of the Greek words for "mind" (nous-masculine) and "intelligence" (epinoia-feminine), this author explains that these powers, joined in union, "are discovered to be duality . . . This is Mind in Intelligence, and these are separable from one another, and yet are one, found in a state of duality."

Proponents of these diverse views agreed that the divine is to be understood in terms of a harmonious, dynamic relationship of opposites-a concept that may be akin to the Eastern view of yin and yang, but remains alien to orthodox Judaism and Christianity.

But the author of the Secret Book has in mind the Hebrew term for spirit, ruah, a feminine word; and so concludes that the feminine Person conjoined with the Father and Son must be the Mother.

In the Gospel of Thomas, Jesus contrasts his earthly parents, Mary and Joseph, with his divine Father-the Father of Truth-and his divine Mother, the Holy Spirit. The author interprets a puzzling saying of Jesus' from the New Testament ("Whoever does not hate his father and his mother cannot be my disciple") by adding that "my (earthly) mother [gave me death], but [my] true [Mother] gave me life." So, according to the Gospel of Philip, whoever becomes a Christian gains "both father and mother" for the Spirit (ruah) is "Mother of many."

Grant Paradise to be the womb; for Scripture teaches us that this is a true assumption when it says, "I am He that formed thee in they mother's womb" (Isaiah 44:2) . . . Moses . . . using allegory had declared Paradise to be the womb . . . and Eden, the placenta . . .

But the author ridicules those literal-minded Christians who mistakenly refer the virgin birth to Mary, Jesus' mother, as though she conceived apart from Joseph: "They do not know what they are saying. When did a woman ever conceive by a woman?" Instead, he argues, virgin birth refers to that mysterious union of the two divine powers, the Father of All and the Holy Spirit.

Genesis 3:20

20 (And the man called his wife's name Eve, because she was the mother of all living)

Beyond Belief, page 164-165:

Thus, Eve symbolizes the gift of spiritual understanding, which enables us to reflect—however imperfectly—upon divine reality.

Another book discovered at Nag Hammadi, On the Origin of the World, says that when the first man and woman recognized their nakedness, "they saw that they were naked of spiritual understanding (gnosis)." But then the luminous epinoia "appeared to them shining with light, and awakened their consciousness."

The Secret Book intends this story to show that we have a latent capacity within our hearts and minds that links us to the divine—not in our ordinary state of mind but when this hidden capacity awakens. Because the term epinoia has no precise equivalent in English, I shall leave it in Greek. To speak of various modes of consciousness susceptible to revelation, the author of the Secret Book invokes a cluster of words related to the Greek verb noein, which means "perceive," "think," or "be aware."

Beyond Belief, page 100:

Finally, echoing what Paul writes in his first letter to the Corinthians, the prayer concludes, "Grant what no angel's eye has seen and what no ruling power's ear has heard, and what has not entered into the human heart . . . since I have faith and hope."

Those who wrote, translated, and carefully copied works such as the Secret Book of James and the Prayer of the Apostle Paul may have known about techniques that certain Jewish groups used to induce a state of ecstasy and invoke visions. For example, one group of Jewish ascetics living in Egypt at the time of Jesus, called the Therapeutae, practiced a rigorous regimen of prayer, celibacy, fasting, and singing to prepare themselves to receive "the vision of God." Some of the Dead Sea Scrolls also offer prayers and rituals apparently intended O help the devout enter God's presence and join in worship with angels. For to this day, many Jews and Christians use mystical language in worship services every week, or even every day, at a culminating moment understood uniting the human congregation with the angels, as they join in singing what the prophet Isaiah says angels sing in heaven: "Holy, holy, holy; Lord God almighty; heaven and earth are full of your glory." Isaiah says that he heard this song when he received a vision and was taken into God's presence.

Genesis 5:24

24 And Enoch walked with God, and he was no more seen: for God took him away.

Author's note:

The Books of Enoch contain details about the roles of the angels and the fate of the fallen angels. The Church Fathers did not believe his work inspired because it wasn't included in the Torah.

Scholars of Jewish history and literature are also investigating an enormous wealth of mystical literature that flourished for about a thousand years preceding kabbalah. Some of these so-called hekalot texts focus upon the figure of Enoch who, according to Genesis, "walked with God" and, without dying, was taken up into God's presence. Even before the first century B.C.E., Enoch had become a paradigm for those seeking access to heavenly wisdom. Other groups of Jews were devoted to the so-called Merkabah literature, which thrived from the second century through the sixth. These writings emerged from Jewish teachers, and their disciples who tried to act upon hints they found in the prophet Ezekiel's marvelous vision of God enthroned upon a chariot shining like fire, borne by winged cherubim, and praised by the angelic host.

The Gnostic Gospel, page 11:

The resurrection, they insisted, was not a unique event in the past: instead, it symbolized how Christ's presence could be experienced in the present. What mattered was not literal seeing, but spiritual vision.

Section 1.2.6

Meditation

The Gnostic Gospels, page 12:

Paul first encountered Jesus in a dramatic vision, and later in a trance (Luke claims to record his words: "When I had returned to Jerusalem and was praying in the temple, I fell into a trance and saw him speaking to me",

Peter, deep in trance, saw Christ, who explained that "I am the intellectual spirit, filled with radiant light." Gnostic accounts often mention how the recipients respond to Christ's presence with intense emotions-terror, awe, distress, and joy.

Gospel of Nazirenes, page xl (Prologue):

This quote from Clement, though somewhat abbreviated, can be found as early as Plato ("Timaeus 90") and in the Gnostic Gospel of Thomas, as well. It can also be found twice in The Gospel of the Nazirenes. Here, are both quotations in their entirety, starting with Chapter 27, verse 4, (The Sermon on the Mount, Part 3):

"Ask, and it shall be given you; seek, and you shall find; knock and it shall be opened to you; for everyone that asks, receives. And he that seeks, will not rest until he finds, and he that has found shall marvel, and he that has marvelled shall reign, and he that has reigned shall rest."

Job 7:13-14

13 When I say, My couch shall relieve me, and my bed shall bring comfort in my meditation,

14 Then fearest thou me with dreams, and astonishest me with visions.

The Second Coming of Christ, page 932:

Thus, Jesus goes on to say: "Every devotee by meditation must saturate salt himself with the fire of realization, that he may be acceptable to God on earth and in the astral world. Everyone who makes a spiritual sacrifice of material indulgences for God-communion will find his soul 'salted' or saturated with divine realization." As salt bestows good flavor on food also preserves it, so when the human consciousness is salted with divine realization it is saved from the delusion of decay and death and savors its native immortality. But if by concentrating on material pleasures and egotism the preservative flavor of the divine salt is lost, so also is lost all goodness it could impart in the seasoning of the soul. "A true disciple is like good salt. He seasons his own life and the lives of others by his spirit of renunciation and his cultivation of divine qualities and realization. Just as, unsavory salt cannot be used for anything, so a disciple who loses the focus of his renunciation and his sense of self-discipline is useless to himself and to others, until he acquires the fresh salt of Self-realization by daily meditation and by absorbing through attentive goodly fellowship the divine peace of the Self-realization expressed by other God-seeking souls."

Second Coming of Christ, page 1209:

If one lives rightly and learns the higher forms of meditation, one develops the spiritual magnetism that neutralizes the animal magnetism of the physical body. With freedom from the "original sin" of sex attraction, one finds the true soul mate in a spiritual marriage on earth, or in a dream or vision, or in the astral world; or supremely, in direct union with God. The love and friendship with the Divine cultivated in the bower of meditation can never be lost. It shall last beyond the portals of the tomb unto Eternity.

The full implication of the words of Jesus, an impossible view for body-bound spiritually nearsighted persons, is best understood by those who meditate deeply and merge their concentration in the Christ Consciousness which Jesus possessed. Otherwise, much truth is lost in misinterpretation, mistranslation, or shallow cognition.

All devotees may find the door to the kingdom of God by concentrating on the spiritual eye, the Christ Consciousness center at the point between the eyebrows. Long and deep meditation as taught by a true guru enables one gradually to convert the consciousness of the material body into that of the astral body, and with the awakened faculties of astral perception to intuit deeper and deeper states of consciousness until one reaches oneness with the Source of consciousness. Entering the door of the spiritual eye, one leaves behind all attachments to matter and the physical body and gains access into the interior infinitudes of God's kingdom.

Matthew 7:7-8

7 Ask, and it shall be given you: seek, and ye shall find: knock, and it shall be opened unto you.

8 For whosoever asketh, receiveth: and he that seeketh, findeth: and to him that knocketh, it shall be opened.

2 Corinthians 4:16

16 Therefore we faint not, but through our outward man perish, yet the inward man is renewed daily.

Philippians 4:5-7

5 Let your patient mind be known unto all men. The Lord is at hand.

6 Be nothing careful, but in all things let your requests be showed unto God in prayer and supplication with giving of thanks.

7 And the peace of God which passeth all understanding, shall preserve your hearts and minds in Christ Jesus.

Galatians 1:16

16 To reveal his son in me, that I should preach him among the Gentiles immediately, I communicated not with flesh and blood.

Isaiah Effect, page 73:

John replied, "Is there any hope?" The voice (Jesus') replies to John, echoing a memory of the greatest possibilities for today and future generations: "There is always hope, O thou for whom heaven and earth were created . . ."

Suddenly the vision of death and destruction fades from view and he is shown another scenario, a second possibility. Rather than the end of all that humanity has grown to know and love, this new possibility illustrates an outcome of a different nature. "But I saw not what befell them, my vision changed, and I saw a new Heaven and a new Earth, for the first heaven and the first earth were passed away, and I heard a great voice saying, there should be no more death, neither sorrow, nor crying, neither shall there be any more pain."

Psalms 119:148

Mine eyes prevent the night watches, to meditate in thy word.

Acts 9:17-18

17 Then Ananias went his way, and entered into that house, and put his hands on him, and saith, Brother Saul, the Lord hath sent me (even Jesus that appeared unto thee in the way as thou camest) that thou mightest receive thy sight, and be filled with the holy Ghost.

18 And immediately there fell from his eyes as it had been scales, and suddenly he received sight, and arose, and was baptized,

2 Corinthians 11:28

Besides the things which are outward, I am cumbered daily, and have the care of all of the churches.

1 Thessalonians 1:8

For from you sounded out the word of the Lord, not in Macedonia and in Achaia only: But your faith also toward God, spread abroad in all quarters, that we need not to speak anything.

2 Corinthians 5:8-9

8 Nevertheless, we are bold, and love rather to remove out of body, and to dwell with the Lord.

9 Wherefore also we covet, that both dwelling at home, and removing from home, we may be acceptable to Him.

1 Corinthians 6:19

19 Know ye not, that your body is the temple of the holy Ghost, which is in you, whom ye have of God? And ye are not your own.

1 Thessalonians 1:3

3 Without ceasing, remembering your effectual faith, and diligent love, and the patience of your hope in our Lord Jesus Christ, in the sight of God, even our Father.

Romans 8:25

25 But if we hope for that we see not, we do with patience abide for it.

Galatians 4:9

9 But now seeing ye know God, yea, rather are of God, how turn ye again unto impotent and beggarly rudiments, where unto as from the beginning ye will be in bondage again.

Ephesians 6:15-20

15 And your feet shod with the preparation of the Gospel of peace.

16 Above all, take the shield of Faith, wherewith ye may quench all the fiery darts of the wicked,

17 And take the helmet of Salvation, and the sword of the Spirit, which is the word of God.

18 And pray always with all manner prayer and supplication in the spirit: and watch thereunto with all perseverance and supplication for all Saints,

19 And for me, that utterance may be given unto me, that I may open my mouth boldly to publish the secret of the Gospel,

20 Whereof I am the ambassador in bonds, that therein I may speak boldly, as I ought to speak.

Romans 8:24

24 For we are saved by hope: but hope that is seen, is not hope: for how can a man hope for that which he seeth.

The Gospel of the Nazirenes, page 97:

Chapter 40, verse 4

4 For in them is fulfilled the prophecy of Isaiah, which said, "And seeing, they shall see and shall not perceive; for this people's heart is waxed gross, and their ears are dull of hearing, and their eyes they have closed, lest at any time they should see with their eyes, and hear with their ears, and should understand with their heart, be converted and healed."

Hebrews 9:28

28 So Christ was once offered to take away the sins of many, and unto them that look for Him, shall he appear the second time without sin unto salvation.

Matthew 16:24

24 Jesus then said to his disciples, If any man will follow me, let him forsake himself: and take up his cross, and follow me.

John 14:7-8

7 If ye had known me, ye should have known my Father also: and from henceforth ye know him, and have seen him.

8 Philip said unto him, Lord, show us thy Father, and it sufficeth us.

John 14:1-4, 13-20

1 Let not your heart be troubled: ye believe in God, believe also in me.

2 In my Father's house are many dwelling places: if it were not so, I would have told you: I go to prepare a place for you.

3 And if I go to prepare a place for you, I will come again, and receive you unto myself, that where I am, there may ye be also.

4 And whither I go, ye know, and the way ye know.

13 And whatsoever ye ask in my Name, that will I do, that the Father may be glorified in the Son.

14 If ye shall ask anything in my Name, I will do it.

15 If ye love me, keep my commandments.

16 And I will pray the Father, and he shall give you another Comforter, that he may abide with you forever,

17 Even the Spirit of truth, whom the world cannot receive, because it seeth him not, neither knoweth him: but ye know him: for he dwelleth with you, and shall be in you.

18 I will not leave you fatherless: but I will come to you.

19 Yet a little while, and the world shall see me no more, but ye shall see me: because I live, ye shall live also.

20 At that day shall ye know that I am in my Father, and you in me, and I in you.

Ephesians 5:8-14

8 For ye were once darkness, but are now light in the Lord: walk as children of light.

9 For the fruit of the Spirit is in all goodness, and righteousness, and truth.

10 Approving that which is pleasing to the Lord.

11 And have no fellowship with the unfruitful works of darkness, but even reprove them rather.

12 For it is shame even to speak of the things which are done of them in secret.

13 But all things when they are reproved of the light, are manifest: for it is light that maketh all things manifest.

14 Wherefore he saith, Awake thou that sleepest, and stand up from the dead, and Christ shall give thee light.

Edgar Cayce on Angels, page 29:

The responsibility for creating either a harmonious or chaotic future rests solely with us. The readings said that ten people can save a city from destruction by sincerely meditating and praying for peace. Twenty can save a nation.

The Gospel of Nazirenes, page 115:

Chapter 47, verse 9

9 The Unbegotten is Spirit, and they who worship the Most High must— worship in Spirit and in Truth, at all times, and in all places.

Section 1.2.7

Fullness

The Gospel of Truth, page 45 of Nag Hammadi Scriptures:

The Father Restores Fullness

This is the Word of the gospel about the discovery of fullness, for those who await salvation coming from above. Their hope, for which they are waiting, is in waiting, and this is their image, the light in which there is no shadow. At this time the fullness is about to come. Deficiency of matter is not from the infinity of the Father, who came to give time to deficiency. In fact, it is not right to say that the incorruptible would actually come in this manner. The Father's depth is profound, and the thought of error is not with him. It is something that has fallen, and something that can readily be set upright through the discovery of the one who has come to what he would restore.

This restoration is called repentance. The reason that the incorruptible breathed out and followed after the one who sinned was so that the sinner might find rest. Forgiveness is what remains for the light in deficiency, the Word of fullness. For a doctor rushes to where there is sickness, since that is the doctor's wish. The person in need does not hide it, because the doctor has what the patient needs. Thus fullness, which has no deficiency but fills up deficiency, is provided to fill a person's need, so that the person may receive grace. While deficient, the person had no grace, and because of this a diminishing took place where there was no grace. When the diminished part was restored, the person in need was revealed as fullness. This is what it means to discover the light of truth that has shone toward a person: it is unchangeable.

Ephesians 3:19

19 And to know the love of Christ, which passeth knowledge, that ye may be filled with all fullness of God.

2 Timothy 1:14

14 That worthy thing, which was committed to thee, keep through the holy Ghost, which dwelleth in us.

Galatians 6:18

18 Brethen, the grace of our Lord Jesus Christ be in your spirit (with your minds and hearts), Amen.

Philippians 3:3

3 For we are the circumcision, which worship God in the spirit, and rejoice in Christ Jesus, and have no confidence in the flesh.

John 14:26-28

26 But the Comforter, which is the holy Ghost, whom the Father will send in my Name, he shall teach you all things, and bring all things to your remembrance, which I have told you.

27 Peace I leave with you: my peace I give unto you: not as the world giveth, give I unto you. Let not your heart be troubled, nor fear.

28 Ye have heard how I said unto you, I go away, and will come unto you. If ye loved me, ye would verily rejoice, because I said, I go unto the Father: for the Father is greater than I.

1 John 3:24

24 For he that keepeth his commandments, dwelleth in Him, and he in Him: And hereby we know that he abideth in us, even by that spirit which He hath given us.

The Gospel of Truth, page 46 of Nag Hammadi Scriptures:

The Place of Rest

All will speak individually about where they have come from and how they were established in the place of rest. They will hasten to return and receive from that place, the place where they stood once before, and they will taste of that place, be nourished, and grow.

Their own place of rest is their fullness. All the emanations from the Father are fullnesses, and all his emanations find their root in the one who caused them all to grow from himself. He assigned their destinies. They all appear so that through their own thought [they might be perfected]. For the place, to which they extend their thought is their root, which lifts them up through all the heights to the Father.

Ephesians 3:18

18 That ye, being rooted and grounded in love, may be able to comprehend with all saints, what is the breadth and length, and depth, and height.

Section 1.3

Kingdom of God

Romans 14:17

17 For the kingdom of God, it is not meat or drink, but righteousness, and peace and joy in the Holy Ghost.

Isaiah 66:1-2

1 Thus saith the Lord, The heaven is my throne, and the earth is my footstool: where is that house that ye will build unto me? and where is that place of my rest?

2 For all these things hath mine hand made, and all these things have been, saith the Lord: and to him will I look, even to him that is poor, and of a contrite spirit, and trembleth at my words.

Luke 12:29-32

29 Therefore ask not what ye shall eat, or what ye shall drink, neither hang you in suspense.

30 For all such things the people of the world seek for: and your Father knoweth that ye have need of these things.

31 But rather seek ye after the kingdom of God, and all these things shall be cast upon you.

32 Fear not, little flock: for it is your Father's pleasure to give you the kingdom

Revelation 21:1

1 And I saw a new heaven, and a new earth: for the first heaven, and the first earth were passed away, and there was no more sea.

Second Coming of Christ, page 1177:

And when he was demanded of the Pharisees, when the kingdom of God should come, he answered them and said, "The kingdom of God cometh not with observation: Neither shall they say, 'Lo here!' or, 'lo there!' for, behold, the kingdom of God is within you" (Luke 17:20-21).

"The kingdom of God—of eternal, immutable, ever-newly blissful Cosmic Consciousness—is within you. Behold your soul as a reflection of the immortal Spirit, and you will find your Self encompassing the infinite empire of God-love, God-wisdom, God-bliss existing in every particle of vibratory creation and in the vibrationless Transcendental Absolute."

The teachings of Jesus about God's kingdom—sometimes in direct language, sometimes in parables pregnant with metaphysical meaning—may be said to be the core of the entirety of his message.

The Gospel records that at the very outset of his public ministry, "Jesus came into Galilee, preaching the gospel of the kingdom of God." His exhortation to "seek ye first the kingdom of God" is at the heart of his Sermon on the Mount. The only prayer he is known to have given his disciples beseeches God, "Thy kingdom come." Again and again he spoke of the kingdom of the Heavenly Father and the method of its attainment: "Except a man be born of water and of the Spirit, he cannot enter into the kingdom of God."(John 3:5).

"Strive to enter in at the strait gate: for many, I say unto you, will seek to enter in, and shall not be able."(Luke 13:24)

"No man hath ascended up to heaven, but he that came down from heaven, even the Son of man which is in heaven. And as Moses lifted up the serpent in the wilderness, even so must the Son of man be lifted up." (John 3:13-14)

"And if thine eye offend thee, pluck it out: it is better for thee to enter into the kingdom of God with one eye, than having two eyes to be cast into hell fire."(Mark 9:47)

"I am the door: by me if any man enter in, he shall be saved, and shall go in and out, and find pasture."(John 10:9)

Many people think of heaven as a physical location, a point of space far above the atmosphere and beyond the stars. Others interpret Jesus' statements about the advent of the kingdom of God as referring to the coming of a Messiah to establish and rule over a divine kingdom on earth. In fact, the kingdom of God and the kingdom of heaven consist, respectively, of the transcendental infinitudes of Cosmic Consciousness and the heavenly causal and astral realms of vibratory creation that are considerably finer and more harmonized with God's will than those physical vibrations clustered together as planets, air, and earthly surroundings.

"If those who lead you say, 'Look! The kingdom is in heaven,' then the birds of heaven will precede you. If they say to you, 'It is in the sea,' then the fish will precede you. But the kingdom is within you and it is outside of you. If you will know yourselves, then you will be known, and you will realize that you are children of the living Father. But if you do not know yourselves, then you dwell in poverty, and you are poverty" (The Gospel of Thomas, verse 3). His disciples said to him, " . . . When will the new world come?" He said to them, "What you are looking forward to have come, but you don't know it" (The Gospel of Thomas, verse 51).

Jesus' disciples said unto him: "When will the kingdom come?" Jesus answered, "It will not come by waiting for it. People will not say, 'Look! Here, it is!' or 'There it is!' But the kingdom of the Father is spread out upon the earth and people do not see it" (The Gospel of Thomas, verse 113).

For every body-circumscribed soul, the Kingdom of God awaits discovery by those who delve in meditation to transcend human consciousness and reach the successively higher states of superconsciousness, Christ Consciousness, and Cosmic Consciousness. Those who meditate deeply, concentrating intensely within their state of silence, or neutralized thoughts, withdraw their minds from material objects of sight, sound, smell, taste, and touch—from all bodily sensations and disturbing mental restlessness. In this focused stillness within, they find an ineffable sense of peace. Peace is the first glimpse of the inner kingdom of God.

Edgar Cayce on Angels, page 161-162:

The reference to the kingdom was not indicating a physical place, but a state of consciousness. Jesus said that the kingdom of heaven is within us.

" . . . O Daniel, a man greatly beloved, understand the words that I speak unto thee, stand upright; for unto thee am I now sent . . . Fear not, Daniel: for from the first day that though didst set thine heart to understand . . . thy words were heard, and I am come for thy words." (10:11-12) The key passage here is "set thine heart to understand." When we desire to comprehend the spiritual nature of our lives, the very thoughts go into the ethers as a message to the celestial hierarchies.

We are just as capable to have communion with God as the prophet Daniel. The problem lies in our feelings of unworthiness.

The coming of the Messiah was foretold again and again in the Old Testament by the prophets. This advent represents not only the physical manifestation of Christ, but the inner awakening which was promised from the beginning to each soul.

The angels had been readied from the beginning for the great redemption of humanity.

Luke 17:21

21 Neither shall men say, Lo here, or lo there: for behold, the kingdom of God is within you.

Edgar Cayce on Angels, page 174:

Further, it reveals that the benefit of understanding it is "a new heaven and a new earth," (21:1) which translates, according to Cayce, to a new state of consciousness of the soul's oneness with God.

Revelation 21:1-4

1 And I saw a new heaven, and a new earth: for the first heaven, and the first earth were passed away, and there was no more sea.

2 And I John saw the holy city new Jerusalem come down from God out of heaven, prepared as a bride trimmed for her husband.

3 And I heard a great voice out of heaven, saying, Behold, the Tabernacle of God is with men, and he will dwell with them: and they shall be his people, and God himself shall be their God with them.

4 And God shall wipe away all tears from their eyes, and there shall be no more death, neither sorrow, neither crying, neither shall there be any more pain: for the first things are passed.

The Gospel of Thomas, page 153 of Nag Hammadi Scriptures:

Verse 113

113 His disciples said to him, "When will the kingdom come?" "It will not come by watching for it. It will not be said,' 'Look, here it is,' or 'Look, there it is.' Rather, the Father's kingdom is spread out upon the earth, and people do not see it."

The Gospel of the Nazirenes, page 234

Chapter 94, verse 5-6

5 And another asked him saying, "Jesus, under the law, Moses clad the Priests with garments of beauty for their ministration in the Temple. Shall we also clothe them to whom we commit the ministry of sacred things as you have taught us?" And Jesus answered, "White linen is the righteousness of the Saints, but truly the time approaches when Zion shall be desolate, and after the time of her affliction is past, she shall rise and put on her beautiful garments as it is written.

6 But seek first the Kingdom of Righteousness, and all these things shall be added unto you. In all things seek simplicity, and give not occasion to vain glory. Seek first to be clothed with charity, and the garment of salvation and the robe of righteousness will follow.

Second Coming of Christ, page 920:

Biblical scholars who profess to find no description of heaven by Jesus in the Gospels do not understand the hidden sense of his words. In this passage, Christ rejects any notion of his kingdom as a limited locality, thus indicating its omnipresent nature—in Christ Consciousness and Cosmic Consciousness.

Second Coming of Christ, page 914:

On this axiom, Jesus taught those who seek greatness on earth or in heaven: "Verily I say unto you, except ye be converted, and become as little children, ye shall not enter into the kingdom of heaven;

Matthew 19:13-15 and Mark 10:14-15: "Suffer the little children to come unto me, and forbid them not: for of such is the kingdom of God. Verily I say unto you, whosoever shall not receive the kingdom of God as a little child, he shall not enter therein."

The Secret Book of James, page 29 of Nag Hammadi Scriptures:

The Last Word

Peter responded to these comments and said, "Sometimes you urge us on toward heaven's kingdom, but at other times you turn us away, master. Sometimes you encourage us, draw us toward faith, and promise us life, but at other times you drive us away from heaven's kingdom."

The master answered and said to us, "I have offered you faith many times—and has revealed myself to you, James—and you have not known me. Now I see you often rejoicing. And although you are delighted about the promise of life, you are sad and gloomy when you are taught about the kingdom."

"Nevertheless, you, through faith and knowledge, have received life. So disregard rejection when you hear it, but when you hear about the promise, be joyful all the more.

"I tell you the truth, whoever will receive life and believe in the kingdom will never leave it, not even if the Father wants to banish him.

The Revelation of Peter, page 495 of Nag Hammadi Scriptures:

The Little Ones Eventually Will Reign

I said, "I am afraid because of what you have told me. Although there are only a few phonies among us, there are many others who lead astray and subdue multitudes of living ones. And when they speak your name, people will believe them."

The Savior replied, "For a specified time proportionate to their error, they will rule over the little ones. And after the completion of error, the being of immortal understanding, who does not grow old, will become new, and the little ones will rule over their rulers. That being will pull out their error by its root, and put it to shame and expose it for all the liberties it has taken. Peter, such people will never change."

Section 1.4

Christian Life and Faith

Second Coming of Christ, page 1027:

And when Jesus saw that he answered discreetly, he said unto him, "Thou art not far from the kingdom of God." And no man after that durst ask him any question (Mark 12:28-34).

The whole purpose of religion—indeed, of life itself—is encapsulated in the two paramount commandments cited by Lord Jesus in these verses. In them lies the essence of eternal truth distinguishing all bona-fide spiritual paths, the irreducible imperative that man must embrace as an individualized soul separated from God if he would reclaim the realization of oneness with his Maker.

"This do, and thou shalt live," Jesus told the lawyer who had asked how to obtain eternal life. That is: "If you can love God wholly in actual communion in daily meditation, and show by your actions your love for your neighbor (your divine brother). [Deuteronomy 6:4-5 and Leviticus 19:18]

The Teachings of Silvanus, page 510, 511 of The Nag Hammadi Scriptures:

Have a good number of friends, but not many counselors. First, examine your counselor, and don't honor anyone who flatters. Their speech is sweet as honey, but their hearts are full of poison. For whenever they think they have become a reliable friend, then they will deceitfully turn against you and throw you down into the mud.

Do not trust anyone as a friend. For the whole world has become deceitful, every person is troubled in vain. All things of the world are without profit; they happen in vain. There is no real friend; not even a brother, since each person seeks his own advantage. My child, do not have anyone as a friend. If you acquire one, do not entrust yourself to him.

Entrust yourself to God alone, both as father and as friend. 'For everyone goes about in deceit.' The whole earth is full of suffering and pain, things in which there is no profit. If you wish to lead your life in tranquility, do not keep company with anyone. Even if you do keep company with them, be as if you do not. Be pleasing to God, and you will not need anyone.

Live with Christ, and he will save you. For he is the true light and the sun of life. Just as the visible sun shines on physical eyes, so Christ illuminates every mind and heart. For if one who is wicked during his lifetime has an evil death, how much more so does one who has a blind mind. For every blind person remains incapable of seeing it, So it is with people who do not have a sound mind. They do not delight in acquiring the light of Christ, which is reason. For everything visible is a copy of what is invisible. As a fire burns in a place without being confined to it, so it is with the sun in the sky: all of its rays extend to places on earth. It is a single being that Christ has, and he gives light to every place.

The Teachings of Silvanus, page 511 of Nag Hammadi Scriptures:

This is also the way he speaks about our mind, using the image of a lamp burning and lighting up the whole place. Existing only in a part of the soul, it still gives light to all the parts of the body.

In addition, I will say something more important. The mind, in terms of its actual being, is in a place, which means it is in the body. But in terms of the thought process, the mind is not in a place. For how can it be in a place when it contemplates every place?

The Teachings of Silvanus, page 504 of Nag Hammadi Scriptures:

Put an end to every kind of immature conduct. Acquire for yourself strength of mind and soul, and strengthen your struggle against every kind of foolishness consisting of the passions of erotic love, base wickedness, love of praise, fondness for strife, tiresome jealousy, wrath, anger, and avaricious desire.

Guard your encampment with weapons and spears. Arm yourself with all the soldiers, which are words, with the commanders, which are counsels, and with your mind as a guiding principle. My child, throw every robber out of your gates. Guard all your gates with torches, which are the words, and by these mean you will acquire a tranquil life.

But the person who will not guard these things will become like a captured city, desolate and trampled by wild animals. For thoughts that are not good are evil beasts. Your city will be filled with robbers, and you will not obtain peace, only all kinds of savage beasts. The evil one, who is a tyrant, is lord over them.

The Teachings of Silvanus, page 499-503 of Nag Hammadi Scriptures:

In what follows, the pupil is warned to beware of the adversary (the devil), whose wiles include "strange kinds of knowledge," "spurious knowledge . . . disguised as mysterious sayings." One should rely on Christ alone. In material that is also attributed to St. Antony, it is asserted that a wise person watches his speech and does not put his trust in human friendship, but trusts in God alone. This section has been labeled "the most Egyptian" of all the material in the Teachings of Silvanus. The second main part of the tractate begins with a discussion of Christ as the "true light and the sun of life." God in his own incorporeal being is impossible to know. He can only be known through Christ, "who bears the image of the Father". As for Christ, "even if he was begotten, he is unbegotten," comprehensible in his human nature but "incomprehensible in terms of his actual being (hypostasis)"—that is, his divine nature. God is ineffable, and speculation as to his being is dangerous. Examine yourself to make sure that you have your mind turned "toward the light of heaven," and walk in the way of Christ.

The teacher then goes on to refer to the descent of Christ to "the underworld", here taken as a reference to Christ's incarnation. One should choose "the gift of Christ" and guard oneself from every kind of evil. In a hymn passage Christ is praised as "Wisdom," "Word," "life," "power," "door," "light," "angel," and "good shepherd." One should entrust oneself entirely to him and gladly drink of "the true vine of Christ". One can avoid sin by fearing and pleasing God, for where Christ is, sin is idle. One should let Christ into the temple of the soul and thus become truly blessed.

In another hymn passage, Christ is again praised for his descent to the underworld, that is, his incarnation on behalf of humanity, which "humanity might become like God". The teacher then alludes to the apostle Paul as the epitome of piety and wisdom. Christ is praised as the one whom, victorious as the first contender, will give the crown to every contender.

In another hymn passage, the teacher praises God, who has glorified his Word. He then launches into a hymn of praise to Christ as "light from the power of God" and "a pure emanation of the glory of the Almighty", a hymn whose first part is a rephrasing of the hymn to Wisdom in the Wisdom of Solomon 7:25-26.

Christ is praised for his efforts on behalf of everyone, helping the contender to "fight the great fight" against the powers of the adversary. He is praised as the hand of God the Father, who fashions all things, for he exists always as Son of the Father, the eternal "image of the Father. It is impossible to know God as he is, and one lacking in self-knowledge will not even be able to know Christ or the angels or other incorporeal beings. The author concludes his teachings with exhortations to his pupil to open the door to the knowledge of God by "knocking" on Him. He should guard the wisdom of Christ in the knowledge that "God's way is always profitable."

My children, do not swim in just any kind of water, and do not allow you to be defiled by strange kinds of knowledge. Don't you know that the schemes of the adversary are not few, and that he has a variety of tricks? They have especially robbed the foolish person of the proverbial snake's shrewdness. For it is right for you to be in agreement with these two, with the snake's shrewdness and the dove's innocence. Otherwise, he will come to you in the guise of a flatterer and true friend, saying, "I advise good things for you." But if you received him as a true friend, you did not recognize this one's deceitfulness.

For he casts into our heart evil thoughts disguised as good ones, hypocrisy as secure shrewdness, avarice as conservative frugality, love of glory as what is beautiful, boastfulness and pride as great austerity, and godlessness as great godliness. For the one who says, "I have many gods," is godless." And he casts spurious knowledge into your heart disguised as mysterious sayings.

Who will be able to comprehend his thoughts and various devices? For those who wish to accept him as king he is a "great mind." My child, how will you be able to comprehend this one's schemes or his soul-killing counsel? For his devices and the schemes of his wickedness are many. And how will you be able to perceive his ways of entry, that is, how he will enter your soul? And how will you be able to perceive in what garment he will enter you?

Accept Christ, who is able to set you free. He has taken on that one's devices, so that through these he might destroy him with guile! For this is the king you have, who is forever invincible. Against him no one will be able to fight or speak a word. This is your king and your father. There is none like him. The divine teacher is with you at all times as a helper. He meets you because of the good you have within you.

Matthew 7:20

20 Therefore by their fruits ye shall know them.

Isaiah 64:4-6

4 For since the beginning of the world, they have not heard nor understood with the ear, neither hath the eye seen another God beside thee, which doeth so to him that waiteth for him.

5 Thou didst meet him, that rejoiced in thee, and did justly: they remembered thee in thy ways: behold, thou art angry, for we have sinned: yet in them is continuance, and we shall be saved.

6 But we have all been as an unclean thing, and all our righteousness is as filthy cloths, and we all do fade like a leaf, and our iniquities like the wind have taken us away.

Colossians 2:8

8 Beware lest there be any man that spoil you through philosophy, and vain deceit, through the traditions of men, according to the rudiments of the world, and not after Christ.

Jeremiah 31:33-34

33 But this shall be the covenant that I will make with the house of Israel, after those days, saith the Lord, I will put my law in their inward parts, and write it in their hearts, and will be their God, and they shall be my people.

34 And they shall teach no more every man his neighbor, and every man his brother, saying, Know the Lord: for they shall all know me from the least of them unto the greatest of them, saith the Lord: for I will forgive their iniquity, and will remember their sins no more.

Section 1.5

Soul, Spirit, Flesh

Section 1.5.1

Creation of Human soul (spirit)

Complete Books of Enoch, page 141:

2 Enoch, Chapter 26

"I summoned the very lowest a second time, and said, 'Let Archas come out hard!' and he came out hard from the invisible. He came out hard, heavy, and very red."

"I said, 'Be opened, Archas, and let there be born from you!' and he came undone, and an age came forth, very great and very dark, bearing the creation of all lower things, and I saw that it was good. I said to him, 'Go down below, and make yourself firm, and be a foundation for the lower things!' It happened. He went down and fixed himself, and became the foundation for the lower things, and below the darkness there is nothing else."

Edgar Cayce on Angels, page 144:

The Creation of Humankind

In order for Amilius to enter into the earth, he would need to create for himself a new kind of body which would not be like the monstrous creations the fallen ones had made for themselves.

A body which would be made of every element of the earth kingdom and yet have the spiritual circuitry to enable it to remain in contact with the realms of God and the angels. In this way, this new being would be of materiality and yet also of God. It would contain earth and spirit-a harmony never before realized.

God worked through Amilius to gradually create, in the realms of spirit, a design for this new body. As the pattern for the body was nearing completion, there were created seven spiritual centers or circuits.

Author's note:

For details on seven spiritual centers, please refer to Figure 1 in Section 4.5.

These centers, called chakras in Sanskrit, created a perfect union between the material and spirit worlds. The three higher centers corresponded to the highest realms of God: Creator Spirit, Son Spirit, and Holy Spirit. Their precise pattern, imprinted within the spiritual consciousness of the soul-body, insured the devotee that the soul would never be out of attunement with the Divine.

Chaos had resulted when souls became trapped in the imperfect bodies of monstrosities because their sensuous desires had cut them off from communion with God. In this new body, however, a soul could always be one step from remembering its divine purpose through those indwelling spiritual centers.

Author's note:

You are considered a born again after you have received the Holy Spirit. Please refer to Section 2.3 for details about Baptism. However, receiving the Holy Spirit is a mystery. You will see you have received one. It doesn't come as a "fuzzy" spirit while you're praying. This fuzziness idea is probably coming from your attunement with the angels. They are there for us. However, the impact by a Holy Spirit is remarkably thorough, and you will remember it. Your whole body "vibrates" once the impact comes. You will immediately test it like you have never experienced before. I felt this while I was asleep during one Fall night in 1999. I had just started meditating at the time.

Edgar Cayce on Angels, page 143-144:

It was a perfect plan, and Amilius had the blessings and promise of the celestial guardians, the archangels, the Creator Himself, that he would not make this journey alone. The sons and daughters of God-144,000 of them-would also assist Amilius in becoming mortal. This consideration had its place in the plan of redemption for if the souls did forget, they would have the intimate guidance of the higher angels and archangels who never left the presence of God, who would, at every turn in the material world, remind them of their original mission.

Until the mission was complete, until every soul who had forgotten God returned, the angels from on high would stand in eternal vigilance, guarding and directing not only the individual souls, but groups, nations, and races. The angels' role would be as messengers of the incarnate souls, and the means for divining messages would include apparitions, dreams and visions, omens and signs.

Author's note:

We just need to keep our praying and desire God to help us; the angels will be there for us. They will only come to help if we "will" for help. Keep in mind; it is all about free will. God does not interfere with your available choices. It's up to you to do the right choice. The power of praying start the progress for the angels to show help. This help is always "just enough" what you want and never to the level of excess or for the wrong reason.

Edgar Cayce on Angels, page 144:

As God existed in a triune of consciousness, so the new human in the earth would also exist with a body, a mind, a spirit. Each element could have separate functions, but would be contained within the one body. First, the soul would be the source of all spiritual knowledge and activity in the earth. Second, the mind would draw from the soul to create circumstances through the power of thought. Yet upon the mind was set the perfect awareness of God-what the readings called the Christ Consciousness. Third would be the physical body itself, the new vehicle with which to carry out the mission of the soul and mind.

The animal kingdom had already been in existence for a long time prior to the arrival of humans, yet the animals did not possess the power to choose.

At last, Amilius had completed the soul pattern of the body, which would be a channel for entities to redeem the material world. It was a glorious moment of the beginning, the beginning of the journey to divine remembrance. The Bible depicts this event as the true origin of the world, "When the morning stars sang together, and all the sons of God shouted for joy." (Job 38:7) The morning stars were the angels who rejoiced that a way had been prepared so that the rest of the celestial family would return to the fold of God.

The entity, known as Amilius in the spiritual realms, would be called Adam, and his coming was glorious in the earth. The Cayce readings confirm that 144,000 souls followed the pattern of Adam, created the humanoid bodies we now occupy, and the races were born.

In building Adam's body in the earth, it was necessary that there be a feminine counterpart. This was done, according to the readings, by Adam going into meditation and traveling in an out-of-body state to the realms where spiritual creation was taking place-the realms of the angels. There, under the direction of God, the soul of Adam separated itself into two. In the story of Genesis, Eve being created from the "rib of Adam" actually refers to the feminine side of his soul manifesting as an individual. In Hebrew "rib" translates as "side."

"God created man and woman first as one, in spirit. Then male and female in flesh. As the mind became aware of its duality in matter, there was the necessity for the positive and negative force to be separate, yet cooperative.

Ephesians 3:16

16 That he might grant you according to the riches of his glory, that ye may be strengthened by his spirit in the inner man.

1 Corinthians 2:9-11

9 But as it is written, The things which eye hath not seen, neither ear hath heard, neither came into man's heart, are, which God hath prepared for them that love him.

10 But God hath revealed them unto us by his Spirit: for the spirit searcheth all things, yea, the deep things of God.

11 For what man knoweth the things of a man, save the spirit of a man, which is in him? even so the things of God knoweth no man, but the Spirit of God.

Revelation 2:4 "Nevertheless, I have somewhat against thee, because thou hast left thy first love."

Author's note:

We were once angels and left God's Kingdom according to Revelation 2:4.

Edgar Cayce on the Akashic Records, page 5-7, 10, 13-15:

Since these records are so complete, so accurate, and so individualized, a logical question might be: Just what is the purpose of the Akashic Records in the first place? Simply put, the answer is to keep track of and assist with each soul's personal growth and transformation. God is essentially love and the Universe is completely orderly. Beyond that concept is the premise that each individual was purposefully created, as a soul, to become a companion with the Creator.

Confirming Scripture, according to the Cayce's readings, we were created in "God's image" (Genesis 1:26) and therefore our natural state is spirit. Life did not begin at the moment of physical birth, rather there was an existence in spirit prior to physicality. God gave to each soul complete freedom of choice and the opportunity to find expression—to find themselves, so to speak. Because souls are created in God's image, it would only through a process of personal experiences—one choice leading to another, and then another, and then another—that God's companions could gain their own individuality, truly being a part of Him and yet individuals in their own right.

Edgar Cayce on the Akashic Records, page 88:

For example, the story of the soul is one in which the soul was with the Creator in the beginning. With our own free will, we have been choosing experiences that have enabled us to develop our own sense of individuality. At the same time, however, we are constantly searching to regain our true relationship with God. That relationship is our destiny. Simply stated, we were with the Creator in the beginning, we went astray, and ultimately we will return to our true home. This pattern—encapsulating our collective past, present, and future—is stored within the database of the Akashic Records. However, that very same theme is related to us in such stories as the Parable of the Prodigal Son.

Edgar Cayce on Angels, page 108:

The Cayce readings indicate that of all the souls that had been created in the beginning, only one-third entered the material world. Many of those who did not enter earthly existence play the roles of guardians, messengers, and bearers of divine decrees for humanity.

The divine angelic hierarchy is more than a collection of celestial beings; they are both inner and outer states of consciousness, constantly presenting an opportunity to us for our divine awakening. For many eons, communication from these beings was not comprehensible to our materialistic consciousness. Now, however, the souls of the earth are being roused from a long spiritual sleep and are being readied for the revealing (at the level of the conscious mind) of a great mystery-that we are part and parcel of the great angels of light and love. This is the reality which is unfolding before us like a flower, right now in our world and in our lives.

Edgar Cayce on Angels, page 150:

One embodiment on earth is not enough for us to fully realize ourselves as spiritual beings. This is evidential of the grace of God who gives souls endless opportunities to work out their spiritual perfection in their own time. The miraculous reality of this idea is that each soul can and will eventually evolve to the perfection which Jesus attained. The following Cayce quotation sums up very well the purpose of each soul's mission in the material world.

We were once conscious of our communion with God and the angels. The whole of spiritual creation was in harmony with every soul. With the "cause of being," as stated in the reading above, it makes sense why there is the beckoning of the spiritual dimensions from the angel kingdoms.

Edgar Cayce on Angels, page 118-119:

John Ronner, in his book 'Know Your Angels', explains the theory of the ancient church teacher Origen, who believed that the varying vibrational patterns of the angels is determined by how close or far from God these angels dwell. "Some intelligences [angels] freely chose to stay close to God, according to plan," he wrote. "They became the highest angels, having ethereal bodies. Others wandered father away and became lower angels, also with ethereal bodies. Still other beings strayed an even greater distance, becoming physical, fleshly human beings. Those who moved out the farthest became devils, with even coarser, cold bodies."

Complete Books of Enoch, page 143-144

2 Enoch, Chapter 30

"On the third day I commanded the earth to grow large fruitful trees, and hills, and seed to sow. I planted the Garden, and enclosed it, and placed as flaming angels as armed guardians, and thus I created regeneration."

"Then came the evening, and then came the morning of the fourth day (Wednesday). On the fourth day I commanded that there should be great lights on the heavenly circles."

"On the first uppermost circle I placed the stars, Kronos, and on the second Aphrodite, on the third Aries, on the fifth Zeus, on the sixth Hermes, on the seventh lesser the moon, and adorned it with the lesser stars. On the lower I placed the sun to light up the day, and the moon and stars to light up the night."

"I made the sun go according to each constellation, of which there were twelve, and I appointed the succession of the months and their names and lives, their thundering, and their hourly movements, and how they should accomplish their courses."

"Then evening came, and then the morning of the fifth day (Thursday) came. On the fifth day I commanded the sea to produce fish, and feathered birds of many varieties, and all animals that went over the earth, on four legs, and soaring in the air, male and female, and every soul breathing the spirit of life."

"Then evening came, and then the morning of the sixth day (Friday) came. On the sixth day I commanded my wisdom to create a human from seven consistencies: one, its flesh from the earth; two, its blood from the dew; three, its eyes from the sun; four, its bones from stone; five, its intelligence from the swiftness of the angels and from cloud; six, its veins and its hair from the grass of the earth; seven, its soul from my breath and from the wind. "I gave it seven natures: hearing for the flesh, sight for the eyes, smell for the soul, the veins for touch, the blood for taste, the bones for endurance, and enjoyment for the intelligence. "I conceived a cunning saying which is: I created humankind from invisible and from visible nature, of both are its death and life and image. It knows speech like some created thing, insignificant in significance and yet significant in insignificance, and I placed it on earth, a second angel, honorable, great and splendid. I appointed it as ruler to rule on earth and to have my wisdom, and there was none like it on earth of all my existing creatures."

"I appointed it a name, from the four component parts, from east, from west, from south, from north. I appointed four special stars for it. I called gave it the name "Adam" and showed it the two ways, the light and the darkness. I told it, "This is good, and that is bad," so that I would learn whether it had love or hatred towards me, so that it would be clear which in the human race loved me."

Section 1.5.2

Creation of Human Flesh

Ephesians 4:18

18 Having their understanding darkened, and being strangers from the life of God through ignorance that is in Him, because of the hardness in their heart.

Romans 8:5-16

5 For they that are after the flesh, savor the things of the flesh: but they that are after the Spirit, the things of the Spirit.

6 For the wisdom of the flesh is death: but the wisdom of the Spirit is life and peace,

7 Because the wisdom of the flesh is enmity against God: for it is not subject to the Law of God, neither indeed can be.

8 So then they that are in the flesh, cannot please God.

9 Now ye are not in the flesh, but in the Spirit, because the spirit of God dwelleth in you: but if any man hath not the Spirit of Christ, the same is not his.

10 And if Christ be in you, the body is dead, because of sin: but the Spirit is life for righteousness sake.

11 But if the Spirit of him that raised up Jesus from the dead, dwell in you, he that raised up Christ from the dead, shall also quicken your mortal bodies, by his Spirit that dwelleth in you.

12 Therefore brethren, we are debtors not to the flesh, to live after the flesh:

13 For if ye live after the flesh, ye shall die: but if ye mortify the deeds of the body by the Spirit, ye shall live.

14 For as many as are led by the Spirit of God, they are the sons of God.

15 For ye have not received the Spirit of bondage, to fear again: but ye have received the Spirit of adoption, whereby we cry, Abba, Father.

16 The same Spirit beareth witness with our spirit, that we are the children of God.

Acts 26:18

18 To open their eyes and turn them from darkness to light, and from the power of Satan to God, so that they may receive forgiveness of sins and a place among those who are sanctified by faith in me.

The Gospel of Thomas, verses 112 from page 153 of Nag Hammadi Scriptures

112 Jesus said, "Woe to the flesh that depends on the soul. Woe to the soul that depends on the flesh." (Isaiah 54:4, Hebrews 1:10-12, Psalms 102:25-27, Rev. 6:13-14)

Galatians 2:16

16 Know that a man is not justified by the works of the Law, but by the faith of Jesus Christ, even we, I say, have believed in Jesus Christ, that we might be justified by faith of Christ, and not by the works of the Law, because that by the works of the Laws, no flesh shall be justified.

The Secret Book of John, page 119 from Nag Hammadi Scriptures:

The Creation of Adam

Yaldabaoth said to the authorities with him, "Come, let's create a human being after the image of God and with a likeness to ourselves, so that this human image may give us light."

They created through their respective powers, according to the features that were given. Each of the authorities contributed a psychical feature corresponding to the figure of the image they had seen. They created a being like the perfect first human, and said, "Let's call it Adam, that its name may give us power of light."

-Revelation of Peter, page 493 of Nag Hammadi Scriptures:

Evil cannot produce good fruit. Everything, wherever it comes from, produces what is like it. Not ever soul is of the truth or of immortality. In our opinion, every soul of these present times is assigned to death and is always enslaved, since this soul is created to serve its own desires. These souls are destined for eternal destruction, in which they are and from which they are, for they love the creatures of matter that came into being with them.

But immortal souls are not like these, Peter. Still, as long as the hour has not yet come, an immortal soul resembles mortal souls. It will not reveal its true nature: it alone is immortal and contemplates immortality, and has faith, and desires to renounce these mortal souls.

People do not gather figs from thistles or thorns, if they are wise, nor grapes from thornbushes. Something always stays in that state in which it exists. If something is in a bad state, that becomes destruction and death for the soul. But the soul abides in the eternal one, the source of life and immortality of life that these resemble.

All that does not really exist will dissolve into nothingness, and those who are deaf and blind associate only with people like them.

The Tripartite Tractate, page 94 of Nag Hammadi Scriptures:

The Various Fates of Psychical People

On the one hand, those that the Word brought forth in his mind after the model of what was preexistent, when he remembered that which is superior and prayed for salvation, have salvation without any uncertainty. They will be completely saved, because of this saving thought, in accordance with what was produced from it. This is also the case with the ones that these in turn brought forth, whether they be angels or humans: because they acknowledge that there is something higher than themselves, and they pray and search for it, they will obtain the same salvation as the ones who brought them forth. For they are of a disposition that is good. They were assigned to the service of the proclamation of the coming of the Savior before it happened as well as of his revelation after he had come. Whether angel or human, these have, by the fact of being nominated for this service, acquired the essence of their being.

On the other hand, those that issued from the thought of lust for domination, who originated from the assault of the ones who opposed him, are the products of that thought. Being, for that reason, mixed, the end they will get is uncertain. Those who rid themselves of the lust for domination that was given them temporarily and for short periods, who give glory to the Lord of glory and who abandon their rage, will be recompensed for their humility by being allowed to endure indefinitely.

Those, however, who arrogantly pride themselves in their vainglorious lust, who love temporary glory, who are oblivious to the fact that the power they have has been entrusted to them only for a limited time and period, and for that reason have not acknowledged that the Son of God is the Lord of the All and the Savior, and who have failed to rid themselves either of their fury or their way of imitating those who are evil—they will receive judgment for their ignorance and their senselessness, namely, suffering.

This applies to those who have gone astray, all those among them who turned away or, even worse, who persisted in such a way that they too committed such indignities against the Lord as the powers on the left committed against him, even to the extent of causing his death, thinking, "We shall become the rulers of the All if he who has been proclaimed king of the All is killed." And those humans and angels who do not originate from the good disposition of the ones on the right, but from the mixture, endeavored to do this. They have willingly chosen for themselves transient honor and lust.

For those on the right who will be saved, the road to eternal rest leads from humility to salvation. After having confessed the Lord, having given thought to what is good for the Church, and having sung together with it the hymn of the humble, they will, for all the good they have been able to do for it, sharing its afflictions and sufferings like people who have consideration for what is good for the Church, partake of the fellowship in hope. This applies to humans as well as to angels.

The Tripartite Tractate, page 93 of Nag Hammadi Scriptures:

The Three Kinds of Human Beings

Now, humanity came to exist as three kinds with regard to essence—spiritual, psychical, and material—reproducing the pattern of the three kinds of disposition of the Word, from which sprung material, psychical, and spiritual beings. The essences of the three kinds can each be known from its fruit. They were never the less not known at first, but only when the Savior came to them, shedding light upon the saints and revealing what each one was.

The spiritual kind is like light from light and like spirit from spirit. When its head appeared, it immediately rushed to it. At once it became a body for its head. It received knowledge straightaway from the revelation.

The psychical kind, however, being light from fire, tarried before recognizing the one who had appeared to it, and still more before rushing to him in faith. Though it was instructed, moreover, only by means of voice, it was content that in this way it was not far from the hope given by the promise, having received, in the form, as it were, of a pledge, the assurance of things to come.

The material kind, however, is alien in every respect: it is like darkness that avoids the shining light because it is dissolved by its manifestation. For it did not accept his coming, and is even <. . .> and filled with hatred against the Lord because he revealed himself.

Now, the spiritual kind will receive complete salvation in every respect. The material kind will perish in every respect, as happens to an enemy. The psychical kind, however, since it is in the middle by virtue of the way it was brought forth as well as by virtue of its constitution, is double, being disposed to good as well as to evil, and the issue that is reserved for it is uncertain < . . . > and to proceed wholly into the things that are good.

The Secret Book of John, page 128 of Nag Hammadi Scriptures:

He answered and said to me, If the spirit descends upon them, by all means they will be saved and transformed. Power will descend upon every person, for without it no one could stand. After birth, if the spirit of life grows and power comes and strengthens that soul, no one will be able to lead it astray with evil actions. But people upon whom the false spirit descends are misled by it and go astray.

I said, "Lord, where will their souls go when they leave their flesh?" He laughed and said to me, The soul in which there is more power than the contemptible spirit is strong. She escapes from evil, and through the intervention of the incorruptible one, she is saved and is taken up to eternal rest.

I said, "Lord, where will the souls go of people who have not known to whom they belong?"

He said to me, "The contemptible spirit has grown stronger in such people while they were going astray. This spirit lays a heavy burden on the soul, leads her into evil deeds, and hurls her down into forgetfulness. After the soul leaves the body, she is handed over to the authorities who have come into being through the archon. They bind her with chains and throw her into prison. They go around with her until she awakens from forgetfulness and acquires knowledge. This is how she attains perfection and is saved."

I said, "Lord, how can the soul become younger and return into its mother's womb, or into the human?" He was glad when I asked him about this, and he said to me, you are truly blessed, for you have understood. This soul will be made to follow another soul in whom the spirit of life dwells, and she is saved through that one. Then she will not be thrust into flesh again."

Author's Note:

This is evidence of reincarnation. Believing in the name of Jesus will save you. However, you'll keep reincarnating until you've found the light in your inner sanctuary. This is when you've attained the Kingdom of God and your soul will no longer see "out".

Revelation 3:12

12 Him that overcometh, will I make a pillar in the Temple of my God, and he shall go no more out: and I will write upon him the Name of my God, and the name of the city of my God, which is the new Jerusalem, which cometh down out of heaven from my God, and I will write upon him my new Name.

The Secret Book of John, page 130, 131 of Nag Hammadi Scriptures:

The first ruler plotted with his powers. He sent his angels to the human daughters so they might take some of them and raise offspring for their pleasure. [Genesis 6:1-4, 1 Enoch 6-11] At first they were unsuccessful. When they had proven unsuccessful, they met again and devised another plan. They created a contemptible spirit similar to the spirit that had descended, in order to adulterate souls through this spirit. The angels changed their appearance to look like the partners of these women, and filled the women with the spirit of darkness that they had concocted, and with evil. They brought gold, silver, gifts, copper, iron, metal, and all sorts of things. They brought great anxieties to the people who followed them, leading them astray with many deceptions. These people grew old without experiencing pleasure and died without finding truth or knowing the God of truth. In this way all creation was forever enslaved, from the beginning of the world until the present day.

The angels took women, and from the darkness they produced children similar to their spirit. They closed their minds and became stubborn through the stubbornness of the contemptible spirit until the present day.

I am the Forethought of pure light,

I am the thought of the Virgin Spirit, who raises you to a place of honor.

Arise, remember that you have heard and trace your root,

which is I, the compassionate.

Guard yourself against the angels of misery,

the demons of chaos, and all who entrap you,

Edgar Cayce on Angels, page 116

The Cayce story of the creation of souls reveals that God desired companionship, desired to experience Himself as individualized states of consciousness. To each of these parts of Himself—the souls—He gave free will. Having given souls the ability to choose, the possibility existed that these minute aspects of God-souls, angels, archangels-could defy even God Himself.

The purpose of the divine plan, according to the readings, is that the souls who forgot their divine heritage have countless opportunities to reawaken from their selfish sleep and return to God through exercising their own free will.

Souls on earth were, as the readings assert, a part of the original rebellion of spirit. But now eons of time later, we are fast approaching a great awakening, the remembrance of God's original plan.

If I take the wings of the morning, and dwell in the uttermost parts of the sea; Even there shall thy hand lead me, and thy right hand shall hold me." (Psalm 139:7-10)

If God's presence exists in all creation, even in the realms of hell, as this biblical verse indicates, then it is reasonable to believe that Satan's legions will eventually return to God.

1 Corinthians 15:42-50

42 So also is the resurrection of the dead. The body is sown in corruption, and is raised in incorruption.

43 It is sown in dishonor, and is raised in glory: it is sown in weakness, and is raised in power.

44 It is sown a natural body, and is raised a spiritual body: there is a natural body, and there is a spiritual body.

45 As it is also written, The first man Adam was made a living soul: and the last Adam was made a quickening spirit.

46 Howbeit that was not first which is spiritual: but that which is natural, and afterward that which is spiritual.

47 The first man is of the earth, earthly: the second man is the Lord from heaven.

48 As is the earthly, such are they that are earthly: and as is the heavenly, such are they also that are heavenly.

49 And as we have born the image of the earthly, so shall we bear the image of the heavenly.

50 This say I, brethren, that flesh and blood cannot inherit the kingdom of God, neither doth corruption inherit incorruption.

Section 1.5.3

Christ Consciousness

Edgar Cayce on Angels, page 54:

Christ Consciousness is defined as the awareness of the soul's oneness with God imprinted in the pattern on the mind. This awareness has always been available for us at the soul level, but it has not been able to be comprehended en masse until now through the collective will of humanity. There was a time, however, in the earth's history when souls knew and remembered their spiritual origins. That era, a time when souls communed with the angelic forces and received direct conscious guidance from God, is now considered mythological and prehistoric.

In that age, souls relied directly upon the spiritual hierarchies for guidance and direction. In the earth's evolution, humanity gradually became so distracted and enmeshed by the material world, social striving, and pursuing creature comforts, etc., that the channel for communion with the angelic forces became clouded, and eventually humans doubted there ever was such a channel available. Today, messages are being given to a new generation from the same archangels who spoke to the old generations written about in the Bible. The times may be different, but the call is essentially the same: Remember where you came from and who you are. You are one with God, and I am here to guide you.

Section 1.5.4

Anti-Christ

Edgar Cayce on Angels, page 112:

In the spirit of that opposed to the spirit of truth, Cayce answered. The fruits of the spirit of the Christ are love, joy, obedience, long-suffering, brotherly love, kindness. Against such there is no law. The spirit of hate, the anti-Christ, is contention, strife, fault-finding, love of self-lovers of praise.

The darkness-the anti-Christ-is in direct opposition to that which is good, harmonious, loving. However, the fallen angels operate in the material world through choices made by human beings. According to the Cayce readings, when Satan was cast out of heaven by Archangel Michael, he was turned loose in the earth realm and could only do evil through the seduction of the human will.

Fundamentalist branches of Christianity, which interpret the Bible literally, look for outward signs of the fulfilling of this coming of the anti-Christ. They closely watch government elections and the rise of world leaders. The possibility does exist that out of the collective evil which people purposely manifest in today's world there might be an individual who will come in our time, drawn into the earth through dark desires, injustices, and evil designs of human folly. The evidence of such evil is before us every day on the news: the killings in war-torn Bosnia and Serbia; the religious war between the Catholics and Protestants in Ireland; the slaughter and starvation in Rwanda. The inner city gang wars have devastated South Central Los Angeles and many other cities. These crises reflect the opposite of harmony, love, balance, and trust. These are the worldly manifestations of the anti-Christ.

Second Coming of Christ, page 1125:

"God resisteth the proud, but giveth grace unto the humble". The sincere devotee is interested in the approbation of the Lord, not the esteem of mortals. James 4:6

Second Coming of Christ, page 734:

That grace is withheld from the devotee who with pride by reason of his spiritual realizations demands of God to surrender Himself. Egotism is the cause of many difficulties in reaching the ultimate spiritual goal; even though one may attain phenomenal powers, there is certain danger of falling from grace without the support of humility.

The Testimony of Truth, Page 626 of Nag Hammadi Scriptures:

Consorting with Demons

Some of them fall into idol worship. Others have demons living with them, as did David the king. It is he who laid the foundation of Jerusalem. [2 Samuel 5:9] And his son Solomon, whom he fathered in adultery, is the one who built Jerusalem. [1 Kings 6:1-7] He did it with the help of the demons, because he got their power.

When he finished building, he imprisoned the demons in the temple, and put them into seven water jugs. They stayed there a long time, left in the water jugs.

When the Romans went up to Jerusalem, they discovered the water jugs, and right away the demons ran out of the water jugs like people escaping from prison. The water jugs remained pure after that. And since those days they live with people who are in ignorance, and have remained on earth.

Edgar Cayce on Angels, page 123-125:

The Cayce readings indicate a philosophy that souls always have free will to choose to do evil or good. God's creatures were not intended to be automated robots who would blindly follow His commands, but it is God's desire that they be willful beings who choose to be one with Him. In many instances the readings emphasized that God has not willed that any soul should perish nor be lost, but has with every temptation prepared a way of escape.

Second Coming of Christ, page 842:

"His flesh is the Word [logos], and his blood is the Holy Spirit," says the third-century gnostic Gospel of Philip. Such views were later replaced by the official church dogma of transubstantiation—the doctrine that the bread and wine used in the Eucharistic rites are mystically transformed into the physical body and blood of Jesus when blessed by an ordained priest during the liturgy of Holy Mass. The esoteric truth behind the church's dogmas and outer rituals, however, was not lost sight of by those of deeper insight, such as Saint Basil the Great, revered Doctor of the Church and bishop of Caesarea (329 to 379 AD). Karen Armstrong, in 'A History of God', describes the distinction between dogma and kerygma made by Basil, who taught that "both kinds of Christian teaching were essential to religion". Kerygma was the public teaching of the Church, based on the Scriptures.

Acts 8:37-40

37 And Philip said unto him, If thou believest with all thine heart, thou mayest. Then he answered, and said, I believe that Jesus Christ is that Son of God.

38 Then he commanded the chariot to stand still: and they went down both into the water, both Philip and the Eunuch, and he baptized him.

39 And as soon as they were come up out of the water, the Spirit of the Lord caught away Philip, that the Eunuch saw him no more: so he went on his way rejoicing.

40 But Philip was found at Azotus, and he walked to and fro preaching in all the cities, till he came to

Caesarea.

Author's note:

Philip was taken up to heaven by a chariot. Also, James, Peter, and Paul have all experienced heaven. They all have written a Gospel or inspirational books that was found hidden at Nag Hammadi. Also, John wrote his Secret Book of John after his encounter with Jesus. See sections 3.2 through 3.4 for details.

Dogma, however, represented the deeper meaning of biblical truth, which could only be apprehended through religious experience and expressed in symbolic form. Besides the clear message, of the Gospels, a secret or esoteric tradition had been handed down "in a mystery" from the apostles; this had been a "private and secret teaching, which our holy fathers have preserved in a silence that prevents anxiety and curiosity . . . so as to safeguard by this silence the sacred character of the mystery. The uninitiated are not permitted to behold these things: their meaning is not to be divulged by writing it down." (Basil, On the Holy Spirit, 28.66.) Behind the liturgical symbols and lucid teachings of Jesus, there was a secret dogma which represented more developed understanding of the faith. Some religious insights had an inner resonance that could only be apprehended by each individual in his own time during what Plato had called theory, contemplation. As Basil said, these elusive religious realities could only be suggested in the symbolic gestures of the liturgy.

According to the great sage Patanjali, the feelings of the heart (chitta) are responsible for all our entanglements in earthly lives.

Yoga (scientific union with God) is the neutralization of the modifications of chitta. Then the beholder (the soul) is established in its own state—i.e., the unconditioned freedom and immortal bliss inherent in the soul as a spark of God-essence.

Jesus' teachings on the emotions parallel those of the more ancient science of yoga. A comprehensive yogic explication of how these energetic forces operate in man's consciousness to promote or impede awareness of the Divine is given in Paramahansa Yogananda's commentary on the first chapter of the Bhagavad Gita (especially verses 4-11). That such teachings were also known and practiced as part of original Christianity is evident in the writings of a number of the early Church Fathers—leading some scholars to refer to them as a kind of "Christian yoga." Among the examples cited is Evagrius Ponticus, a fourth-century Desert Father whose writings were influential in the early mystical traditions of both Roman and eastern Orthodox Christianity, and later among the Sufi mystics of Islam. In Lost Christianity (New York: Tarcher/Penguin 2003), Professor Jacob Needleman says of Evagrius's teaching: "The key term is the word apatheia, which translates into our word 'apathy' but which is as far from the meaning of our English word as diamonds are from broken glass . . . . Apatheia means, literally, 'without emotions'—or, more precisely, freedom from emotions . . . . Evagrius himself writes, 'Now this apatheia has a child called agape (love of God) who keeps the door to deep knowledge of the created universe. Finally, to this knowledge succeed theology (experiential knowledge of God) and the supreme beatitude.'"

Professor Needleman continues: "The most influential of Evagrius' practical writings may be taken as general guidelines for the arduous inner struggle to break free from the sufferings and illusions brought to man by the emotions. Emotions and the thoughts that support them are often given the name demons.' This term, which sounds so naive to the modern mind, has a meaning that is anything but naive. Man is a microcosmic being; he lives and moves within a field of forces and influences spanning the entire ontological range of forces in the universe. These forces have a direction—a vertical direction toward or away from unity with God. And the transactions of these forces take place within the mind and heart, within the soul,' as well as in the external universe . . . .

"The Praktikos of Evagrius begins with the listing of eight kinds of 'evil' or 'passionate' thoughts: gluttony, impurity, avarice, sadness, anger, acedia, vainglory, and pride. By calling them 'thoughts,' Evagrius is referring to an exceedingly important element in the early-Christian teaching about the emotions. It is not in our power, Evagrius writes, 'to determine whether we are disturbed by these thoughts, but it is up to us to decide if they are to linger within us or not and whether or not they are able to stir up our passions.' In short, thoughts, impulses, associations appear within the psyche, but as such they are not yet emotions. It is only when these thoughts are given something by ourselves, some energy, some specific psychic force, that they take on the nature of emotion—passion—and assume their overwhelming power in our inner and outer lives."

Jesus defends the action of his disciples of partaking of food without observing the ritual washing of hands as having no ill effect on the purity of their hearts and souls. The Pharisees and scribes who religiously practiced outward customs without corresponding inner efforts at godliness gained nothing more than a hypocritical pretense of spirituality.

Second Coming of Christ, page 898:

"Faith is the substance of things hoped for, the evidence of things not seen—through faith we understand that the worlds were framed by the word of God, so that things which are seen were not made of things which do appear." [Hebrews 11:1-3] The phenomena of material creation can be apprehended by man's intellect and senses, but not the supersensory astral and causal vibratory forces that underlie and structure the physical world. The light of intuition is required to reveal the subtle workings of the heavenly powers.

That light is the soul's realization of truth, which expresses itself through intuitive knowing, and the resultant conviction is faith. Thus, faith is the term used by Jesus to denote that which perceives the invisible cosmic creative powers, and God as the final Substance. Faith in, i.e., intuitive knowledge of, Cosmic Consciousness as the prime mover of all atomic creation bestows power to act on any portion of the universal structure. The sense-dependent, matter-worshiping man is a consummate infidel—disavowing, because he has no "evidence of things not seen," the invisible forces of an invisible God that would bestow on him all "things hoped for." Nevertheless, even ignorance-blinded individuals possess some degree of faith: a latent intuition of God's presence and power within that gives birth to all human hopes and incentive to achieve. This unconscious faith is the secret fountainhead of man's expectations of fulfillment of his copious dreams. Human hope, if used rightly as motivation to cultivate higher potentials of mind, imagination, and will, ultimately produces true faith, the intuitive realization of the divine powers in the soul.

Second Coming of Christ, page 904:

In Jesus, there was no trace of ego with its body-identified attachments and enslavement to desires, anger, and vengefulness. By gradual steps, each man has a soul destiny to rise to a Christlike life—to practice the universal Christ principles at all times. Life is a laboratory and testing ground in which man is to learn his divine potentials. And how to be happy even when bruised by trials and grievous offenses. Man's tests are not sent by God as punishment; His law is not "an eye for an eye and a tooth for a tooth." If God fights man, then He is not God. He knows He got us into this mess, and He wants us to get out, and the way is to endure our tests and conquer. Each person must learn to bear his cross while never losing faith in God. When the body suffers and one are yet able to say, "I am all right," he is transcending the body.

Second Coming of Christ, page 915-916:

Heavenly beings find supreme joy in helping one another serve the universal order as God's angels and in aiding in the upliftment and liberation of souls.

Egotism is the surest sign of an ignorant man. A childlike humble nature in a wise man is the surest sign that he contacts God.

Second Coming of Christ, page 912, 913:

If any devotee aspires to be favored in God's eyes, he should desire to be the least and humblest in the world's estimation, utterly forswearing egotism and selfishness. He should outwardly keep his consciousness ready to be of loving service to all, and inwardly endeavor, as long as he lives, to contact in meditation the Christ Consciousness inherent in the Holy Ghost Cosmic Vibration. Anyone who by ecstatic communion absorbs in his Cosmic Vibration-saturated consciousness the divine childlike qualities— humility, purity, love, joy—receives me; that is, gradually attunes himself with and manifests my Christ Consciousness. And he who receives my Christ Consciousness pervading the finite cosmos ultimately receives the transcendent Cosmic Consciousness that sent the Christ Intelligence as Its pure reflection in vibratory creation. That soul, having been released from its egoistic body consciousness and having become united with the infinite Cosmic Consciousness is, in the eyes of metaphysical law, the greatest in the kingdom of heaven—one with the Peerless Spirit.

There is none greater than God, yet He does not push Himself forward as foremost in the cosmos. He silently serves all creation and all creatures to the end of eternity, without asking anything in return. His nonpareil greatness lies in His being in love with all and feeling His oneness with the throb of life in all things and creatures. Anyone who seeks acclaim in the universal order will be so judged if he is humble like God and eternally attuned with Him. The egotist is soon cast down from the lofty seat of commendation in others' hearts and set at the lowest point of their estimation. But the person whose character bespeaks his unconditional love and spirit of service without selfish motive becomes a consummate emperor of benevolent power enthroned on all hearts within his kingdom of influence. There is nothing greater than love to draw to the worthy the love and esteem of others. Love, affirmed by humility, conquers human hearts and wins the heart of God. In the consciousness made humble and receptive through devotion, God and the Great Ones will manifest.

Humility and love alone can attract the divine response—nothing else. [Isaiah 57:15]

Isaiah 57:15

15 For thus saith he that is high and excellent, he that inhabiteth the eternity, whose Name is the

Holy one, I dwell in the high and holy place: with him also that is of a contrite and humble spirit to revive the spirit of the humble, and to give life to them that are of a contrite heart.

—lack of egotism, body consciousness, selfishness, and attachment; and presence of purity, guilelessness, innocence, obedience, humbleness, meekness, love, trust, and joy. Only when a devotee becomes possessed of these qualities through deep meditation and practice of self-discipline does he prepare himself to receive and manifest Christ Consciousness.

The pure child's mind is by nature centered in the paradise, the elevated consciousness, of the spiritual eye; but with sexual arousal and the strong urgings of the senses for gratification, the mind is thrown out of the higher potentials of paradise and descends into identification with the fleshly senses and their absorption in the physical world.

As a result, "Adam and Eve" (reason and feeling) are being expelled from Eden with each new generation of children as they are ensnared by delusion. The heavenly consciousness with which souls were intended to enjoy earth life devolves into the dualistic perceptions of good and evil with their fleeting pleasures and recurring pains that are the fated lot of the body-bound.

Section 1.5.5

Fruit of the Holy Spirit

Gospel of Truth, page 41 of Nag Hammadi Scriptures:

On the other hand, the fruit that has not yet appeared knows nothing and does nothing. Thus, each realm in the Father comes from what is, but what has set itself up is from what is not. For whatever has no root has no fruit, and although thinking, "I have come into being," it will perish by itself. So whatever does not exist will never exist.

What, then, does he want such a one to think? It is this: "I have come into being like shadows and phantoms of the night." When the light shines, the person knows the terror that had been experienced was nothing.

Second Coming of Christ, page 734:

The harvest of cosmic consciousness is plenteous, nay endless, but very few are the devotees who will labor in meditation to sow the seeds of this harvest in order to reap its fruits. Pray, therefore, that God, the giver of cosmic consciousness, may bless you to become true aspiring devotees that through His grace and your spiritual efforts you may attain the full measure of that divine harvest." The harvest of God-realization is abundant beyond measure: eternal wisdom, eternal ever new bliss, eternal consciousness and immortality. But there are extremely few human beings who will live a life of discipline and continuity in meditation. From which they may reap in the short season of life the everlasting harvest of God-contact. God-realization comes to the devotee not only of owing to his efforts to manifest Self-realization, but also because of the Lord's divine compassion.

Galatians 5:22-26

22 But the fruit of the Spirit is love, joy, peace, longsuffering, gentleness, goodness, faith,

23 Meekness, temperancy: against such there is no law.

24 For they that are Christ's, have crucified the flesh with the affections and the lusts.

25 If we live in the Spirit, let us also walk in the Spirit.

26 Let us not be desirous of vainglory, provoking one another, envying one another.

Edgar Cayce on Angels, page 153:

The Bible indicates that humankind was created a little lower than the angels, yet when the souls who went astray return to the conscious awareness of their relationship with God, they will be the rulers of the kingdom of angels. Jesus was the first to complete the journey and return to conscious reunion with God. When Jesus commanded the storm to be still, He was commanding the angels who govern the earthly elements. His mystical education as Enoch was put into practical application as Jesus.

There is a compelling theory in the cabala, the Jewish mystical tradition, which indicates that the angel Metatron was formerly Enoch in the earth. In the Talmud, Metatron (which translates to "closest to the throne") is considered to be the link between the angelic world and the physical world and is charged with the sustenance of humankind.

Metatron did not remain with the rest of the angels. He went to earth to evolve to human perfection in Christ. The readings indicate that between lives souls often act as guides and guardian angels to those still in the earth.

The Tripartite Tractate, page 96 of Nag Hammadi Scriptures:

For not only earthly humans need the redemption, but the angels need the redemption as well, and the image, and even the Fullnesses of the aeons and those marvelous luminous powers needed it, so as to leave no doubt with regard to anyone. And even the Son, who constitutes the type of the redemption of the All, needed the redemption, having become human and having submitted himself to all that was needed by us, who are his Church in the flesh. After he, then, had received the redemption first, by means of the word that came down upon him, all the rest who had received him could then receive the redemption through him. For those who have received the one who received, have also received that which is in him.

For the redemption began to be given among the humans who were in the flesh, with his firstborn and his love, the Son, coming in the flesh, and the angels who were in heaven having been found worthy of forming a community, a community in him upon the earth—for this reason it is called the Father's angelic redemption—and with him comforting those who had suffered on behalf of the All for the sake of his knowledge, for he was given grace before anyone else.

Edgar Cayce on Angels, page 133:

We have the Son (Christ), then the other sons or celestial beings (angels) that are given their force and power. The original battle of the angels of light with the angels of darkness is now fought upon the battleground of the human psyche. All that happened in spiritual realms of consciousness have their pattern imprinted upon our souls.

1 Thessalonians 1:4

4 Knowing, beloved brethren, that ye are elect of God.

Section 1.5.6

Holy Land

Isaiah Effect, page 218:

It is within our body-temple that the forces of the cosmos unite as an expression of time, space, spirit, and matter. More precisely, it is within the experience of time and space that the spirit works through matter to find the fullest expressions honoring life. Interestingly, the Qumran scholars focused upon a particular place within the body, rather than on the body itself as the landscape of divine expression. In the words of a fragment found in the Dead Sea Scrolls, we are reminded that through our bodies we have "inherited a holy land . . . this land is not a field to be plowed, but a place within us where we may build our holy temple." The innermost portion of our living temples represents the sacred place where the body of the matter is touched by the breath of spirit.

In the temples of Egypt, for example, the holiest chapel is nestled deep in the interior of the complex. Timeworn scriptures refer to the single room, often small in comparison the rest of the structure, embedded within winding corridors and preparatory shrines as beth elohim, the holy of holies. It is in the holy of holies that the invisible world of spirit touches the physical matter of the world.

Ezekiel 37:14

14 And shall put my Spirit in you, and ye shall live, and I shall place you in your own land: then ye shall know that I the Lord have spoken it, and performed it, saith the Lord.

Author's note:

Your own land is your body temple where your spirit resides.

Revelation 21:1

1 And I saw a new heaven, and a new earth: for the first heaven, and the first earth were passed away, and there was no more sea.

The Secret Book of James, page 28 of Nag Hammadi Scriptures:

Few Find Heavens Kingdom

When we heard this, we were delighted. We had become gloomy because of what we said earlier. But when he saw us happy, he said: "Woe to you who are in need of an advocate. "Woe to you who stand in need of grace. "Blessed will they be who have spoken out and acquired grace for themselves. "Compare yourselves to foreigners. How are they viewed in your city? Why are you anxious to banish yourselves on your own and distance yourselves from your city? Why abandon your dwelling on your own and make it available for those who want to live in it? You exile and runaways, woe to you, for you will be captured. "Or maybe you think that the Father is a lover of humanity, or that he is won over by prayers, or that he is gracious to one because of another, or that he tolerates whoever is seeking?" He knows about desire and what the flesh needs. Doesn't it desire the soul? The body does not sin apart from the soul just as the soul is not saved apart from the spirit. But if the soul is saved from evil and the spirit too is saved, the body becomes sinless. The spirit animates the soul, but the body kills it. The soul kills itself. "I tell you the truth, he certainly will not forgive the sin of the soul or the guilt of the flesh, for those who have worn the flesh will be saved. Do you think that many have found heaven's kingdom? "Blessed is one who has seen oneself as a fourth one in heaven."

Edgar Cayce on Akashic Records, page 81:

And let that prayer or meditation be something like this, though always put it in your own words: "I am the child of the Infinite Life that flows within me, has built for me a perfect temple to live in. When I live and move and have my being in it, with Faith and Love, it guides me, protects me and watches over me, day and night. So, I am renewed each day, filled with Health, Wealth, Love, Freedom, Peace of mind, Serenity of Soul. And now I thank Thee, Father, and the rest in Peace for all are Well." Something like that in your own words not merely said each night and morning, but said in such manner that you feel His Presence, will change your health, and your outlook on life. Won't you give it a try?

Isaiah Effect, page 218:

Essene masters viewed our body as a convergence point through which the forces of creation join to express the will of God. They considered the time together as an opportunity to share the very experiences of anger, rage, jealousy, and hatred that we sometimes shun and judge in our lives. It is through the same bodies that we hone the qualities of love, compassion, and forgiveness that elevate us to the greatest expressions of our humanness. For this reason, they regarded our body as a sacred place, a soft and vulnerable temple for our soul.

Apocalypse of Peter, page 169:

Psalms 24.4-6 give an answer to this question. First, it sets out the ethical requirements 'He who has a clean hand and a pure heart, who does not lift up his soul to what is false, and does not swear deceitfully'. Secondly, it gives words of blessing to those who are qualified to enter the temple, 'He will receive the blessing from YHWH, and vindication from the God of his salvation. Such is the generation of those who seek the face of God of Jacob'.

Psalms 24:4-6

3 Who shall ascend into the mountain of the Lord? And who shall stand in his holy place?

4 Even he that hath innocent hands, and a pure heart; which hath not lifted up his mind unto vanity, nor sworn deceitfully.

5 He shall receive a blessing from the Lord, and righteousness from the God of his salvation.

6 This is the generation of them that seek him, of them that seek thy face, this is Jacob. Selah.

It may be clear that Apocalypse of Peter 17.4 reflects the alternative reading of the Septuagint and the Peshitta. Whereas in the biblical text 'Such are the generation refers to worshipper with clean hands,' who is about to enter the temple. In Apocalypse of Peter, 'this generation' refers to 'the men who were in the flesh', waiting in the first heaven before entering the second heaven. Although the text does not explain who these men in the flesh are, the reference to Psalms 24 makes clear that they are the righteous, probably not yet covered with their heavenly clothes, and not yet having entered the sanctuary. They are waiting in a hall, before they enter, in the following of Jesus, into the real sanctuary. It is clear that Psalms 24 does not receive historical interpretation. The righteous people are waiting after their death in the first heaven.

Edgar Cayce on the Akashic Records, page 167, 168:

Because of Cayce's frequent emphasis on the Creator, the Creative Forces, or God, it may be instructive to point out that the readings never focused on the importance of one's religion. From the readings' perspective, any religion which taught the parenthood of the Creator and the brother/sisterhood of all humanity could be helpful in the growth of the soul. In Cayce's cosmology, no one is automatically destined for "heaven," and no one is ever relegated to "hell." Ultimately, all souls will receive the same reward: an awareness of their individuality and their oneness with God.

. . . COORDINATE the teachings, the philosphies of the east and the west, the oriental and occidental, the new truths and the old . . . Correlate not the differences, but where all religions meet—THERE IS ONE GOD! "Know, O Israel, the Lord thy God is ONE!"

For Cayce, the importance of life was not a matter of one's religion; rather, it was a matter of whether an individual could grow in his or her awareness of the living spirit. Heaven was not so much a place, as it is a state of being which all souls will eventually manifest. As one individual was told, "For you grow to heaven, you don't go to heaven. It is within thine own consciousness that ye grow there"

Chapter 2

Saved

There are nine sections in this Chapter. Section 2.1 contains several verses about the Grace of God. The Father, through his grace, provides you the Holy Spirit. This Spirit will help to return to the Kingdom of God. Section 2.2 gives you a better understanding of what drives you away from God. The importance of Baptism is discussed in Section 2.3, and from the Gospel of Philip, there is a deeper meaning of it. Section 2.4 talks about Salvation and the importance of your inner sanctuary. Section 2.5 describes "Gabriel Trumpet" and what it does for your soul right after you die and after some time in the spiritual world, it sounds again for your return to another body. Section 2.6 has details from the Secret Book of James about being saved, and some verses from the Gospel of John regarded this issue. Section 2.7 contains quotes from Jesus in the Gospel of Thomas. Section 2.8 contains responses from Jesus to Peter regarding Peter's questions about "second death". Finally, some details about heaven and purification of the souls are given in Section 2.9. These details came from the references of The Apocalypse of Peter and The Book of Enoch.

Section 2.1

Grace of God

2 Thessalonians 2:13

13 But we ought to give thanks always to God for you, brethren beloved of the Lord, because that God hath from the beginning chosen you to salvation, through sanctification of the Spirit, and the faith of truth,

Acts 2:38-39

38 Then Peter said unto them, amend your lives, and be baptized every one of you in the Name of Jesus Christ for the remission of sins: and ye shall receive the gift of the holy Ghost.

39 For the promise is made unto you, and to your children, and to all that are afar off, even as many as the Lord our God shall call.

Titus 3:4-7

4 But when that bountifulness and that love of God our Savior toward man appeared,

5 Not by the works of righteousness, which we had done, but according to his mercy he saved us, by the washing of the new birth, and the renewing of the holy Ghost,

6 Which he shed on us abundantly, through Jesus Christ our Savior,

7 That we, being justified by his grace, should be made heirs according to the hope of eternal life.

Romans 10:9

9 For if thou shalt confess with thy mouth the Lord Jesus, and shall believe in thine heart, that God raised Him up from the dead, thou shalt be saved.

Ephesians 2:8

8 For by grace are ye saved through faith, and that not of yourselves: it is the gift of God,

John 3:3-7

3 Jesus answered and said unto him, Verily verily I say unto thee, Except a man be born again, he cannot see the KINGDOM OF GOD.

4 Nicodemus said unto him, How can a man be born which is old? Can he enter into his mother's womb again, and be born?

5 Jesus answered, Verily, verily I say unto thee, except that a man be born of water and of the Spirit, he cannot enter into the KINGDOM OF GOD.

6 That which is born of the flesh, is flesh: and that is born of the Spirit, is spirit.

7 Marvel not that I said to thee, Ye must be born again.

Galatians 3:11-27

11 And that no man is justified by the Law in the sight of God, it is evident: for the just shall live by faith.

12 And the Law is not of faith: but the man that shall do those things, shall live in them.

13 Christ hath redeemed us from the curse of the Law, made a curse for us, (for it is written, Cursed is everyone that hangeth on tree.)

14 That the blessing of Abraham might come on the Gentiles through Christ Jesus, that we might receive the promise of the Spirit through faith.

15 Brethren, I speak as men do: though it be but a man's covenant, when it is confirmed, yet no man doth abrogate it, or addeth anything thereto,

16 Now to Abraham and his seed were the promises made. He saith not, and to the seeds, as speaking of many: but, And to thy seed, as of one, which is Christ.

17 And this I say, that the covenant that was confirmed afore of God in respect of Christ, the Law which was four hundred and thirty years after, cannot disannul, that it should make the promise of none effect.

18 For if the inheritance be of the Law, it is no more by the promise, but God gave it freely unto Abraham by promise.

Author's note:

430 year countdown began when God gave prophecy to Abraham when he was 75, to Exodus (210 years in Egypt).

19 Wherefore then serveth the Law? It was added because of the transgressions, till the seed came, unto the which the promise was made: and it was ordained by Angels in the hand of a Mediator.

20 Now a Mediator is not a Mediator of one: but God is one.

21 Is the Law then against the promises of God? God forbid: For if there had been a Law given which could have given life, surely righteousness should have been by the Law.

22 But the Scripture hath concluded all under sin, that the promise by the faith of Jesus Christ should be given to them that believe.

23 But before faith came, we were kept under the Law, as under a garrison, and shut up unto that faith, which should afterward be revealed.

24 Wherefore the Law was our schoolmaster to bring us to Christ, that we might be made righteous by faith.

25 But after that faith is come, we are no longer under a schoolmaster.

26 For ye are all the sons of God by faith, in Christ Jesus.

27 For all ye that are baptized into Christ, have put on Christ.

2 Peter 3:9

9 The Lord of that promise is not slack but is patient toward us and would have no man to punish, but would all men to come to repentance.

The Apocalypse of Peter, page 163:

The end of quotation of Apocalypse of Peter 4.9 could mean ' . . . and soul and spirit, and the great Uriel gave at the command of God'. It can be considered as an interpretation of Ezek 37.12-14, where it is God who put the spirit into the resurrected bodies, so that they shall live. In Apocalypse of Peter, this action is attributed to the angel Uriel.

Ezekiel 37:12-14

12 Therefore prophesy, and say unto them, Thus saith the Lord God, Behold, my people, I will open your graves, and cause you to come up out of your sepulchers, and bring you into the land of Israel,

13 And ye shall know that I am the Lord, when I have opened your graves, O my people, and brought you up out of your sepulchers,

14 And shall put my Spirit in you, and ye shall live, and I shall place you in your own land: then ye shall know that I the Lord have spoken it, and performed it, saith the Lord.

1 Thessalonians 4:15

15 For this say we unto you by the word of the Lord, that we which live, and are remaining in the coming of the Lord, shall not prevent them which sleep.

The Gospel of Truth, page 38-40 of Nag Hammadi Scriptures:

Those whose names he knew at the beginning were called at the end, as it is with every person who has knowledge. Such names the Father has uttered. One whose name has not been spoken is ignorant, for how could a person hear if that person's name had not been pronounced? Whoever remains ignorant until the end is a creature of forgetfulness and will perish with it. Otherwise, why do these wretches have no name, why no voice?

So whoever has knowledge is from above. If called, that person hears, replies, turns to the one who is calling, and goes up to him. He knows how he is called. That person has the knowledge and does the will of him who called. That person wishes to please him, finds rest, and has the appropriate name. Those who have knowledge in this way know where they come from and where they are going. They know as one who, having become intoxicated, has turned from his drunkenness and, having come to his senses, has gotten control of himself.

He has brought many back from Error. He went before them to the places from which they had turned when they followed Error, because of the depth of him who surrounds every place, though nothing surrounds him. Indeed, it is amazing that they were in the Father without knowing him and that they could leave on their own, since they were not able to contemplate or know the one in whom they were.

For if his will had not come from him. He revealed it as knowledge that is in harmony with the expressions of his will—that is, knowledge of the living book, which he revealed to the eternal realms at the end as his letters. He showed that they are not merely vowels or consonants, so that one may read them and think them devoid of meaning. Rather, they are letters of truth; they speak and know themselves. Each letter is a perfect truth like a perfect book, for they are letters written in unity, written by the Father for the eternal realms, so that by means of his letters they might come to know the Father.

Thus, the Father's Word goes out in the All as the fruition of his heart and expression of his will. It supports all and chooses all. It also takes the expression of all and purifies it, bringing it back to the Father, to the Mother, Jesus of infinite sweetness.

The Father opens his bosom, and his bosom is the Holy Spirit. He reveals his hidden self, and his hidden self is his Son, so that through the Father's mercy the eternal realms may know him, end their wearying search for the Father, and rest in him, knowing that he is rest. For he has filled what was deficient and has done away with its appearance. The mere appearance of what was deficient is the world, and mere appearance serves in the world.

For where, there is envy, and strife there is deficiency, but where there is unity, there is completeness. Since deficiency came about because the Father was not known, from the moment when the Father is known, deficiency will cease to be. From then on the world of appearance will no longer be evident, but rather it will disappear in the harmony of unity.

Now the works of all lie scattered. In time, unity will make the heavenly places complete, and in unity all individually will come to themselves. By means of knowledge, they will purify themselves from the multiplicity into unity, devouring matter within themselves like fire, darkness by light, death by life.

Since these things have happened to each of us, it is right for us to see to it above all that this house be holy and silent for the sake of unity.

The Gospel of Truth, page 43-45:

He is the shepherd who left behind the ninety-nine sheep that had not strayed and went in search of the one that was lost. He rejoiced when he found it. For ninety-nine is a number expressed with the left hand, but when another one is found, the numerical sum is transferred to the right hand. In this way what needs one more—that is, the whole right hand—attracts what it needs, takes it from the left and brings it to the right, and so the number becomes one hundred. This is the meaning of the pronunciation of these numbers.

The Father is like that. He labored even on the Sabbath for the sheep that he found fallen into the pit. He saved the life of the sheep and brought it up from the pit.

Understand the inner meaning, for you are children of inner meaning. What is the Sabbath? It is a day on which salvation should not be idle. Speak of the heavenly day that has no night and of the light that does not set because it is perfect. Speak from the heart, for you are the perfect day and within you dwells the light that does not fail. Speak of truth with those who seek it and of knowledge with those who have sinned in their error.

Steady the feet, of those who stumble and extend your hands to the sick. Awaken those who wish to arise and rouse those who sleep, for you embody vigorous understanding. If what is strong acts like this, it becomes even stronger. Focus your attention upon yourselves. Do not focus your attention upon other things—that is, what you have cast away from yourselves. Do not return to eat what you have vomited. Do not be moth-eaten, do not be worm-eaten, for you have already gotten rid of that. Do not be a place for the devil, for you have already destroyed him. Do not strengthen what stands in your way, what is collapsing, to support it. One who is lawless is nothing. Treat the lawless one more harshly than the just one, for the lawless does what he does because he is lawless, but the just does what he does with people because he is righteous. Do the Father's will, then, for you are from Him.

The Father is sweet and His goodness is in his will. He knows what is yours, in which you find rest. By the fruit one knows what is yours. For the Father's children are his fragrance; they are from the beauty of his face. The Father loves his fragrance and disperses it everywhere, and when it mixes with matter, it gives his fragrance to the light. Through his quietness, he makes his fragrance superior in every way to every sound. For it is not ears that smell the fragrance, but it is the spirit that possesses the sense of smell, draws the fragrance to itself, and immerses itself in the Father's fragrance. Thus it cares for it and takes it to where it came from, the original fragrance, which has grown cold in psychical form. It is like cold water that has sunk into soft soil, and those who see it think there is only soil. Later the water evaporates when the wind draws it up, and it becomes warm. Cold fragrances are from division. For this reason faith came, did away with division, and brought the warm fullness of love, so that what is cold may not return, but the unity of perfect thought may prevail.

Because of the coming of Christ it was said openly, "Seek, and the troubled will be restored, and he will anoint them with the ointment." The ointment is the mercy of the Father, who will have mercy on them, and those anointed are the perfect. For filled jars are usually sealed with wax. But when the seal of a jar is broken, it may leak, and the cause of its defect is the lack of a seal. For then a breath of wind and the power that it has can make it evaporate. Bit on the jar that is without defect the seal is not broken, nor does it leak, and the perfect Father fills again what it lacks.

Section 2.2

Contemptible Spirit vs. Holy Spirit

Complete Books of Enoch, page 61:

1 Enoch, Chapter 49, verse 1-4

Wisdom is poured out like water, and magnificence does not fail in his presence for evermore, for all his just secrets are powerful. But wickedness disappears like a shadow, and does not continue, for the chosen one stands in the presence of the Lord of spirits, and his splendor lasts forever and ever, and his power lasts for all generations.

The spirit of wisdom lives in him, as does the spirit which gives understanding and power, and the spirit of those who have fallen asleep justly. He will judge secret things. No one will be able to tell a lie in his presence, for the chosen one is in the presence of the Lord of Spirits, in accordance with his wish.

The Secret Book of John, page 128-130 of Nag Hammadi Scriptures:

I said to the Savior, "Lord, will all the souls then be led safely into pure light?" He answered and said to me, these are great matters that have arisen in your mind, and it is difficult to explain them to anyone except those of the unshakable generation.

Those upon whom the spirit of life will descend and whom the spirit will empower will be saved, and will become perfect and worthy of greatness, and will be cleansed there of all evil and the anxieties of wickedness, since they are no longer anxious for anything except the incorruptible alone, and concerned with that from this moment on, without anger, jealousy, envy, desire, or greed for anything.

They are affected by nothing but being in the flesh alone, and they wear the flesh as they look forward to a time when they will be met by those who receive them. Such people are worthy of the incorruptible, eternal life and calling. They endure everything and bear everything so as to finish the contest and receive eternal life. I said to him, "Lord, will the souls of people be [rejected] who have not done these things, but upon whom the power and the spirit of life have descended?"

He answered and said to me, if the spirit descends upon them, by all means they will be saved and transformed. Power will descend upon every person, for without it no one could stand. After birth, if the spirit of life grows and power comes and strengthens that soul, no one will be able to lead it astray with evil actions. But people upon whom the false spirit descends are misled by it and go astray.

I said, "Lord, where will their souls go when they leave their flesh?" He laughed and said to me, the soul in which there is more power than the contemptible spirit is strong. She escapes from evil, and through the intervention of the incorruptible one, she is saved and is taken up to eternal rest.

I said, "Lord, where will the souls go of people who have not known to whom they belong?"

He said to me, "the contemptible spirit has grown stronger in such people while they were going astray." This spirit lays a heavy burden on the soul, leads her into evil deeds, and hurls her down into forgetfulness. After the soul leaves the body, she is handed over to the authorities who have come into being through the archon. They bind her with chains and throw her into prison. They go around with her until she awakens from forgetfulness and acquires knowledge. This is how she attains perfection and is saved.

The Secret Book of John, page 165 of Nag Hammadi Scriptures:

But according to the Secret Book it is, above all, the "luminous epinoia" that conveys genuine insight. We might translate this as "imagination," but many people take this term as Irenaeus did, to refer to fantasy rather than conscious awareness. Yet as the Secret Book envisions it, epinoia (and related modes of awareness) remains an ambiguous, limited—but indispensable—gift. When John asks, whether everyone receives the luminous epinoia, the Savior answers yes. "The power will descend upon every person, for without it, no one can stand." Epinoia strengthens those who love her by enabling them to discriminate between good and evil, so that moral insight and ethical power are inseparable from spiritual understanding: "When the spirit of life increases, and the power comes and strengthens that soul, no one can any longer deceive it with works of evil."

The Secret Book of John, page 129-130 of Nag Hammadi Scriptures:

I said, "Lord, where will the souls go of people who had knowledge but turned away?" He said to me, they will be taken to the place where the angels of misery go, where there is no repentance. They will be kept there until the day when those who have blasphemed against the spirit will be tortured and punished eternally.

I said, "Lord, where did the contemptible spirit come from?"

He said to me, The Mother-Father is great in mercy, the Holy Spirit, who in every way is compassionate, who sympathizes with you, the Insight of enlightened Forethought. This one raised up the offspring of the perfect generation and their thought and the eternal light of the human. When the first ruler realized that these people were exalted above him and could think better than he, he wanted to grasp their thought.

He did not know that they surpassed him in thought and that he would be unable to grasp them. He devised a plan with his authorities, who are his powers. Together they fornicated with Sophia, and through them was produced bitter fate, the final, fickle bondage. Fate is like this because the powers are fickle. To the present day fate is tougher and stronger than what gods, angels, demons, and all the generations have encountered. For from fate have come all iniquity and injustice and blasphemy, the bondage of forgetfulness, and ignorance, and all burdensome orders, weighty sins, and great fears.

Thus, all of creation has been blinded so that none might know the God that is over them all. Because of the bondage of forgetfulness, their sins have been hidden.

They have been bound with dimensions, times, and seasons, and fate is master of all. The first ruler regretted everything that had happened through him. Once again he made a plan, to bring a flood upon the human creation. The enlightened majesty of Forethought, however, warned Noah. Noah announced this to all the offspring, the human children, but those who were strangers to him did not listen to him. It did not happen the way Moses said, "They hid in an ark."

Genesis 6:5-9

5 When the Lord saw that the wickedness of man was great in the earth, and all the imaginations of the thoughts of his heart were only evil continually,

6 Then it repented the Lord, that he had made man in the earth, and he was sorry in his heart.

7 Therefore the Lord said, I will destroy from the earth the man, whom I have created, from man to beast, to the creeping thing, and to the fowl of the heaven: for I repent that I have made them.

8 But Noah found grace in the eyes of the Lord.

9 These are the generations of Noah: Noah was a just and upright man in his time: and Noah walked with God.

Author's note:

Noah got his message from God by meditation while he "walked" with God in spirit.

Rather, they hid in a place, not only Noah, but also many other people from the unshakable generation. They entered that place and hid in a bright cloud. Noah knew about his supremacy. With him was the enlightened one who had enlightened them, since the first ruler had brought darkness upon the whole earth.

Gospel of Philip, page 184 of Nag Hammadi Scriptures:

Let each of us also dig down after the root of evil within us and pull it out of our hearts from the root. It will be uprooted if we recognize it. But if we are ignorant of it, it takes root in us and produces fruit in our hearts. It dominates us. We are its slaves, and it takes us captive so that we do what we do not want and do not do what we want. It is powerful because we do not recognize it. As long as it exists, it stays active.

Section 2.3

Baptism

The Gospel of Philip, page 175 of Nag Hammadi Scriptures:

The holy place is baptism; the holy of the holy is redemption; the holy of holies is the bridal chamber. Baptism entails resurrection and redemption, and redemption is in the bridal chamber. The bridal chamber is within a realm superior to what we belong to, and you cannot find anything like it . . . . These are the ones who worship in spirit and in truth, for they do not worship in Jerusalem. There are people in Jerusalem who do worship in Jerusalem, and they await the mysteries called the holy of holies, the curtain of which was torn. Our bridal chamber is the image of the bridal chamber above. That is why its curtain was torn, from top to bottom, for some people from below had to go up.

Matthew 27:51

51 And behold, the veil of the Temple was rent in twain, from the top to the bottom, and the earth did quake, and the stones were cloven.

Hebrews 9:3

3 And after the second veil was the tabernacle which is called the holiest of all.

Hebrews 10:19-20

19 Seeing therefore, brethren, that by the blood of Jesus we may be bold to enter into the Holy place,

20 By the new and living way, which he hath prepared for us, through the veil, that is, his flesh.

The Gospel of the Nazirenes, page 20:

Chapter 6 verse 27

27 Now all the while Jesus was abroad, his brother James and cousin John were of a purpose to amass and teach The Way to a growing number of followers, each of their own: James being in and around Jerusalem, and John all around and about the outlying and surrounding areas of Judea.

The Gospel of the Nazirenes, page 23:

Chapter 8 verse 6-8

6 And they which were sent were of the Pharisees, and they asked him and said to him, "Why do you baptize then, if you are not the Messiah, neither that Prophet of whom Moses spoke?"

7 John answered them saying, "I baptize with water; but there is one among you, whom you know not, who shall baptize with water and with fire."

8 These things were done in Bethebara, beyond Jordan, where John was baptizing. And Jesus began at this time to be thirty years of age, being after the flesh indeed the son of Joseph and Mary; but after the Spirit, the Anointed One, a Son of the Most High.

The Apocalypse of Peter, page 106:

In Apocalypse of Paul, on the other hand makes no mention of intercession at all. The crucial act is the repentance of the soul prior to death. Repentance of souls after they are already experiencing the punishments, even when coupled with the intercession of Paul and archangel Michael, does not lead to the baptism of these souls in the Acherusian Lake. These souls gain only a brief annual ease of their torments. The souls that are washed in the Acherusian Lake are those souls who repent while they are still alive:

From Apocalypse of Paul;

This is Acherusian Lake; the city of the Saints, which the father built for his only begotten son Jesus Christ, is east of all these things. It is not allowed for everyone to go into it. It is on account of this that the Acherusian Lake is on the way. If (one is) a fornicator or a sinner and he turns and repents (metanoein) and produces fruit worthy of repentance (metanoia) and (then) he leaves the body, he first worships God and (then) he is given into the hands of Michael. He (Michael) washes him in Acherusian Lake, and he is taken into the city to those who have not sinned.

Repentance is a recurring motif throughout Apocalypse of Paul. Elsewhere in Apocalypse of Paul, when the soul is brought before God in heaven, God does not allow the angel to relate the soul's bad deeds from its youth, only from the last year of its life. If the soul, repents in that final year, God forgives it. The repentant soul is washed in the Achuresian Lake and brought into the city of Christ. The overarching emphasis placed on repentance in Apocalypse of Paul suggests that this text describes a final ritual ablution of the repentance soul, a mark that, unlike the first baptism, cannot be undone through sin since the soul is now dead.

Beyond Belief, page 130:

According to the Gospel of Philip, Philip suggested that baptism is not the same for everyone. There are many people whose baptism simply marks initiation: such a person "goes down into the water and comes up without having to receive anything and says "I am Christian," but sometimes, Phillip continues, the person who undergoes baptism "receives the holy spirit . . . this is what happens when one experiences a mystery." What makes a difference involves not only the mysterious gift of divine grace but also the intimate capacity for spiritual understanding. So, Philip writes, echoing Paul's Letter to the Galatians, many believers see themselves as God's slaves than as God's children; but those who are baptized, like newborn infants, are meant to grow in faith toward hope, love, and understanding (gnosis):

Beyond Belief, page 132:

Philip quotes Paul's famous teaching on resurrection "flesh and blood shall not inherit the kingdom of God," (1 Corinthians 15:50) to show that those who receive the holy spirit in baptism are not only "born again" but also "raised from the dead." After all, he asks, "what is flesh?" In answer, he quotes from John's gospel to show that when Jesus told his disciples to "eat my flesh and drink my blood" (John 6:53), he was speaking in metaphor, since what he meant was that they were to partake of the sacred meal of bread and wine, which conveys Jesus' "flesh", that is. Philip suggests, his divine word, and his "blood," the holy spirit.

Philip thus discriminates between nominal Christians—those who claim to be Christians simply because they were baptized—and those who, after baptism, are spiritually transformed. He sees himself among the latter but does not congratulate himself for belonging to a spiritual elite; instead, he concludes by anticipating that ultimately all believers will be transformed, if not in this world then in eternity. Whoever undergoes such transformation, he says "no longer is a Christian, but a Christ."

The Gospel of Philip, page 178 of Nag Hammadi Scriptures:

Chrism Is Superior to Baptism

Chrism is superior to baptism. We are called Christians from the word "chrism," not from the word "baptism." Christ also has his name from chrism, for the Father anointed the Son, the Son anointed the apostles, and the apostles anointed us. Whoever is anointed has everything: resurrection, light, cross, Holy Spirit. The Father gave all this to the person in the bridal chamber, and the person accepted it. The Father was in the Son and the Son was in the Father. This is heaven's kingdom.

The Gospel of Phillips, page 175 of Nag Hammadi Scriptures:

Baptism

We are born again through the Holy Spirit, and we are conceived through Christ in baptism with two elements. We are anointed through the Spirit, and when we were conceived, we were united.

No one can see oneself in the water or in a mirror without light, nor can you see yourself in the light without water or a mirror. So it is necessary to baptize with two elements, light and water, and light is chrism.

The Tripartite Tractate, page 97 of Nag Hammadi Scriptures:

As for the true baptism, into which the members of the All descend and where they come into being, there is no other baptism except the one—and that is the redemption—which takes place in God the Father, the Son, and the Holy Spirit, after confession of faith has been made in those names which are the single name of the good tidings and after one has believed that the things one has been told are real.

And on account of this, whoever believes in their reality will obtain salvation, and that means to attain, in an invisible way, the Father, the Son, and the Holy Spirit, but only after one has borne witness to them in unfaltering faith and if one grasps them in a firm hope. In this way, it may happen that the fulfillment of what one has believed becomes a return to them, and that the Father becomes one with him—the Father, God, whom he has confessed in faith, and who has granted him to be united with himself in knowledge.

The baptism we have spoken about is called "the garment" that is not taken off by the ones who put it on and that is worn by the ones who have received redemption. And it is called "the confirmation of truth," which never fails in its constancy and stability and holds fast those who have obtained restoration while they hold on to it. It is called "silence" because of its tranquility and unshakability. It is also called "the bridal chamber" because of concord and the inseparability of the ones whom he has known and who have known him. It is also called "the unsinking and fireless light," not because it sheds light, but rather because those who wear it, and who are worn by it as well, are made into light. It is also called "the eternal life," which means immortality.

The Gospel of Philip, page 177 of Nag Hammadi Scriptures:

People who say they will first die and then arise are wrong. If they do not receive the resurrection first, while they are alive, they will receive nothing when they die. So it is said of baptism, "Great is baptism," for if people receive it, they will live.

Author's note:

According to page 84 of "Embraced By The Light", Betty Eadie quoted, "it is important for us to acquire knowledge of the spirit while we are in the flesh."

The Testimony of Truth, page 618 of Nag Hammadi Scriptures:

There are some who, upon entering the faith, receive baptism on the ground that they have that as a hope of salvation. They call it the "seal," not realizing that the fathers of the world are manifest there. But he, for his part, knows that he is sealed. The Son of Humanity did not baptize any of his disciples. As for those who are baptized, if they were headed for life, the world would be emptied. But the fathers of baptism were defiled.

But the baptism of truth is something else; it is by renunciation of the world that it is found. But those who say only with their mouths that they are renouncing it are lying, and they will wind up in the terrible place, where they will also be treated with contempt. They are habitually wicked in their actions.

The Gospel of the Nazirenes, page xxxiv:

Only Begotten provides historical proof that there was at least one school of thought strongly opposed to what ultimately became official Church doctrine on the matter.

Further research reveals that this idea was one of the first and ultimately most tragic departures from traditional Nazirene thought (as espoused by Jesus' brother James) by the Church promulgated by Saul of Tarsus, later known as Paul. By reference to Jesus as the First Begotten, we are led to believe that there may be a Second Begotten, Third Begotten and so on. Following further through the implications of these references, we may glimpse into the nature of Nazirene beliefs on the matter: i.e. That Jesus (the human) received the fullness of God consciousness when baptized with the Holy Spirit at the river Jordan by John. In this manner, because he had devotedly prepared and nurtured this state within his soul throughout his experiences (known in Naziritic terms as "The Way"), Jesus was augmented to fulfill the Divine potential of humanity. On this "rock", lies the basis of what has been in the past an unbridgeable gulf between true Nazirene (sometimes erroneously designated as Gnostic) belief and what ultimately became "New Testament" Christianity.

The most important aspect of this point cannot go unmentioned. The history of the two main Essene sub sects (Nazirenes and Ebionites) records that they believed: a) The Holy Spirit entered Jesus officially upon his baptism by John in Jordan and not at conception; and b) as the later Gnostics contended, the term "First Begotten" as opposed to "Only Begotten" links Jesus with the reincarnation of Adam as a mortal, striving to an achievable initiate perfection which was reached at his baptism by John rather than an immortal being (i.e. God's or The Unbegotten's Only Begotten) made flesh.

With this information in mind, it becomes more difficult for a Paulianic-based approach to explain this difference in nomenclature away, especially that a significant number of important Church Fathers through the Fourth Century support the fact that the "ringleaders" behind these so-called heretical Jewish groups that held these beliefs were called Nazirenes!

Isn't that what they called Jesus and his closest followers? The next quote is from the earliest of this group of Church Fathers, Papias (60-140 A.D.), who was First Bishop of Hurapolis. Papias, who claimed to have been a disciple of John the apostle in his (Papias') youth, in quoting from this original Aramaic scroll, begins to set the tone for that which is unmistakably Nazirene philosophy:

The next to shed light on the evidence is Eusebius, a highly respected Church Father historian of the Nicean era, who wrote the most complete Church history of his time. He is quoted here from his work Theophania:

Himself taught the reason for the separation of souls . . . as we have found somewhere in the Gospel that is spread abroad among the Jews in the Hebrew tongue, in which it is said: "I choose for myself the most worthy. The most worthy are those whom my Father in heaven has given me."

Jerome, likewise, in his Commentary on Matthew, says:

The Jewish Gospel here reads as follows: "If ye be in my bosom, and do not the will of my Father in heaven, I will cast you out of my bosom."

The Gospel of the Nazirenes, page 226-227:

Chapter 91, verse 3-10

3 And Jesus answered and said, "Verily I say to you, Mary, the Kingdom is within you. But the time approaches when that which is within shall be made manifest in the without, for the sake of the world."

4 Order indeed is good, and needful, but before all things is love. Love one another and all creatures of the Earth, and by this shall all men know-that you are disciples of The Way.

5 And one asked him saying, Jesus shall infants be received into the Congregation in like manner as Moses commanded by circumcision? And Jesus answered, "For those who are in The Law there is no cutting of the flesh, nor shedding of blood."

6 Let the infant of eight days be presented to the Most High with prayer and thanksgiving, and let a name be given to it by its parents, and let the Priest sprinkle pure water upon it, according to that which is written in the Prophets, and let its parents see to it that it is brought up by Nazirite tradition in The Way of The Law, neither eating flesh nor drinking strong drink, nor touching things impure, nor hurting the creatures given by the Creator into the hands of man to protect.

7 Again one said to him, Jesus, how will it be when they grow up? And Jesus said, "After seven years, or when they begin to know the evil from the good, and learn to choose good, let them come in Spirit and receive the blessing at the hands of the Priest or the Angel of the Congregation with prayer and thanksgiving, and let them be admonished to keep from flesh-eating and strong drink, and from hunting the innocent creatures of the Earth; or shall they be lower than the horse or the sheep to whom these things are against nature?"

8 And again he was asked, if there come to us any that eat flesh and drink strong drink, shall we receive them? And Jesus said to him "Let such abide in the outer court till they cleanse themselves from these grosser evils; for till they perceive, and repent of these, they are not fit to receive the higher mysteries."

9 And another asked him saying, "when shall they receive Baptism?" And Jesus answered, "After another seven years, or when they know the doctrine, and do that which is good, and learn to work with their own hands, and choose a craft whereby they may live, and are steadfastly set on

The Way, then let them ask for initiation, and let the Angel or Priest of the Congregation examine them and see if they are worthy, and let him offer thanksgiving and prayer and bury them in the waters that they may rise to newness of life, confessing the Lord as their Father and Mother, choosing to obey The Holy Law, and keep themselves free from the evil in the world.

10 And another asked him, Jesus, "at what time shall they receive the anointing?" And Jesus answered, "When they have reached the age of maturity, and manifested in themselves the sevenfold gifts of the Spirit, then let the Angel offer prayer and thanksgiving and seal them with the seal of the Anointed. It is good that all be tried in each degree seven years. Nevertheless let it be to each according to their growth in the Love, and the Wisdom of the Lord.

Section 2.4

Salvation

Romans 10:10

10 For with the heart man believeth unto righteousness, and with the mouth man confesseth to salvation.

The Treatise on Resurrection, page 50 of Nag Hammadi Scriptures:

Because the Savior assumed the physical existence of humans, they on their part acquired access to his spiritual form of being. This is their spiritual resurrection. Access to the resurrection depends on faith. The author stresses that the resurrection cannot be proven by philosophical arguments. Faith is a truth and wisdom that has been received, and it cannot be understood by everybody. One is chosen and predestined for this knowledge. Faith in the Savior is not primarily an intellectual act; it is a substantive relationship with the divine. Those who recognize the truth can do so because they are of the same spiritual substance as the Savior himself. When they attain knowledge, they are revealed, and they come forth as spiritual beings.

This idea is related to another important theme in the text: spiritual existence is fundamentally the only real form of existence. The world is, in fact, an illusion. This implies that the resurrection is thought of not just as the return to and the restoration of an original spiritual existence, but also as an act of knowledge in which one realizes that spiritual essence is something that one already has, hidden within oneself as one's true self. From this perspective, the salvific act of the Savior takes on a new significance. On the one hand, it was an event in history, in which the Savior put an end to corruptible existence by himself assuming a human body and subsequently discarding it through his resurrection. On the other hand, the event of salvation is also understood as an awakening, whereby the mission of the Savior was to make the elect realize that they possess their spiritual nature already. From this point of view, salvation is no longer primarily seen as the liberation from the body and the attainment of spiritual existence in the sense of a redemptive event taking place in time and space. Rather, resurrection in this case means the realization that spiritual existence is something one already possesses and that time and space as such are illusions. Thus, a change of focus is discernible in the text as it moves from the representation of salvation as a narrative, with fall and return as its main themes, to a perspective in which everything that takes place in time and space is regarded as unreal. This change of focus is not arbitrary, but follows logically from the basic concept of salvation in the Treatise on Resurrection: if salvation means the elimination of the physical world, it also means the elimination of the categories of time and space within which salvation as a narrative is represented.

John 6:53-61, 64-66

53 Then Jesus said unto them, Verily, verily I say unto you, Except ye eat the flesh of the Son of man, and drink his blood, ye have no life in you.

54 Whosoever eateth my flesh, and drinketh my blood, hath eternal life, and I will raise him up at the last day.

55 For my flesh is meat indeed, and my blood is drink indeed.

56 He that eateth my flesh, and drinketh my blood, dwelleth in me, and I in him.

57 As that living Father hath sent me, so live I by the Father, and he that eateth me, even he shall live by me.

58 This is that bread which came down from heaven: not as your fathers have eaten Manna, and are dead. He that eateth of this bread, shall live forever.

59 These things spake he in the Synagogue, as he taught in Capernaum.

60 Many therefore of his disciples (when they heard this) said, This is an hard saying: who can hear it?

61 But Jesus knowing in himself, that his disciples murmured at this, said unto them, Doth this offend you?

64 But there are some of you that believe not: for Jesus knew from the beginning, which they were that believed not, and who should betray him.

65 And he said, Therefore said I unto you, that no man can come unto me, except it be given unto him of my Father.

66 From that time, many of his disciples went back, and walked no more with him.

Hebrews 6:19-20

19 We have this hope as an anchor of the soul, unfailing and trustworthy. It enters the inner sanctuary behind the veil,

20 Where Jesus, our forerunner, has entered on our behalf. He has become a high priest from the line of succession of Melchizedek.

The Secret Book of James, page 28 of Nag Hammadi Scriptures:

When we heard this, we became sad. But when he saw that we were sad, he said, "I say this to you that you may know yourselves. Heaven's kingdom is like a head of grain that sprouted in a field. And when it was ripe, it scattered its seed, and again it filled the field with heads of grain for another year. So, with you, be eager to harvest for yourselves a head of the grain of life that you may be filled with the kingdom.

"And as long as I am with you, pay attention to me and trust in me, but when I am far from you, remember me. And remember me because I was with you and you did not know me. Blessed will they be who have known me. Woe to those who have heard and have not believed. Blessed will they be who have not seen but yet have believed. Once again I appeal to you. I am disclosed to you as I am building a house useful to you when you find shelter in it, and it will support your neighbors' house when theirs threatens to collapse. I tell you the truth, woe to those for whom I was sent down here. Blessed will they be who are going up to the Father. Again I warn you, you who exist. Be like those who do not exist that you may dwell with those who do not exist."

"Do not let heaven's kingdom become a desert within you." Do not be proud because of the light that enlightens. Rather, act toward yourselves as I myself have toward you. I have put myself under a curse for you that you might be saved.

The Treatise on Resurrection, page 49-51 of Nag Hammadi Scriptures:

The doctrine of the resurrection taught in this text takes its point of departure from Christological and soteriological considerations. The Savior was divine and human at one and the same time. This duality in the Savior's nature was a function of his redemptive task: in order to save humanity from its fallen condition, the Savior himself had to assume human nature, but because of his divinity he was also able to overcome the human fate of death. In this way, the Savior "swallowed death" an expression from Paul.

This Christology of two natures and understanding of redemption as an act of substitution is clearly in line with mainstream Christian theology (even anticipating later orthodox dogma), though this Christology also agrees with basic tenets of Eastern Valentinian soteriology. However, the soteriology of the Treatise on Resurrection differs notably from later orthodox doctrine with regard to its views about the condition from which the Savior saved humanity. The "death" that the Savior brought to naught is not primarily a state of sin, but the condition of physical existence in a corruptible material world. The Savior's death and his incarnation are basically one and the same redemptive act. The fact that he entered this world and assumed a human body means that he accepted death. When the Savior later rose from the dead, he also freed himself from the body he had put on when he descended into the world and became once more a purely spiritual being. During this process, he "swallowed" the entire visible world: it was revealed as nothing.

Section 2.5

Gabriel's Trumpet

Second Coming of Christ, page 358:

"Marvel not at this: for the hour is coming, in the which all that are in the graves shall hear his voice, and shall come forth; they that have done good, unto the resurrection of life; and they that have done evil, unto the resurrection of damnation" (John 5:28-29)).

This age of logic, having struggled out of a long night of superstition, belies belief in a literal interpretation of Christ's words, in this verse from John 5. The word "graves" used by Jesus gave Biblical interpreters of little or no direct intuitional perception the thought that after death man's soul waits with its cold corpse entombed, able to rise only on Resurrection Day when archangel Gabriel blows his trumpet. It appears that, for twenty centuries, Gabriel has not sounded his trumpet, because the skeletons of millions can be found still in their graves.

This misconception of resurrection, that God would keep living souls refrigerated for years beneath the cold sod, and then suddenly warm them up to be sent to Hades or Heaven, is baseless, revolting, injurious, and unreasonable. If that is the plan, what injustice it is that sinners and the virtuous alike, without discrimination, have been kept waiting for centuries. The law of "cause and effect" has something better for those who strived to live a righteous life. Are we to believe that an autocratic God, without rhyme or reason, dumps all souls after death under a clod of earth and keeps them sleeping peacefully or dreaming in nightmares for centuries until His mood suddenly chooses to command Gabriel to blow the trumpet and wake the dead? And what of those highly spiritual souls whose bodies are not buried but were cremated and the ashes scattered to the winds and seas?

The traditional Christian belief that the Resurrection on the last day will be heralded by the angel Gabriel blowing his trumpet is not specifically mentioned in the Bible. In various New Testament passages, the Resurrection is said to be heralded by an unnamed angel sounding a celestial trumpet or the voice of Christ or both. For example, in Matthew 14:30-31, speaking of "the end of the world," Jesus says: "He shall send His angels with a great sound of a trumpet." Saint Paul wrote that at the time of the Resurrection "the trumpet shall sound" (1 Corinthians 15:51), also of the Lord's coming "with the voice of the archangel, and with the trump of God." (1 Thessalonians 4:16-17).

Revelation 3:12

12 Him that overcometh, will I make a pillar in the Temple of my God, and he shall go no more out: and I will write upon him the Name of my God, and the name of the city of my God, which is the new Jerusalem, which cometh down out of heaven from my God, and I will write upon him my new Name.

Second Coming of Christ, page 364:

"Now this I say, brethren, that flesh and blood cannot inherit the kingdom of God; neither doth corruption inherit incorruption. Behold, I shew you a mystery; we shall not all sleep, but we shall all be changed, in a moment, in the twinkling of an eye, at the last trump, for the trumpet shall sound, and the dead shall be raised incorruptible, and we shall be changed. For this corruptible must put on incorruption, and this mortal must put on immortality. So when this corruptible shall have put on incorruption, and this mortal shall have put on immortality, then shall be brought to pass the saying that is written, 'Death is swallowed up in victory. O death, where is thy sting? O grave, where is thy victory? The sting of death is sin; and the strength of sin is the law.

But thanks be to God, which giveth us the victory through our Lord Jesus Christ" (1 Corinthians 15:50-57). Saint Paul thus describes the "trumpet" of Cosmic Vibration, which resurrects man's consciousness at the end of each earthly incarnation from mortal confinement to the greater freedom after death. Ultimately, "at the last trumpet," the soul is raised to liberation in God through the Christ Consciousness inherent in the Holy Ghost Vibration, "the victory through our Lord Jesus Christ," after repeated incarnations of spiritual advancement have destroyed all "corruption," mortal consciousness and desires, and their resultant karma. Then "death is swallowed up in victory," the karma-compelled cycles of birth and death are over for that soul.

The Gospel of the Nazirenes, page 91:

Chapter 37, verse 1-8

1 Jesus sat on the porch of the Temple, and some came to learn his doctrine, and one said to him, "Rabbi, what do you teach concerning life?"

2 And he said to them, "Blessed are they who endure many experiences, for they shall be made perfect through them; they shall be as the Angels of the Most High and shall die no more, neither shall they be born any more, for death and birth have no more dominion over them.

3 They who have endured and overcome shall be made Pillars in the Temple of the Lord, and they shall go out no more. Verily I say to you, except you be born again of water and fire, you cannot see the Kingdom.

4 And a certain Rabbi (Nicodemus) came to him by night for fear of the Sanhedrin, and said to him, "How can a man be born again when he is old? Can he enter a second time into his mother's womb and be born again?"

5 Jesus answered, "Verily I say to you except a man be born again of flesh and of Spirit, he cannot enter into the Kingdom." The wind blows where it will, and you hear the sound thereof, but cannot tell from where it comes or where it goes.

6 The light shines from the East even to the West; out of the darkness the Sun rises from beyond our sight and returns from whence it came. So is it with humanity, from the ages unto the ages.

7 When Life comes from beyond our sight, it is that we have lived before, and when it returns from whence it came, it is that we may rest for a little, and thereafter be reborn unto the flesh.

8 So through many changes must we be made perfect, as it is written in the book of Job, I am a wanderer, changing place after place and house after house, until I come to the city and mansion which is eternal.

The Apocalypse of Peter, page 49-50:

As we have seen, in Buchholtz' opinion the main theme of the work is God's mercy to the sinners. This is undoubtedly true. But let us examine the question more closely. The real teaching of our treatise seems to be the following. There are two judgments, and the first one takes place directly after death. It is just: everybody is condemned according to his or her sins. Mercy has no place in it; it is God's justice that prevails. Adam, too, when he sinned, was punished accordingly: death came upon him and he was expelled from Paradise. But God created everything for his glory, it would not be logical to destroy it afterwards. If something does not work as it should, God will reconstruct and not annihilate it. This means that sins are requited, but the sinners themselves will not be destroyed by a second death meaning eternal torture in the underworld. The notion comes from Rev 20:14-15, 'And death and hell were cast into the lake of fire. This is the second death. And whosoever was not found written in the book of life was cast into the lake of fire.' The second judgment takes place after the resurrection, and this time mercy will reign in: in this judgment there will be no division, all believers in Christ will receive eternal life and enter God's Kingdom.

Author's note:

The second death is an end of the soul. More details about second death are provided in Section 2.8.

Second Coming of Christ, page 1148-1153:

According to the law of cause and effect, in the after-death develop spiritual state such persons will live for a karmically determined time in a self-created hell in the astral world, bemoaning the loss of their sensate physical body, its comforting breath, sensory pleasures, unfulfilled desires, and the accustomed sustenance of favored tasty foods (referred to in the parable in which the rich man "fared sumptuously every day"). They are unable to enjoy the divine state of ever new heavenly bliss they could have realized in the after-death state. Shortsighted people of the world pursue God's ephemeral mundane gifts of material objects and pleasures in complete neglect of the Giver who is everlastingly useful to His seeking children. Wise children of the Heavenly Father who discover that they are made in His image seek first His kingdom of eternal happiness hidden within, and material things afterwards, realizing that no spurious material substitutes can ever alleviate the true happiness-thirst of the soul. That is why Jesus had said, "Bread the men of the world seek after; but ye who are wise, seek ye the kingdom of God first." He counseled all souls on earth to learn to live "not by bread alone, but by every word that proceedeth out of the mouth of God," so that in the after-death state they would be already consciously familiar with living by the word of God, or Cosmic Vibration, and Cosmic Bliss.

Most persons can look forward to a glorified experience of peace, freedom, and blessed relief from life's burdens and afflictions when the spirit leaves the body at the time of death. However, those such as the rich man in this parable who are strongly attached to their physical forms are aghast at being wrenched away from their bodily instrument with its much-indulged materialistic capacities. As the life energy empowering all the senses and organs moves toward the medulla and then out of the physical form, desires urge the ego-bound soul to try to draw the consciousness back into the body. Such persons try again and again unsuccessfully to operate the lungs and other organs or to move the muscles with their disembodied will, but at last surrender their fruitless effort and enter a sort of dreamless sleep, a period of rest from the travails of life.

After the initial astral sleep, souls who left the body with powerful bad habits and dissipation of the senses of the physical form partially awaken in intermittent dreamlike astral experiences of unrequited craving to indulge the sense-desires of the lost physical vehicle. This frustration of unfulfillment and unslaked mortal thirsts causes a mental agony that is the real hell experienced in the afterlife. When the karmically ordained period of astral suffering or reward is over, the soul wakes up in another body in a new incarnation on earth, endowed with the physical instrumentalities to pursue once again its desires and learning experiences—this time, it is to be hoped, with at least a little more wisdom learned from previous painful lessons.

The physical body and world are perceived through the two physical eyes; the heavenly astral body and cosmos are purely seen through the intuitional power of the one spiritual eye. "If therefore thine eye be single, thy whole body shall be full of light."(Matthew 6:22) It is by opening the "single" or spiritual eye that one can perceive the luminous prank forces that compose the astral body and astral cosmos. Extremely materialistic persons, those who have led a terrible life, are unable after death to awaken fully into the consciousness of the wondrous potentials of their astral body. Their beclouded consciousness remains aware only of a region of darkness and mental distress. Even while incarnate on earth, advanced souls who meditate deeply experience through their spiritual eye the all-knowing intuition of the soul as an illuminating lightless light that dispels the darkness of closed eyes; with that single power they can see, hear, smell, taste, and touch in the inner astral world. Thus, when they die, intuition comes to their aid as a revealing light by which they can perceive the shining beauty of the astral world and their astral body. Only those who have developed soul intuition and have cultivated before death, the body transcendence of God-consciousness can attain conscious ascendence into, and full awareness of, the highest regions of the heavenly astral world; and they can also, if they so desire, see across the vibrational gulf that divides heaven from earthly life.

Author's note:

Astral world (heaven) is defined as a universe of light and color composed of finer-than-atomic forces. At physical death, the soul of man, clothed in an astral form of light, remains there until physical rebirth.

Everything one has done to develop the "sixth sense" of intuition while on earth helps one after death. Since it is the degree of realization and the amount of virtue one has expressed on earth that determines one's experience in the astral region, there is much work to be done to purify the indwelling consciousness by God-contact and by persistence in exercising the godly virtues. In depicting the astral ascension of the afflicted beggar Lazarus, Jesus gives comfort to suffering virtuous persons by the assurance that they should not feel discouraged, nor should they envy those with material advantages. Earthly blessings, if improperly used, may be followed by experiences of extreme discomfort in the after-death state. Righteous persons who retain their goodness until the end of their lives, no matter what suffering or deprivation they endure, will find when they leave the body that they have earned a heavenly freedom and joy in the astral kingdom. God does not wish suffering on His children, and certainly has not made it a prerequisite for attaining His kingdom; nevertheless, no pain that one suffers consciously goes without reward, the purifying effect of having burned off a measure of past karma or of having kindled an inner illumination that awakened and consolidated a nascent soul virtue. Every sacrifice performed on the altar of the body is recognized by God. Those who suffer in the course of service to God and His children, and willingly sacrifice all for Him as Jesus did, will surely attain God-bliss.

Jesus explains in the parable, through Abraham's comments to the rich man, why Lazarus could not be sent to solace him in his astral sufferings. Abraham makes reference to the "gulf" of dividing vibration separating the astral vibratory spheres one from the other. As the material universe is divided into the principal vibratory regions of earth, water, air, and fiery energy, so there are several distinct regions of the subtler cosmos, each of which has many subdivisions, with the exception of the highest plane—all is one.

Ether-filled space acts as a vibratory rampart that prevents materialistic persons on earth from entering the heavenly astral kingdom; likewise, increasingly subtle vibratory forms of etheric space divide the lower from the higher astral regions, and the even finer causal realm from the astral. Thus, the astral realm to which the rich man was consigned was separated by a vibrational barrier from the finer heavenly abode to which Lazarus's spiritual karma had drawn him, "so that they which would pass from hence to you cannot; neither can they pass to us, that would come from thence."

The more advanced a soul is, the freer its movement within the vast territory of God's kingdom. Fully liberated souls have no boundaries of movement. But karma-restricted souls cannot move freely from one sphere into another sphere. People who are dark with delusive ignorance, crimes, or other wrong acts and have thus attracted temporary residence in the "slums" of the astral land after death would not even be able to stand the finer vibrations of a higher sphere and its residents of spiritual souls, just as in this world evil ones can not bear to be in spiritual environs or company of saintly persons. On earth people cannot touch a high-voltage electric current without being burned; similarly, in the astral realm souls whose consciousness is of low vibrational quality experience energy shocks when they come in contact with higher vibrations. As man suffers in this world from collision with matter, so the astral body suffers in that world from collision with vibrations higher than its own.

Nevertheless, God in His mercy does not leave suffering souls in any region of creation bereft of help. In the astral world, there are advanced good souls who help repentant bad ones to work out their karmic penances— as also do the prayers and goodwill that reach them from their loved ones on earth. Only those who have sufficiently developed their spiritual consciousness and the enlightenment of intuition during their earthly incarnations are consciously able to devote themselves to the good works of helping others in the astral world and are also able to give invisible assistance to souls on earth.

In the afterlife, as on earth, souls must either ascend or descend none can remain stationary until the permanence of God-union is attained. Those who have gone into the astral world at physical death with material desires must return to the gratifying playground of the physical world. Souls who have freed themselves from earthly karma and who continue to develop in God-consciousness in the astral world, ascend into the supernally blissful causal heaven.

Most average persons, those whose sins are venial and few, are reborn on earth relatively sooner than more advanced souls; after their soul-renewing sojourn in the astral, they wake up in a new physical body with fresh opportunities to progress. Sinful persons are often confined longer by the force of their karma to whatever astral sphere is most conducive to learning the lessons that will prepare them for ultimate redemption. Virtuous souls may stay longer in the astral than do ordinary souls, reaping the blessed rewards of their good karma.

Although the rich man in the parable was caught in the self-create hades of his dissolute ways and unfulfilled desires and failed to gain alleviation of his miseries, he was generous enough in spirit to ask Abraham to send Lazarus to warn his wayward brothers and thereby save them from a similar fate. Even though divine law did not permit Abraham to comply with that wish, the implicit lesson in the story is that the rich man's repentance and marked unselfishness in thinking of his brothers' freedom, even while in the throes of his own torment, would aid in working out the effects of his own profligate actions and help to liberate him from his lower-astral suffering. As in the physical world man can either act wrongly and move toward the dungeon of ignorance and misery or act rightly and thus move toward freedom, so souls in the astral world can either intensify their evil by rebellious thoughts or expiate their evil karma by repentance, prayer, and conscious virtuous resolution.

1 Corinthians 15:52

52 In a moment, in the twinkling of an eye at the last trumpet. for the trumpet shall blow, and the dead shall be raised up in corruptible, and we shall be change.

Complete Books of Enoch, page 61-62:

1 Enoch, Chapter 50, verse 1-5

He will show this to others so that they will change their minds and stop what they are doing. They will have no honor in the presence of the Lord of spirits, but by his name, they may be rescued. The Lord of spirits will have compassion on them, as he has much compassion. His judgment is just, and wickedness will not be able to stand against his judgment. The one who does not change their mind will perish. "From then on I will not have compassion on them," says the Lord of spirits.

Second Coming of Christ, Page 354:

Jesus, the man, could feel his consciousness, not only as residing in and governing his mortal body, but also as the Christ Intelligence pervading all the space cells of his vast cosmic body. As God helps to resurrect souls from entombment within the delusive sepulchre of the three bodies, so also, a true son—a master or God-realized guru—can raise any devoted, aspiring disciple into the omnipresent Spirit. The guru, who is one with the Father, can help the deeply meditating disciple to expand his consciousness and life from the limited sensations of the body out into unlimited space to feel all life in omnipresence. That is the meaning of the "Son quickeneth" or the "Father quickeneth."

Devotees who by constant meditation and spiritual ecstasy feel Christ in all creation are the real Christ-ians. Through direct experience they know and believe in Christ Intelligence and the Father who reflected that Intelligence in all creation, and they know Christ as manifested in the Cosmic Vibration. That is why it is emphasized "he that heareth my word . . . hath everlasting life"; that is, he who listens to the Cosmic Vibration and intuitively feels Christ-wisdom flowing into him not only knows and believes in God and Christ, but becomes one with the imperishable life emanating from Them.

Such souls who are one with Cosmic Vibration and the Christ Intelligence in it, and with God's Intelligence beyond creation, are free from condemnation; that is, from the law of action and its inscrutable judgment that governs man's life.

The devotee seeking everlasting life needs to practice the consciousness-expanding technique of listening to the Cosmic Vibration and feeling Christ Consciousness within it. When he is consciously able to do that and to lift his soul from perceiving the sensations of the physical body, the power and energy of the astral body, and lastly, the thought confinement of the causal body, he raises himself from the tomb of the metaphysically dead three bodies to pass on into the perception of perpetual freedom in Spirit.

Ordinary persons who have no direct knowledge or experience of the Cosmic Vibration—the comforting Holy Ghost, which Jesus promised to send and which devotees can feel by practicing Self-Realization methods—actually have relatively little conscious awareness after death during their deep peaceful rest between incarnations.

But the time will come to such persons, and verily the time has arrived now for advanced disciples, when by the guru's help and by meditation they shall hear the cosmic sound of the Holy Ghost Vibration and feel their expanding wisdom as emanating from the Son of God, the Christ Consciousness. Those devotees who commune with the all-comforting Holy Ghost Vibration (as taught in Lahiri Mahasaya's technique and in which Christ instructed his close disciples) shall not experience the ordinary oblivion of death, but shall live in a continuity of consciousness in the everlastingness of life that flows from God the Father, linking their life with the omnipresent life in all creation.

Author's note:

I was brought closer to Christ Consciousness while I recited Aum (OM). The sacred Cosmic Sound of Aum or Amen is the testimony of the manifested Divine Presence in all creation. You can follow this from the Self-Realization Fellowship.

An ordinary person appears to live only once, in his present lifetime, because he cannot remember his identity during the process of transition from one life to another, as his soul passes through many incarnations. In that sense, man does not live forever, even though his immortal soul never dies.

Only during nocturnal sleep or during the big sleep of death may a soul rest for a while from external stimuli and the ceaseless activating force of desire; but though its bodily instruments sleep, the ever conscious soul keeps stirring all the time. If one sleeps peacefully or fretfully, then, on waking, one feels peaceful or worried, as the case may be. So, in deathly sleep, man's deep consciousness keeps stirring—the life and intelligence is continuously invigorating itself. After he has had sufficient respite from external stimuli, his unfulfilled desires begin to revive, increasing in strength until they cause him to reawaken—either in an astral environment or a new physical incarnation, depending on his karma and the inclination of his desires.

Any stir of intelligence during life or death is vibratory change, the motion of which creates sound—as all vibration is manifested from the Holy Cosmic Vibration and all sound from its sound of Amen or Aum. The great uplifting vibratory change instilled by Cosmic Law at the karmically appointed time of death to release physically captive souls into the freedom of the diseaseless, accident less, painless astral sphere is one meaning of the "resurrection after Gabriel blows his trumpet." Gabriel's trumpet sounds again after a soul's pre-allotted time in the astral world: The Cosmic Intelligent Vibration, "his voice," leads that soul—encased in an astral body wherein its past good and bad karmic tendencies are stored—to enter into a newly built protoplasmic home of a united sperm and ovum cell, which then develops into the embryo and a new physical body.

Thus, they who have done good come forth resurrected into a higher life of better circumstances; and they who have done evil come forth on earth "unto the resurrection of damnation," to face and work out the consequences of their misdeeds, in a new life and opportunity to learn and change their ways. The Cosmic Law and Cosmic Holy Ghost Vibration are only guides to help both good and bad to their respective new-life destinations, Nature's secretive way of working to carry out God's creative plan in a wondrous, mysterious dignity.

The law of resurrection, or reincarnation, thus teaches man that he must never give up, even if old, discouraged, or at death's door. He should try every minute of his existence to improve himself, knowing that life continues after death into the better land of the astral plane, and thence into new, encouraging surroundings on the physical plane.

At last he will wake up to Gabriel's trumpet call of ultimate wisdom in the spiritual kingdom, from which there is no forced return to earth. Even as Jesus by overcoming mortal consciousness attained supreme power over life and death, so every man, by the right method of deep meditation, can learn consciously to lift the soul from body consciousness into the presence of God. When the last trumpet sounds for that soul, death will hold no mystery. The prodigal soul is taken back from its wanderings in matter to its ever-blessed spiritual home in God.

John 6:62, 63

62 What then if ye should see that Son of man ascend up where he was before?

63 It is the spirit that quickeneth: the flesh profiteth nothing: the words that I speak unto you, are spirit and life.

Job 8:19-22

19 Behold, it will rejoice by this means, that it may grow in another mold.

20 Behold, God will not cast away an upright man, neither will he take the wicked by the hand,

21 Till he have filled thy mouth with laughter, and thy lips with joy.

22 They that hate thee, shall be clothed with shame, and the dwelling of the wicked shall not remain.

Job 14:12-14

12 So man sleepeth and riseth not: for he shall not wake again, nor be raised from his sleep till the heaven be no more.

13 Oh that thou wouldest hide me in the grave, and keep me secret, until thy wrath were past, and wouldest give me term, and remember me!

14 If a man die, shall he live again? All the days of mine appointed time will I wait, till my changing shall come.

Second Coming of Christ, page 1145:

God-knowing sages have declared that the three strongest temptations of man are money, sex, and intoxicants. In earlier eras in undeveloped civilizations, sex and wine were the primary pitfalls; in our industrial age, with its dependence on finance in individual life and society at large, it may be said that money is the principal tool of delusion, for it buys wine, stimulates indulgence in evil sensory passions, and exerts a powerful hypnosis of self-importance and false security. Scriptural wisdom, which condemns worship of "unrighteous mammon," needs to be heeded by money-mad modern man.

Saint Paul echoed the teachings of Jesus: "They that will be rich fall into temptation and a snare, and into many foolish and hurtful lusts, which drown men in destruction and perdition. For the love of money is the root of all evil but thou, O man of God, flee these things; and follow after righteousness, godliness, faith, love, patience, meekness. Fight the good fight of faith, lay hold on eternal life, whereunto thou art also called." (1 Timothy 6:9-11)

1 Timothy 6:9-11

9 For they that will be rich, fall into temptation and snares, and into many foolish and noisome lusts, which drown men in perdition and destruction.

10 For the desire of money is the root of all evil, which while some lusted after they erred from the faith, and pierced themselves through with many sorrows.

11 But thou, O man of God, flee these things, and follow after righteousness, godliness, faith, love, patience, and meekness.

Second Coming of Christ, page 925-928:

Man did not create anger, greed, selfishness, lust; their potential was implanted in him by Satan to counter the divine qualities bequeathed to him in his God-created soul. But each human being has free will to make a choice: either to follow the wisdom of the soul and embrace its attributes of goodness or to align himself with the evil passions stimulated within him by cosmic delusion. Everlasting joy and liberation are the blessings of goodness. Woe and threefold misery are the lot of the physically identified the man who, acting in response to the urges of delusion, vents the evil propensities within him and lets them flow outward as noxious actions. "That is why whenever your hands, feet, eyes, or any other organ of sensation and action are used or incited to be used as instruments of evil, you should cut off the attention and currents of life energy that actuate them, employing will power and inner self-control."

"Wherefore if thy hand or thy foot offend thee, cut them off, and cast them from thee: it is better for thee to enter into life halt or maimed, rather than having two hands or two feet to be cast into everlasting fire. And if thine eye offend thee, pluck it out, and cast it from thee: it is better for thee to enter into life with one eye, rather than having two eyes to be cast into hell fire" (Matthew. 18:8-9).

Matthew 18:8-9

8 Wherefore, if thy hand or thy foot cause thee to offend, cut them off, and cast them from thee: it is better for thee to enter into life, halt, or maimed, than having two hands, or two feet, to be cast into everlasting fire.

9 And if thine eye cause thee to offend, pluck it out and cast it from thee: it is better for thee to enter into life with one eye, than having two eyes to be cast into hell fire.

"I am not telling you to dismember yourself if you have committed wrong actions; for by doing so you would destroy only the instruments of evil, not the mental tendencies and desires that willed and actuated the offense. Physically maiming innocent bodily organs might preclude some physical acts of evil, but would not neutralize or prevent mental evils, the real cause of physical evils and the subversion of the godly qualities of the soul. Evil must be destroyed from within. Cut off the mental impulse that activates the motor nerves ('hands and feet') and pluck it from the sensory nerves ('eye') when you are led to see and desire evil or to act evilly. By self-control and the power of concentration that lifts the thoughts to divine perceptions, switch off the delusive inclinations that would offend or obstruct your indwelling God-consciousness, and then forever cast them off from your being."

"It is better for you to be halt or maimed of temporary sense pleasures in material life by sacrificing desire for these indulgences in order to enter into the consciousness of divine joy and eternal life, rather than to remain slavishly identified with the body, allowing the sense organs and nervous system to burn continuously with physical lust, greed, and, material cravings."

Douglas F. Grady

Second Coming of Christ, page 931-932:

The orthodox notion of eternal hellfire and damnation is an utterly false precept; it arises not from God or His true prophets but man's own unforgiving wrath against the evil actions of his brethren. It is nothing but satanic delusion that makes man ascribe to the all-loving God, who is equally the Father of all, a revengeful, vindictive spirit that creates hells and purgatories. As Jesus himself pointed out, the truth is that God in His Infinite Love is helping His children continuously to come back to His eternal kingdom of Bliss.

"Hellfire" is self-created by the wrongs perpetuated by a man. Those who act evilly create evil tendencies that smolder unseen in the brain, ready to pour out fiery suffering at a suitable time. The word hell is from the Anglo-Saxon root helan, "to conceal." Therefore, the word hellfire is very appropriate to depict the concealed flames of agony which stored-up tendencies can produce in earthly life or the afterlife in the astral world. Just as an evildoer with any iota of rationality burns with evil conscience during wakefulness and subconscious terror during sleep, so the consciousness of a man of an evil conscience suffers from hellfire or agony in the "wakeful" state of human life, and after death suffers the effects of bad karma in the form of "fiery" nightmare-like experiences in the astral world. Physical misery ends with death; but spiritual misery born of ignorant actions continues in the after-death state and on into new physical incarnations, until by virtuous deeds and renunciation of evil that bad karma is expiated.

Complete Books of Enoch, page 48
1 Enoch 22:1-14

Then Raphael, one of the sacred angels who was with me, answered, "The beautiful places have been created for this very purpose, for the spirits of the souls of the dead to assemble in them, so that all the souls of humans should assemble here. They will stay in these places until the day of their judgment, until their appointed time. Their appointed time will be long, until the great judgment." And I saw the spirits of humans who were dead, and their voices reached heaven in complaint. Then I asked Raphael, the angel who was with me, "Whose spirit is that, the voice of which reaches heaven in complaint?" He answered me, "This is the spirit of Abel who was slain by his brother Cain, and who will accuse that brother, until his descendants are wiped off the face of the earth, until his descendants are annihilated from the descendants of the human race."

Author's note:

The souls of the just are kept separated from the souls of the wrongdoers after the end of their physical bodies.

At that time, I asked about him, and about the general judgment, "Why is one separated from another?" He answered, "These three have been made so that the spirits of the dead might be separated. This division has been made for the spirits of the just, in which there is the bright spring of water. And this has been made for wrongdoers when they die and are buried in the earth when judgment has not been executed on them in their lifetime. Here, their spirits will be separated in this great pain, until the time of the great judgment, the scoldings, and the torments of the accursed, whose souls are punished and bound there forever. Thus, has it been from the beginning of the world. "And this division had been made for the spirits of those who make complaints, who give information about their destruction, when they were killed in the days of the wrongdoers. This has been made for the spirits of unjust humans who are wrongdoers, those who have committed crimes, and are godless associates of the lawless. But their spirits will not be annihilated in the day of judgment, nor will they arise from this place."

Then I blessed the splendid Lord, "Blessed are you, just Lord, who reigns over everything for ever and ever!"

Section 2.6

Saved

The Secret Book of James, page 30 of Nag Hammadi Scriptures:

I pray that the beginning may come from you. This is how I can be saved. They will be enlightened through me, by my faith, and through another's that is better than mine. I wish mine to be the lesser. Do your best to be like them, and pray that you may acquire a share with them. Beyond what I have said, the Savior did not disclose any revelation to us on their behalf. We proclaim a share with those for whom the message was proclaimed, those whom the lord has made his children.

John 1:12

12 But as many as received him, to them he gave prerogative to be sons of God, even to them that believe in his Name.

Romans 5:1

1 Then being justified by faith, we have peace toward God through Lord Jesus Christ.

Romans 5:9

9 Much more then, being now justified by his blood, we shall be saved from wrath through Him.

Romans 10:13

13 For whosoever shall call upon the name of the Lord, shall be saved.

John 3:15-21

16 For God so loveth the world, that he hath given his only begotten Son, that whosoever believeth in him, should not perish, but have everlasting life.

17 For God sent not his Son into the world, that he should condemn the world, but that the world through him might be saved.

18 He that believeth in him, is not condemned: but he that believeth not, is condemned already, because he hath not believed in the Name of that only begotten Son of God.

19 And this is the condemnation, that that light came into the world, and men loved darkness rather than that light, because their deeds were evil.

20 For every man that evil doeth, hateth the light, neither cometh to light, lest his deeds should be reproved.

21 But he that doeth truth, cometh to the light, that his deeds might be made manifest, that they are wrought according to God.

John 5:22-24

22 For the Father judgeth no man, but hath committed all judgment unto the Son,

23 Because that all men should honor the Son, as they honor the Father: he that honoreth not the Son, the same honoreth not the Father which hath sent him.

24 Verily, verily I say unto you, he that heareth my word, and believeth him that sent me, hath everlasting life, and shall not come into condemnation, but hath passed from death to life.

John 6:36-40

36 But I said unto you, that ye also have seen me, and believe not.

37 All that the Father giveth me, shall come to me: and him that cometh to me, I cast not away.

38 For I came down from heaven, not to do mine own will, but his will which hath sent me.

39 And this is the Father's will which hath sent me, that of all which he hath given me, I should lose nothing, but should raise it up again at the last day.

40 And this is the will of him that sent me, that every man which seeth the Son, and believeth in him, should have everlasting life: and I will raise him up at the last day.

John 20:29-31

29 Jesus said unto him, Thomas, because thou hast seen me, thou believest: blessed are they that have not seen, and have believed.

30 And many other signs also did Jesus in the presence of his disciples, which are not written in this book.

31 But these things are written that ye might believe, that Jesus is that Christ that Son of God, and that in believing ye might have life through his Name.

John 6:45-47

45 It is written in the Prophets, And they shall be all taught of God. Every man therefore that hath heard, and hath learned of the Father, cometh unto me:

46 Not that any man hath seen the Father, save he which is of God, he hath seen the Father.

47 Verily, verily I say unto you, he that believeth in me, hath everlasting life.

John 11:25

25 Jesus said unto her, I am the resurrection and the life: he that believeth in me, though he were dead yet shall he live.

John 12:44-50

44 And Jesus cried, and said, He that believeth in me, believeth not in me, but in him that sent me.

45 And he that seeth me, seeth him that sent me.

46 I am come a light into the world, that whosoever believeth in me, should not abide in darkness.

47 And if any man hear my words, and believe not, I judge him not: for I came not to judge the world, but to save the world.

48 He that refuseth me, and receiveth not my words, hath one that judgeth him: the word that I have spoken, it shall judge him in the last day.

49 For I have not spoken of myself: but the father which sent me, he gave me a commandment what I should say, and what I should speak.

50 And I know that his commandment is life everlasting: the things therefore that I speak, I speak them so as the Father said unto me.

The Secret Book of James, page 30 of Nag Hammadi Scriptures:

"I have spoken my last word to you; I shall depart from you, for a chariot of spirit has carried me up, and from now on I shall strip myself that I may clothe myself. "So pay attention: blessed are those who have proclaimed the Son before he came down, so that, when I did come, I might ascend. "Blessed three times over are those who were proclaimed by the Son before they came into being, so that you might share with them."

When he said this, he left. Peter and I knelt down, gave thanks, and sent our hearts up to heaven. We heard with our ears and saw with our eyes the noise of wars, a trumpet blast, and great turmoil.

When we passed beyond that place, we sent our minds up further. We saw with our eyes and heard with our ears hymns, angelic praises, and angelic rejoicing. Heavenly majesties were singing hymns, and we rejoiced too. Again after this we wished to send our spirits up to the Majesty. When we ascended, we were not allowed to see or hear anything. For the other disciples called to us and asked us, "What did you hear from the teacher? What did he tell you? Where did he go?" We answered them, "He ascended. He gave us his right hand, and promised all of us life. He showed us children coming after us and commanded us to love them, since we are to be saved for their sakes." When they heard this, they believed the revelation, but they were angry about those who would be born.

Not wishing to give them reason to take offense, I sent each of them to a different location. I myself went up to Jerusalem, praying that I might acquire a share with the loved ones who are to appear.

Section 2.7

Statements from Jesus

Beyond Belief, page 227:

The Gospel of Thomas

These are the secret sayings that the living Jesus spoke and Judas Thomas the Twin wrote down.

1 And he said, "Whoever finds the interpretation of these sayings will not taste death."

2 Jesus said, "Let one who seeks not stop seeking until he finds. When he finds, he will be troubled. When he is troubled, he will be astonished and will rule over all."

3 Jesus said, "If your leaders say to you, 'Look, the Kingdom is in heaven,' then the birds of heaven will precede you. If they say to you, 'It is in the sea,' then the fish will precede you. Rather, the Kingdom is inside you and outside you. When you know yourselves, then you will be known, and you will understand that you are children of the living Father. But if you do not know yourselves, then you live in poverty, and you are poverty."

4 Jesus said, "The man old in days will not hesitate to ask a little child seven days old about the place of life, and that person will live. For many of the first will be last and will become a single one."

5 Jesus said, "Recognize what is before your eyes, and the mysteries will be revealed to you. For there is nothing hidden that will not be revealed."

25 Jesus said, "Love your brother like your soul; protect him like the pupil of your eye."

27 "If you do not fast from the world, you will not find the Kingdom. If you do not observe the sabbath day as a sabbath day, you will not see the Father."

28 Jesus said, "I took my stand in the midst of the world, and in flesh I appeared to them. I found them all drunk, and I did not find any of them thirsty. My soul ached for the children of humanity, because they are blind in their hearts and do not see, for they came into the world empty, and they also seek to depart from the world empty. But meanwhile they are drunk. When they shake off their wine, then they will repent."

29 Jesus said, "If the flesh came into being because of spirit, that is to them, 'We have come from the light, from the place where the light came into being by itself, established [itself], and appeared in their image.' If they say to you, 'Who are you?' say, 'We are its children, and we are the chosen of the living Father.' If they ask you, 'What is the sign of your Father in you?' say to them, 'It is movement and rest.'"

51 His disciples said to him, "When will the rest for the dead take place, and when will the new world come?" He said to them, "What you look forward to has already come, but you do not recognize it."

52 His disciples said to him, "Twenty-four prophets have spoken in Israel, and they all spoke of you." He said to them, "You have disregarded the living one who is in your presence and have spoken of the dead."

53 His disciples said to him, "Is circumcision beneficial or not?" He said to them, "If it were beneficial, their father would produce children already circumcised from their mother. Rather, the true circumcision in spirit has become profitable in every respect."

54 Jesus said, "Blessed are the poor, for yours is the Kingdom of Heaven."

57 Jesus said, The Kingdom of the Father is like a person who had good seed. His enemy came during the night and sowed weeds among the good seed. The man did not let the workers pull up the weeds, but said to them, "No, otherwise you might go to pull up the weeds and pull up the wheat along with them." For on the day of the harvest the weeds will be conspicuous and will be pulled up and burned.

Section 2.8

First Death, Second Death

Numbers 16:29-30

29 If these men die the common death of all men, or if they be visited after the visitation of all men, the Lord hath not sent me.

30 But if the Lord make a new thing, and the earth open her mouth, and swallow them up with all that they have, and they go down quick into the pit: then ye shall understand that these men have provoked the Lord.

The Apocalypse of Peter, page 42-43:

The revelation takes place on the Mount of Olives and is initiated by a question or remark from Peter: it were better for the sinners that they had not been created. Christ answers rebuking Peter: "Thou resistest God. Thou wouldest not have more compassion than he for his image . . ." and promises Peter to show him the works of the sinners 'in which they have sinned against the Most High'. There follows the description of the judgement, Christ being established judge by God: 'my Father will place a crown upon my head, that I may judge the living and the dead and recompense every man according to his work'. For the sinners there is eternal torture, in accordance with their sins, while the righteous are introduced into a sort of Paradise. The message of this revelation is expressed by the tortured sinners themselves: 'Righteous is the judgement of God: for we have heard and perceived that is judgement is good, since we are punished according to our deeds'. The central notion of this part is God's justice, meaning retribution to everyone according to his own deeds.

'The Father will judge nobody, but he will give the judgement to his Son (John 5:22) in order that he might give eternal life to those who believe in him.'

Jesus replied as follows: "Did you understand what I told you first? It is permitted to you not to know in your heart what you have asked. It would not be useful to tell the sinners what you have heard so that they should not multiply their sins and evil deeds." Hearing this, Peter falls to the feet of the Lord crying and imploring to him for a long time. At last Jesus has pity on him and answers his question, but his answer is an enigmatic one: "for He maketh his sun rise on the evil and on the good, and sendeth rain on the just and unjust". Because the mercy of my Father is like this: "as the sun rises and the rain falls in the same way, so shall we have mercy and compassion for all of our creatures."

The third part begins again with Peter crying and imploring Jesus with the words: "this is the second death which I am afraid of!" Jesus gives the same answer as at the beginning of the first revelation: "you will have no more mercy on the sinners than I do." Then Jesus adds, "for I was crucified because of the sinners, in order to obtain mercy for them by my Father."

The third revelation was for Peter. The mystery Jesus now reveals to him is not known to anybody, except Jesus and the Father, not even to the angels, the righteous, the martyrs, or the prophets. Jesus admonishes Peter to hide it in a box and not to tell it anybody, except the sages.

Then Jesus reveals that at the Last Judgement the sinners who believe in Christ will be pardoned, because Christ assumed their body and that they ate his body and drank his blood. "The Father will grant to all of them life, glory and eternal kingdom, and his judgement will not be divided." This is the mystery revealed to Peter: had he not cried and wept, Jesus would not have told him. Peter must not speak about this to sinners: even when they hear about the punishment of the fire, they kill one another, so they knew about the mercy, would do what is right. Better to threaten them with fire.

The revelation continues: God created Adam for his glory; he surely does not want to destroy him. Jesus quotes here Psalms 36:5,

Psalms 36:5

5 Thy mercy, O Lord, reacheth unto the heavens, and thy faithfulness unto the clouds.

Adam sinned and was punished for it: he was expelled from Paradise and death came upon him common death, that is, the separation of the soul from the body). But God will not destroy by a second death which he has created.

Douglas F. Grady

Author's note:

Second death is the end of the soul.

After revealing all this, Jesus asks Peter whether he has any doubts left. Peter answered: "Really, when I asked you concerning the sinners who are like me, you told me and explained to me very carefully the words of David, indicating that God's mercy is great. My heart was burning when I was thinking of it that after the resurrection of the dead where would be the second death for the sinners which means descending into the Sheol. Because of this you explained this word to me, and I am convinced and I have no more doubts."

Thus they can be considered as three degrees in the acquisition of a secret knowledge, or three phases of initiation into a mystery. Each revelation is provoked by a question from Peter: "Were it not be better for the sinners, that they had not been created?" in the first revelation and "Would it not have been better for the sinners if they had not been created at all, because they die a second death?"

Section 2.9

Afterlife / Paradise / Purification

The Apocalypse of Peter, page 76-77:

These are the descriptions of paradise (Apocalypse of Peter 16.2-4; see 1 Enoch 32, the opening of the gates of) heaven, and the reference to the second heaven (Apocalypse of Peter 17.3,6; see 1 Enoch 13-16; Levi 2.6-12, 5.1). Note also that the description of Moses and Elijah in Apocalypse of Peter 15.2-7 closely resembles the description of Noah in 1 Enoch 106. The reference to the one heavenly temple, and the short notice that 'we saw and were rejoiced' (Apocalypse of Peter 16.9) makes sense if one locates the event in the same area where Enoch was brought to the heavenly temple, and Levi saw the holy temple.

The Apocalypse of Peter, page 79-80:

And the Lord showed me a widely extensive place outside this world, all gleaming with light, and the air there was flooded by the rays of the sun, and the earth itself budding with flowers which fade not, and full of spices and plants which blossom gloriously and fade not and bear blessed fruit. So great was the fragrance of the flowers that it was borne thence even unto us. The inhabitants of that place were clad with the shining raiments of angels and their raiment was suitable to their place of habitation. Angels walked among there amongst them. All who dwell there had an equal glory, and with one voice they praised God the Lord, rejoicing in that place. The Lord said unto us, "This is the place of your high-priests (brothers), the righteous men."

Veilhauer claims that it would lack any religious character, were it not for the inhabitants who with one voice praised God. His statement is true but the reason for this is that the description of paradise has a Greek background— as Albrecht Dieterich demonstrated at the end of the nineteenth century. However, chapter of the Eithiopic text has a Greek background, too, as the terms 'Acherusian Lake' and 'Elysian Fields' suggest.

The Acheron is a river of Thesprotia in southern Epirus, which breaks through an impenetrable gorge into the Acherusian plain where there was a lake in ancient times.

The Acherlon is mentioned by Herodotus, too, concerning Periander's divination for buried treasure: 'Periander had mislaid something which a friend had left in his charge, so he sent to the oracle of the dead, amongst the Thesproti on the river Acheron, to ask where he had put it'. The Acheron flows through profound and gloomy gorge, one of the darkest and deepest of the glens of Greece. Hence it was a spot likely to be accounted a descent into hell, where the ghost might be summoned back as was Samuel by the witch of Endor (1 Samuel 28).

1 Samuel 28:7

7 Then said Saul unto his servants, Seek me a woman that hath a familiar spirit, that I may go to her, and ask of her. And his servants said to him, Behold, there is a woman at En Dor that hath a familiar spirit.

The Apocalypse of Peter, page 81-82:

Tibullus provides the first surviving description of the Elysian Fields in Roman literature. He adapts the common Greek and Roman picture of the Elysian Fields to the young lovers. Venus will lead Tibullus to the Elysian Fields because he was always addicted to gentle love. There are dances, singing, the birds wander freely; there are aromatic shrubs, sweet-smelling roses. There is no more labour in Elysium than there was in the golden age. Groups of youths hold hands and dance with garlands on their heads. Hell is described as a deep night, contrasting with the dancing series and the reds and greens of the preceding lines. So the phrase referring to hell, at 'scelerata iacet sedes in nocte profunda', means that in hell there is deep darkness; it suggests that in the Elysian Fields, in turn, there is brightness and lightness. Tibullus shortly describes hell: 'there is no crop of standing corn below, no cultivated vineyard'. Putnam is right when he comments on this statement, 'The sentiment suits the poet's present mood of devotion to the quiet life on the land and complements his description of the Elysian Fields at 1.3.61. Putnam's reading of Tibullus parallels the Apocalyse of Peter, which also mentions as vineyard in the description of paradise.

In Virgil's description, the Elysian Fields are flourishing, there is a charming area of greenery and joyful places, all brilliantly illuminated by rich celestial light, a special sun, and stars. Here the heroes, statemen, and artists—such as Orpheus—practice their former profession. This Elysium is particular because only a few distinguished souls remain there forever; the rest, after completing their period of cleansing, accept their tainting bodies again. The concept of the body as a prison for the soul of Orphic origin, and entered literature through Plato's works. It is philosophy and comtemplation that is able to set us free from contaminating effect of the body. Plato, too, teaches the purification of some souls: ' And those who are found to have lived neither well or ill, go to Acheron and, embarking upon vessels provided for them, arrive in them at the lake; there they dwell and are purified'.

The Apocalypse of Peter, page 82:

If we now compare the Elysian Fields of the Apocalyse of Peter with those of Greek and Roman writers and poets, we find that the description of the scene is Greek, but the inhabitants and their activities are different. The inhabitants of the Elsian Fields of the Apocalyse of Peter are clad with shining raiment and praise God. The special emphasis on light and praise of God is Jewish-Christian. Both motifs appear in Psalms 104:1-2 and Ezekiel 1:28;

Psalms 104:1-2

1 My soul, praise thou the Lord: O Lord my God, thou art exceeding great, thou art clothed with glory and honor.

2 Which covereth himself with light, as with a garment, and spreadeth the heavens like a curtain.

Ezekiel 1:28

28 As the likeness of the bow, that is in the cloud in the day of rain, so was the appearance of the light round about.

Complete Books of Enoch, page 63:

1 Enoch 52:1-9

"There will be no iron for war, no material for a breastplate. Bronze will be of no use, tin will be of no use and will count for nothing, and lead will not be wanted. All these things will be rejected, and destroyed off the face of the earth, when the chosen one appears in the presence of the Lord of spirits."

The Apocalypse of Peter, page 84:

The text is written in vulgar Greek, nevertheless it can be interpreted on the basis of Plato's following statement: ' And those who are found to have lived neither well or ill, go to the Acheron and, embarking upon vessels provided for them, arrive in them at the lake; there they dwell and are purified, and if they have done any wrong they are absolved by paying the penalty for their wrong doings, and for their good deeds they receive awards, each according to his merits'. Here is the case of those who have lived neither well or ill and therefore after death their souls go to Acherusian Lake as to Purgatory where they are purified. The idea of Purgatory is to be found both in Old and New Testament, for example, in Zechariah 13:9;

Zechariah 13:9

9 And I will bring that third part through the fire, and will fine them as the silver is fined, and will try them as gold is tried: they shall call on my Name, and I will hear them: I will say, It is my people, and they shall say, The Lord is my God.

The Apocalypse of Peter, page 103:

Although the role of the intercessor is not as powerful in Apocalypse of Paul as in other texts, Apocalypse of Paul agrees with them that the only souls of sinners are washed in the Acherusian Lake. There is no mention of those 'who have not sinned' being washed into the Acherusian Lake. They are merely led into the city of Christ, sailing, no doubt, over the Acherusian lake as Paul does in his outwardly tour: 'And the angel answered and said to me: Follow me and I shall lead you into the city of Christ. And he stood by Lake Acherusia and put me in a golden boat and about three thousand angels were singing a hymn before me until I reached the city of Christ'.

Paul's journey over the Acherusian Lake recalls another forth century text, Paul of Tamma's treatise on the Cell. Paul of Tamma tells his spiritual son: 'My son, obey God and his commandments and be wise and remain in your dwelling place, which is dear to you, as your cell remains with you in your heart while you are seeking after its grace. And the labor of your cell will come with you to God. Your cell will take you over the Acherusian Lake, and it will take you into the church of the firstborn' (Hebrews 12:23)

Hebrews 12:23 And to the assembly and congregation of the first born, which are written in heaven, and to God the judge of all, and to the spirits of just and perfect men,

Here as in other Christian texts there is no mention of the Acherusian Lake being the lake of fire or a place of punishment, yet Paul of Tamma teaches his spiritual son that it is necessary to pass over it. Reading the Cell in the light of the aforementioned Christian apocrypha raises the strong possibility that, for Paul of Tamma, the goal is to be righteous enough not require washing in the Acherusian Lake. In all of these texts, the washing has been reserved only for sinners. Devotion to one's cell should render one's soul pure enough to pass over the Acherusian Lake, as Paul is able to in Apocalypse of Paul.

Edgar Cayce on Angels, page 95-96:

The Seraphim represent the highest order, the angels of love, light, and fire. Their name originates from the Hebrew word, seraphs, meaning "love." The mystical significance of fire is cleansing. It is a symbol of purification, according to the Edgar Cayce readings. The biblical verse which states, that all shall "be tried with fire" (1 Peter 1:7) means that all will be cleansed and purified from any earthly distraction.

This is particularly evident in the Book of Isaiah, for when the prophet sees the Seraphim, he proclaims, "Woe is me! For I am undone; because I am a man of unclean lips . . ." (6:5)

At this point an angel of the Seraphim places a burning coal upon the lips of Isaiah and says, "Lo, this hath touched thy lips; and thine iniquity is taken away, and thy sin purged." (6:7) Fire, in this case, is a purifying activity, not a destructive force.

Chapter 3

Doctrines, Lost Books of the Bible

Chapter 3 contains details about the Lost Books that were left out from the Bible. These books were written, in my opinion, by God's messengers.

I have chosen these books because they contain useful information to understanding the truth. Details about "The Gospel of the Nazirenes" are given in Section 3.1. Some scholars have considered this work as the true Gospel. Section 3.2 is "The Secret Book of John" where John wrote about the secret teachings revealed by Christ in a post-resurrection appearance to the apostle John the son of Zebedee. It, therefore, constitutes a continuation of the Fourth Gospel, whose departure dialogues between the pre-crucifixion Jesus and his uncomprehending disciples Peter, Thomas, and Philip. Section 3.3 is about the book, "Secret Book of James", that apostle James wrote. Lastly, Section 3.4 is about the book, "Apocalypse of Peter", which has fascinating details about afterlife.

Section 3.5 contains quotations from Jesus and Peter regarding the operation of the church. Then, for the last section of this Chapter, section 3.6, in it shows a verse from The Book of Revelation Chapter 12 that made a metaphorical reference to "woman".

Section 3.1

Gospel of the Nazirenes

The Gospel of the Nazirenes, page xvii:

This book was published in London in 1870 as 'The Gospel of the Holy Twelve'. This Gospel is one of the most ancient and complete of early (pre-) Christian fragments. It was preserved in one of the Monasteries of the Buddhist monks in Tibet, where it was hidden by some of the Essene community for safety from the hands of corrupters and now for the first time translated from the Aramaic. The contents clearly show it to be an early Essenian (Nazirene) writing. This ancient community of the Jewish [sect] called Yessenes, Iessenes, Nazirites, or Nazirs strongly resembled the Therapeutae, Pythagoreans, and the Buddhists.

The Gospel of The Nazirenes, page xxxix:

In The Gospel of the Nazirenes parts of both quotes are found in the same chapter (18:1):

I choose for myself the most worthy. The most worthy are those whom the All-Parent has given me. Therefore, if you be in my bosom, and do not the will of the Lord, which is The Law, being self-condemned; you shall be cast out.

One might consider going back to a time machine and asking the Roman Empire sometimes between the sacking of Jerusalem in 70 A.D. and the council of Nicea in 325 A.D.

The Romans themselves say that Constantine the Great, at the behest of God, ordained a clique of priests and scribes to decide which manuscripts and scrolls of the period should go into the Bible. The Gospel of the Nazirenes was considered as a "heresy" because it contradicts to the teaching of the Roman Church. To think they stopped there would be naive. They proceeded over the next two hundred years to add and delete at will, in spite of what the foreboding epitaph at the end of "Revelations" says—which curiously wasn't added until sometime later.

The unfortunate culmination of all this came in 527 A.D. Emperor Justinian's first official edict concerning the Church was to outlaw all teachings considered to be departures from official Church Canon: In particular, anything considered to be of a heathen persuasion, (i.e. Buddhist, Hindu or Eastern), was forbidden.

The impact of this was that any individual or group caught teaching such things as: the teachings of cause and effect (i.e. Karma); the immortality of the soul (reincarnation, etc.); vegetarianism (or any related forms of asceticism); compassionate treatment of animals; and most importantly of all, anti-slavery could be arrested and horrifically executed. (Slavery was not only legal, but upon Justinian's arrival, the manual for proper treatment and pricing was promptly upgraded.) As history bears out, many from sects such as the Appolinarians, the Eutychesians, and most specifically the Nestorians (all of whom had ties to one form or another of neo-Gnosticism, and who taught or practiced some or all of the previously listed condemnations) were mercilessly pursued and persecuted under Justinian's regime.

Gospel of Nazirenes, page xlix:

It is evident that the views during the reign of Iranaeus (who died in 220 A.D.) were "written in stone" at the Council of Nicea in 325 A.D. Those views were a sharp departure from the edicts and principles of "The Way" as espoused by the original Nazirene movement, whose leadership was passed on by Jesus to his brother James and Simon Peter.

Another scholar writes:

The Nazarene Gospel belongs to an early stage of evangelical literature, which scholars, believe that it was earlier than the canonical Matthew. It is interesting to note that Jerome, who accepted the view prevalent in the early Church that St. Matthew's gospel was originally written in Hebrew, was at first disposed to think that in the Nazarene gospel he had discovered the lost original of the canonical book. One of the most important of the noncanonical writings . . . he found it in use among the Nazarenes, in a Jewish-Christian community in Syria . . . it was written in Aramaic.

This statement, from "The Apocryphal Gospels" section of The History of Christianity—In The Light of Modern Knowledge by Rev. Adam Findlay, M.A., D.D., though posed by numerous predecessors, nevertheless sets both a tone and a standard for twentieth-century scholarship on the subject. In another statement, Findlay reiterates and expands:

The most primitive of the noncanonical gospels, the Gospel of the Nazirenes, was in use up to the end of the fourth century in a community which set special store by it; another, a Gospel of Peter which was episcopally condemned at the close of the second century, was found in an Egyptian grave.

We follow Findlay with another early-to-mid-twentieth-century biblical historian, Dr. Edgar J. Goodspeed, who is best known for his scholarly apocryphal translations. From his History of Early Christian Literature:

Eusebius lists this gospel among the "disputed"—or nonconforming books. Jerome, toward the close of the century, could not find a Greek copy of it, but saw an Aramaic text of it in Palestine, which, he says, he translated into Greek and Latin, probably meaning for the parts he wished to copy or use in his works. This Aramaic version, so often regarded as "the original," was . . . for the use of the Jewish Christian sects—perhaps Ebionites, more probably Nazarenes—who in the third century were using the book, and finally gave their name to it, so that it came to be known as the "Gospel of the Nazarenes." Epiphanius says that the "Nazarenes," or Gnostic Jewish Christians, used a gospel resembling Matthew . . . . This gospel disappeared probably sometime during the latter part of the third or early part of the fourth century.

Gospel of the Nazirenes, page xii:

Without a historically accurate account of the times and teachings of Jesus, one is easily subjected to the distorted information propagated at the Council of Nicea and later in the fourth century. The Nicene Creed and all its related dogma (transmitted through the ages as historical and spiritual truth) have been perpetuated ever since.

A gospel referred to under a number of different titles (The Gospel of the Nazirenes being one of them) has also persisted through the centuries. This

Gospel was referred to by a number of Church Father Historians: Papias, Hegesippus, Iranaeas, Clement, Origen, Basil, Epiphanius, Eusebius, and St. Jerome, among others.

The Way of Jesus the Nazirene as taught in this gospel is the ancient way of life taught since the time of Enoch and Noah. It's historical authenticity is validated by its total alignment with ancient teachings found in the Torah and the Talmud. Although it may appear shocking to those brought up on the "King James," there is strong historical evidence that these teachings are essentially the same as the Bet Hillel school of Pharisees and the Essenes of that time. There is also some historical evidence that Jesus studied with Hillel the Elder, who founded the Bet Hillel branch of Pharisees. Jesus and the members of the Bet Hillel School, which was a slight minority to the Bet Shammai School, "were persecuted by the Bet Shammai Pharisees who were in control at that time. Yes, Jesus was brought up not only as a Jew, but in the Nazirite-Essene or Nazirene sect of the Essene branch of Judaism. Many of the Essenes at that time were previously Hillel Pharisees who were forced to leave the sect because of the bitterness of the attacks by the Shammai Pharisees.

The teachings of the Essenes included vegetarianism, negation of sacrifice/cruelty to animals, karma/reincarnation—immortality of the soul, love of neighbor as self, and the mission to share the One Lord Creator (a common term used for Diety in this period) with all nations. For example, there is an account of Menahem the Essene who in 20 B.C.E. lead 160 Essenes in teaching the One Lord Creator to the nations. They did not, as conquerors, forced a religion on the population. They respected the right of each nation to develop their own personal way to come to know the One without beginning or end.

It is not surprising, in this historical context, and is validated in The Gospel of the Nazirenes, that Jesus also taught the importance of vegetarianism, noncruelty to animals, love of neighbor as self, reincarnation, and the mission to share these teachings with all the nations.

In this Gospel, there is also an emphasis on the universality of truth.

Beyond Belief, page 15:

One of the earliest sources, for example, the Teaching of the Twelve Apostles to the Gentiles (Gospel of the Nazirenes), shows that members of certain early groups of Jesus' followers did not think themselves as Christians—as we think of Christians—as separate from Jews, but as God's people—by which some apparently meant Jews who revered Jesus as the great interpreter of God's law, the Torah. Written in Syria about 10 years before the New Testament gospels of Matthew and Luke, this writing, known as Didache (Greek for "teaching"), opens with a succinct summary of God's law, along with a negative version of the so-called golden rule: "The Way of Life is this: First you shall love the God who made you, and your neighbor as yourself;

The main sources from which these quotes arise are available to all who would search through the countless volumes of reference material on the text referred to by past and present historians as an original "Aramaic Matthew." There is no doubt that further information will be forthcoming when access to more material becomes available. This Gospel has been mentioned and quoted from numerous times by many of the early Church historians. These references have contributed greatly to our understanding of Nazirene traditions in first-century Palestine. This "Aramaic Matthew" has been called by a number of variant titles: Gospel of the Hebrews, Gospel of the Nazirenes, Gospel of the Ebionites and most recently, though less frequently, Gospel of the Holy Twelve.

Isaiah Effect, page 46:

Dating to the fourth century A.D., the Nag Hammadi Library begins at the approximate time that the Dead Sea Scrolls leave off. The Gnostic traditions originated during a time when early Christian doctrines were reshaped and were taking on a new identity. Gnostic identified with central teaching of Christianity, in their original form, and chose to separate, rather than follow the tide of change that was leading Christian traditions from the original basis of their belief. As the Roman Empire converted to conventional Christianity, Gnostic followers were first relegated to the status of a radical sect and eventually eradicated from the consideration of Christianity entirely. Books such as the Gospel of Mary, the Apocalypes of Paul, James, and Adam, and the book of Melchizedek survive today as a testament to the Gnostic wisdom of preserving rare teachings for future generations.

Of special note, among the Nag Hammadi documents, is a rare text known as the Apocalype of Adam. A collection of teachings that were divinely inspired and transmitted, this book is the account of Adam that we read of in the Book of Genesis. What makes the Apocalypse of Adam unique is the apparent absence of any relationship to earlier material. It appears that this text was already complete and well established as an earlier form of Gnosticism long before the time of Christian literature.

Adam began his account by describing the presence of three visitors from heaven, guides that led him through his visions into the futures of humankind. Shortly before his death, he dictated his revelations to his son Seth. Similar to the teachings of the prophet Enoch, who dictated the secrets of Creation to his son, Methuselah, at an advanced age, the texts begin with Adam teaching his son in the seven hundredth year. Establishing a brief history of his life with Eve, Seth's mother, Adam shared his visions of events that are yet to occur. Now then, my son Seth, I will reveal the things which those men whom I saw at first revealed to me. Adam tells of the time of the great flood of Noah, still to come in his future, complete with accurate references to Noah's family and the ark that saves them.

Perhaps the most powerful among the Nag Hammadi works is a rare text written by a woman of the Gnostic traditions, titled "The Thunder: Perfect Mind". This work is virtually unique in the Nag Hammadi Library and very unusual. Written in the first person, the manuscript is in the form of a dialogue in which the unnamed author proclaims herself to have experienced many dichotomies of human experience. "For I am the first and the last. I am the honored one and the scorned one. I am the whore and the holy one. I am the wife and the virgin. Of I am barren one and many are her sons."

Through collections of words that are reminiscent of the poetry found in the Dead Sea Scrolls, she reminds us that within every person lives all possibilities of all experience, from the lightest of light to the darkest of the dark. The text continues with final verse admonishing readers to remember that as men go to their resting place, "There they will find me, and they will live, and they will never die again."

One of the most controversial of the Nag Hammadi texts is the document known as the Gospel of Thomas. At least the portion of this manuscript is identified as being translated from Greek into Coptic Egyptians, the language used in Christian monasteries of Egypt early in the first millennium. The Gospel of Thomas is a rare collection of sayings, parables, stories, and direct quotes from Jesus, believed to have been recorded by the brother of Jesus, Didymos Judas Thomas. This is the same Thomas who later founded Christian churches in the East.

Portions of this gospel are very similar to the manuscript of the Gospel Q, a source manuscript, believed to date to the first century. The "Q" texts are known to have been used as a reference by New Testament authors. However, many portions of the Gospel of Thomas are not found in the Gospel Q, suggesting that it is an independent resource that may confirm and validate other texts dating from the same time.

With this formula in mind, the Essene masters invite us to heal the memories of our most painful experiences by changing the emotion of the experience itself. An ancient basis for the modern axiom "energy follows attention," a concise parable from the lost Gospel Q describes this concept: "Whoever tries to protect his life will lose it." These deceptively brief words explain why we sometimes attract into our lives those experiences that we least choose to have. In recent times, affirmations have become very popular with followers of some spiritual and esoteric teachings. In these traditions, it is suggested that by affirming the things that we choose to experience in our lives, often many times each day, they will come to pass. The ancient model of thought, emotion, and feeling may help those people to understand what has happened or failed to happen.

Section 3.2

The Secret Book of John

The Secret Book of John, page 100 of Nag Hammadi Scriptures:

Discovered in the Berlin Gnostic Codex 8502 in 1896 but not published until 1955, the Secret Book (Apocryphon) of John is probably the most widely known of all the Sethian treatises. The popularity and importance of the Secret Book of John in antiquity is clearly evident. It now survives in no fewer than four separate manuscripts, a huge number of copies, compared with what we have for most Gnostic texts. Two manuscripts (Nag Hammadi Codices II and IV) contain a somewhat longer version of the Secret Book of John, while the other two (Nag Hammadi Codex III and the Berlin Gnostic Codex 8502) contain somewhat shorter versions. All four codices contain other writings, but in the three Nag Hammadi codices, the Secret Book of John is always the first tractate copied into the codex. "In Against Heresies 1.29", the late second-century anti-Gnostic Christian bishop Irenaeus summarized a work very similar to the first part of the Secret Book of John.

The Secret Book of John, page 104 of Nag Hammadi Scriptures:

The Secret Book contains what purport to be secret teachings revealed by Christ in a post-resurrection appearance to the apostle John the son of Zebedee. It thus constitutes a continuation of the Fourth Gospel, whose farewell dialogues between the pre-crucifixion Jesus and his uncomprehending disciples Peter, Thomas, and Philip. The dialogues concerning Jesus's promised return to the Father are now supplemented by John's post-ascension encounter with the very Savior who had indeed returned to the Father just as he had predicted. The veiled references to the many rooms of his Father's house to which the earthly Savior had promised to take his followers are now described in detail, and the unity between the Father and the Son is now clarified: Jesus is the Father, Mother, and Son; indeed, in his primordial capacity as the blessed Mother-Father, Christ had already raised up the seed of Seth to the Father's many-roomed house, namely, the four eternal realms, or aeons, which he had previously prepared before this world had ever come to be. In contrast to a future parousia at the end of days envisioned by John 21 and the Johannine letters, the Secret Book of John portrays this parousia as occurring shortly after the events described in the gospel and effect challenges the leadership role John 21 assigns to Peter by having the postascension Jesus appoint John as the teacher of his fellow disciples.

Christ's ensuing lengthy discourse, punctuated at certain points by John's requests for clarification, consists of two parts, the Savior's lengthy monologue on theogony and cosmogony and a subsequent dialogue between John and the Savior on anthropogony and soteriology. According to Michael Waldstein, with respect to its rapprochement with Jewish Genesis traditions, the first part tells of pre-Genesis realities and events about which Moses provides no information, and the second offers a rereading of Genesis 1-7. With respect to its rapprochement with Platonic traditions, especially Plato's Timaeus, the Jewish creator god is split "into an upper God of pure goodness, who is personally identified as the transcendent God of Middle Platonic theology who retained some central features of the God of Israel, and an evil lower God who was personally identified as the God of Israel, but is portrayed as a parody of the Platonic demiurge."

Nehemiah 1:5

5 And said, O Lord God of heaven, the great and terrible God, that keepeth covenant and mercy for them that love him, and observe his commandments,

Author's note:

How could God be considered "terrible"? Could this relate to what Jesus Christ was explaining to John about the "pre-Genesis realities and events about the cosmic rulers which Moses provided no information?"

In the first part, Christ reveals to John the nature of the supreme deity (the primal divine triad, Father, Mother, and Child), the divine realm brought into being by him (the All or Pleroma of light organized into Four Luminaries, Harmozel, Oroiael, Daveithai, and Eleleth), and its relation to the created order—how the creation, with its flaws and shortcomings originated (through the fall of Sophia/Wisdom and the creation of a lower world at the hands of her ill-begotten son, Yaldabaoth, and his demonic underlings) and became dominated by the inferior powers that now control it. This part concludes with Yaldabaoth's boast, "I am a jealous god and there is no other god beside me" (Isaiah 45:5-6, 21), which marks the point of transition to the second part of the revelation, a dialogue wherein Christ makes the first of many textual allusions to Genesis. What makes the work distinctively Sethian is the understanding of the Four Luminaries as the respective aeonic dwellings of the archetypal Adam, Seth, his primordial seed (the seven Semite generations from Seth through Noah), and Seth's postdiluvian progeny.

The second part of the Secret Book of John contains Christ's explanation of the true meaning of Genesis 1-9, revealing how Yaldabaoth created Adam as an initially weak copy, not yet spiritual, of the image of the archetypal human projected below from the divine world. John then asks the first often questions, introducing an element of dialogue not found in the first part; and the subject matter shifts from theogony and cosmogony to soteriology and anthropogony. This part goes on to reveal how Adam acquired his true spiritual nature and was enlightened by Insight (Epinoia) appearing in the form of the spiritual Eve and by eating of the tree of knowledge, was expelled from paradise, and begot Seth. After a short dialogue on the salvation of various types of souls from the incarnational cycle and the origin of the wicked spirit, Christ's revelation concludes with the story of Yaldabaoth's further enslavement of the human race through the origination of fate, the coming of the flood, and (note the reverse of the biblical order) how intercourse between the angels and human women led to humanity's sexual enslavement. The Savior then departs to the aeonic world with a reminder that salvation is certain, since the divine Mother has already enlightened her seed.

Beyond Belief, page 126:

The Gospel of John inspired yet another example of "evil exegesis"—the famous and influential Secret Book of John, which Ireneaus apparently read. The Secret Book opens after Jesus' death, when John, the brother of James, the son of Zebedee, walking toward the Temple, is accosted by a Pharisee, who charges "this Nazerene" has decieved John and his fellow believers, "filled your ears with lies, closed your hearts, and turned away from the traditions of your fathers." John turns away from the Temple and flees to a desolate place in the mountains, "grieving greatly in his heart." There, as he struggles alone in fear and doubt, he says that "suddenly the heavens opened, and the whole creation shone, and the world was shaken." John is astonished and terrified to see an unearthly light, in which changing forms appear, and to hear Jesus' voice saying, "John, John, why are you astonished, and why are you afraid? . . . I am the one who is with you always. I am the Father; I am the Mother; and I am the Son." After a moment of shock, John recognizes Jesus as the one who radiates the light of God and appears in various forms, including Father, Son, and Holy Spirit—the last envisioned as feminine (suggested by the gender of the Hebrew term for spirit, ruah) and so as Divine Mother.

But after Jesus consoles John with this vision, he says that "the God and Father of all things" cannot actually be apprehended in anthropomorphic images, since God is "the invisible, unimaginable, wholly beyond human comprehension. How, then, can one speak of God at all? To answer this question, the author of the Secret Book borrows the language of John's gospel: "To the point that I am able to comprehend him—for who will ever be able to comprehend him? . . . God is the light, the one who gives the light; the life, the one who gives the life." "John, the disciple of the Lord, wanting to set forth the origin of all things, how the Father brought forth all things," reveals in his opening lines—the original structure of divine being. This, he says, is the "primary ogdoad," which consists of the first eight emanations of divine energy, rather than what kabbalists later will call the divine sephirot; thus, when Valentinus and his disciples read the opening of John's gospel, they envisioned God, the divine word, and Jesus Christ as, so to speak, waves of divine energy flowing down from above, from the great waterfall to the local creek.

Ireneaus rejects this attempt to find the hidden meaning in John's prologue and explains to his reader that he has quoted this commentary at length so that "you can see, beloved, the method by which by which those using it to deceive themselves, and abuse the Scriptures by trying to support their own invention from them." Had John meant to set forth the primordial structure of divine being, Ireneaus says, he would have made his meaning clear; thus, the "fallacy of their interpretation is obvious", and he then, as we shall see, offers the true interpretation of John's gospel.

Beyond Belief, page 164-175:

The Secret Book intends this story to show that we have a latent capacity within our hearts and minds that links us to the divine—not in our ordinary state of mind but when this hidden capacity awakens. Because the term epinoia has no precise equivalent in English, I shall leave it in Greek. To speak of various modes of consciousness susceptible to revelation, the author of the Secret Book invokes a cluster of words related to the Greek verb noein, which means "perceive," "think," or "be aware."

The Secret Book explains that, although God is essentially incomprehensible, the powers that reveal God to humankind include pronoia (anticipatory awareness), ennoia (internal reflection), and prognosis (foreknowledge or intuition), all personified as feminine presences, presumably because of the gender of the Greek words.

The author of the Secret Book stresses that the insights this spiritual intuition conveys are neither complete nor certain; instead, epinoia conveys hints and glimpses, images and stories, that imperfectly point beyond themselves toward what we cannot now fully understand. Thus, the author knows that these very stories—those told in the Secret Book—are to be taken neither literally nor too seriously; for these, too, are merely glimpses that, as Paul says, we now know only "in a mirror, darkly." Yet, however incomplete, these glimpses suffice to reveal the presence of the divine, for the Secret Book says that, apart from spiritual intuition, "people grow old without joy . . . and die . . . without knowing God."

How is it, then, that many people remain oblivious to epinoia?

To answer this question, the Secret Book tells a story intended to show that although the creator-god pictured in Genesis is himself only an anthropomorphic image of the divine Source that brought forth the universe, many people mistake this deficient image for God.

This story tells how the creator-god himself, being unaware of the "blessed one, the Mother-Father, the blessed and compassionate One" above, boasted that he was the only God ("I am a jealous God; there is none other besides me"). Intent on maintaining sole power, he tried to control his human creatures by forbidding them to eat the fruit of the tree of knowledge. But when Adam and Eve disobeyed him, and chose to seek knowledge of the divine Source above, he realized that they had listened to their inner resource, the luminous epinoia. As soon as the creator-god realized what they had done, he retaliated; first he punished them both, and even cursed the earth itself because of them; then he tried to force the woman to subject herself to the man, saying, "Your husband shall rule over you"; and, finally, "all his angels cast them out of Paradise," burdening them with "bitter fate" and with daily cares to make them oblivious to the "luminous epinoia."

But this is a mythical explanation. Can we find a more practical reason for the suppression of the "luminous epinoia"? I suggest that the author of the Secret Book knew how Christians like Irenaeus challenged those who spoke of the "God beyond God," and insisted that everyone worship only the creator. But while Valentinus's followers often met such challenges with silence, But it would take more than theological argument for Irenaeus's viewpoint to prevail in churches throughout the world: it would take, in fact, the revolution initiated by the Roman emperor Constantine. In his famous History of the Church, Eusebius of Caesarea, a bishop in Palestine who survived years of persecution in which many of his friends and fellow Christians died, wrote how God miraculously intervened on October 28, 312, by revealing Christ's sign in the heavens to the pagan emperor Constantine and gaining his allegiance. Eusebius then tells how, in the years that followed, Constantine declared amnesty for Christians and became their imperial patron. But this practical military leader chose to recognize only those who belonged to what may have become, by his time, the best-organized and largest group, which he called the "lawful and most holy" catholic church."

Constantine's recognition carried with it, of course, enormous benefits. In 313 A.D., the emperor ordered that anyone who had confiscated property from "the catholic church of the Christians in any city, or even in other places," during the persecutions of the previous decades must return it immediately to "these same churches" and offer compensation for any damages. Eusebius of Caesarea marveled that in this astonishing new era, "bishops constantly received even personal letters from the emperor, and honors, and gifts of money." Eusebius includes in his history a letter Constantine wrote the same year to the proconsul of Africa to say that he was exempting Christian clergy from financial obligations incumbent on ordinary citizens; only to those he called the "ministers of the lawful and most holy catholic religion." The emperor also offered tax relief and, later, tax exemptions to clergy who qualified—while threatening to increase taxes for anyone guilty of founding "heretical" churches. About ten years later, apparently responding to what he considered abuses of these privileges, he wrote a new order to specify that the privileges that have been granted in consideration of religion must benefit only the adherents of the catholic faith [or "law"]. It is our will, furthermore, that heretics and schismatics shall not only be alien from these privileges but also shall be bound and subjected to various compulsory public services.

Besides allocating money to repair damaged churches, Constantine ordered new ones to be built, including, tradition says, a magnificent Church of St. Peter on the Vatican hill in Rome and the Church of the Holy Sepulcher in Jerusalem. In 324A.D., he wrote to the eastern bishops, urging them to "ask without hesitation whatever [funds] you find to be necessary" from the imperial treasury. He assured them that he had already ordered his finance minister to give them whatever they asked to build new churches and fit them with the splendor appropriate to honor the God of the universe. Constantine also delegated to certain bishops the distribution of the imperial grain supply and other necessities to support people in need, so that they might fulfill Jesus' admonitions to care for the sick, the needy, and the destitute, as well as those who had suffered torture, imprisonment, or exile during the years of persecution. Furthermore, while transforming the status of Christians, Constantine's revolution changed the status of Jews. As Timothy Barnes, one of the foremost contemporary historians of these events, writes, "Constantine translated Christian prejudice against Jews into legal disabilities." He forbade Jews to enter Jerusalem, except on the one day a year they were to mourn for having lost it, and ordered them not to seek or accept converts to Judaism. Moreover, Constantine "prescribed that any Jew who attempted forcibly to prevent conversion from Judaism to Christianity should be burned alive."

To strengthen his own alliance with church leaders and to unify fractious Christian groups into one harmonious structure, Constantine charged bishops from churches throughout the empire to meet at his expense at Nicaea, an inland city, near a large lake, to work out a standard formulation of Christian faith. From that meeting and its aftermath, during the tumultuous decades that followed, emerged the Nicene Creed that would effectively clarify and elaborate the "canon of truth," along with what we call the canon—the list of twenty-seven writings, which would, become the New Testament. Together these would help establish what Irenaeus had envisioned—a worldwide communion of "orthodox" Christians joined into one "catholic and apostolic" church.

How that happened, is far more complex than can be related here. I hesitate even to mention the extraordinary events of the fourth century, since no short sketch can adequately describe them; yet I offer one, since these events no doubt are linked to the history we have been exploring. Fortunately, several outstanding historians have written accounts available for the interested reader. For our purposes here, even the briefest summary would have to note how, during the transitional decades after 312, Constantine subjected the Roman empire to a massive restructuring and shifted the underpinnings of imperial power. What he did—and did gradually, in order to minimize opposition from powerful senators—was transfer the empire's basic allegiance from the traditional guardians of its welfare, the gods of Rome, to the foreign god worshiped by those whom his predecessors had persecuted for atheism. It was at this critical time that Constantine convened the international council of bishops to meet at Nicaea, "because of the excellent temperature of the air," in the early days of June 325. The emperor himself attended the council and participated in it, telling his guests at one of the lavish state dinners that he believed God had appointed him "bishop [the Greek term means "supervisor"] of those outside the church." Although in the past, many historians assumed that Constantine directed and even dictated the entire proceedings, more careful historical investigation has shown that he not only allowed but expected the bishops themselves to arbitrate disputes and to forge a working consensus among rival parties. When he addressed those who gathered at Nicaea, he urged them to resolve their differences "lest private animosities interfere with God's business."

When Alexander and Athanasius received Constantine's summons to Nicaea, to formulate a creed for the "universal" church, they arrived determined to make sure that the carefully chosen—and hotly contested—theological phrases placed there would confess Christ, the Word, as God. They must have been pleased with the result: the formula upon which the majority finally voted, after intense argument, proclaimed that Jesus Christ was "God from God, Light from Light, true God from true God"; that he was "begotten, not made," that is, borrowing John's term, God's "only begotten" offspring (not "made," as were all beings whom God created, angels and humans alike).

The next phrase, upon which Alexander and his allies had agreed in advance, proved explosively controversial. To exclude Arius's view that Christ was divine but not in the same sense as God, they insisted on adding that Christ was "of one being with"—essentially no different from—God the Father. While the great majority of bishops "were prepared to accept almost any formula that would secure harmony within the church," those who opposed this phrase pointed out that it occurs neither in the Scriptures nor Christian tradition. Is it not extreme, they asked, and contrary to the gospels, to say that Jesus Christ is essentially "the same" as God the Father? But those who insisted that he was carried the day; and no doubt it mattered that Constantine, perhaps frustrated by so much time spent wrangling over a phrase, urged the bishops to include it and end the argument.

Now that Constantine had endorsed the term, anyone who challenged it might seem to be questioning the orthodoxy of the emperor himself. In any case, all those present signed the document except the few who chose instead to leave: Arius himself, along with some priests and two bishops from Libya who remained loyal to him. Later, however, the inclusion of this phrase intensified controversy among Christians that continued for decades—indeed, for generations (and, some would say, for centuries).

Eventually the Nicene Creed, approved by the bishops and endorsed by Constantine himself, would become the official doctrine that all Christians henceforth must accept in order to participate in the only church recognized by the emperor—the "catholic church." A year before the bishops met at Nicaea, Constantine had tried to legislate an end to "heretical sects," which, by one estimate, may have included about half the Christians in the empire. The emperor ordered all "heretics and schismatics" to stop meeting, even in private houses, and to surrender their churches and whatever property they owned to the catholic church. Although many Christians associated with teachers such as Valentinus, Marcion, and the prophet Montanus ignored the law, and magistrates often failed to enforce it, such legislation lent enormous support to the network of catholic churches.

Constantine believed that all people should be Christian, but that Christians might legitimately hold divergent opinions on theological questions, and that sensible Christians could disagree about doctrine in a spirit of brotherly love.

Some scholars have suggested that these theological disputes were essentially political. The historian Erik Peterson points out that many Christians associated God the Father with the emperor, Jesus Christ with the bishops, and the holy spirit with "the people." Thus, he suggests, Athanasius's claim that the Son is entirely equal with the Father implies that the bishops' authority is equal to that of the emperor himself. Peterson says that this position correlates with Athanasius's refusal to take orders from any emperor, and pervaded the power struggles that characterized the relationship between emperors and bishops in the West throughout the middle ages.

Section 3.3

The Secret Book of James

Beyond Belief, page 97:

The Egyptian monks who treasured the secret writings in their monastery library even two hundred years after Irenaeus had denounced them. But in 367 C.E., Anthanasius, the zealous bishop of Alexandria—an admirer of Irenaeus—issued an Easter letter in which he demanded that Egyptian monks destroy all such writings, except for those he specifically listed as acceptable, even canonical—a list that constitutes virtually all of our present "New Testament". But someone—perhaps monks at the monastery of St. Pachomius—gathered dozens of books Athanasius wanted to burn, removed them from the monastery library, sealed them in a heavy, six-foot jar, and intending to hide them, buried them on a nearby hillside near Nag Hammadi. There an Egyptian villager named Muhammad Ali stumbled upon them sixteen hundred years later. Now we can read for ourselves some of the writings that Ireneaus detested and Athanasius banned, we can see many of them express the hope of receiving revelation, and encourage "those who seek God." The author of the Secret Book of James, for example, reinterprets the opening scene we noted from the New Testament Acts, in which Luke tells how Jesus ascended into heaven and departed.

The Secret Book says that Jesus astonished his disciples by suddenly coming back—a year and a half after he had departed—and explained that he had not actually removed himself from his disciples. Jesus invited James and Peter to travel with him to heaven, perhaps in the kind of ecstatic trance that John of Patmos said he experienced before he wrote the book of Revelation.

Beyond Belief, page 100:

Those who wrote, translated, and carefully copied works such as the Secret Book of James and the Prayer of the Apostle Paul may have known about techniques that certain Jewish groups used to induce a state of ecstasy and invoke visions. For example, one group of Jewish ascetics living in Egypt at the time of Jesus, called the Therapeutae, practiced a rigorous regimen of prayer, celibacy, fasting, and singing to prepare themselves to receive "the vision of God." Some of the Dead Sea Scrolls also offer prayers and rituals apparently intended to help the devout enter God's presence and join in worship with angels. For to this day many Jews and Christians use mystical language in worship services every week—or even every day—at a culminating moment understood to unite the human congregation with the angels, as they join in singing what the prophet Isaiah says angels sing in heaven: "Holy, holy, holy; Lord God almighty; heaven and earth are full of your glory." Isaiah says that he heard this song when he himself received a vision and was taken into God's presence.

The Secret Book of James, page 19-21 of Nag Hammadi Scriptures:

The Secret Book of James follows the ancient epistolary style for the opening of a letter (name of the sender, name of the addressee, salutation, and greeting of peace) as well as its conclusion. The letter has been sent by James, it is said, at the request of his addressee, and it contains an account of a secret revelation the Savior gave to James and Peter. James recalls that he wrote the letter, which is esoteric in its content, in Hebrew letters, and he asks his addressee not to share this writing with many: even the Savior did not want to deliver his message to the twelve disciples, but only to two of them. Doubtless the addressee is worthy of receiving this secret teaching, as is shown by the title James gives him: "a minister of the salvation of the saints" (the saints can be the members of a Gnostic community or, more generally, the elect believers who are deserving of salvation). And faith given through this discourse (logos) will automatically confer salvation upon them.

In the literary fiction of the Secret Book of James, the events depicted happen 550 days after the Savior's resurrection, at a time when the twelve disciples, all sitting together, are writing down in books what they remember of the words Christ told to each of them during his earthly life.

This constitutes an important piece of information about how the disciples shaped Christ's logia, a process also recorded elsewhere in early Christian literature (e.g., in 1 Clement 13.1-2). The gap of 550 days between the resurrection and the second coming of the Savior can be compared with a tradition recorded in the Ascension of Isaiah, a Jewish apocryphal text with Christian interpolations, which speaks of a period of 18 months, or 540 days.

The intention of the Savior is to draw James and Peter apart from the other disciples and help them to "be filled"—a technical phrase in Gnostic thought linked to Pleroma and "fullness"—through his revelation. James is receptive to the words of the Savior, but Peter shows no understanding. The two figures have been interpreted as opposing symbols of the Gnostic community and the emerging orthodox church: members of the Gnostic community have no need of an intermediary to obtain salvation, while the members of the great church are grounded in an ecclesial structure that they need if they are to be saved. Such ideas are advanced in Secret Book of James. The Savior's teachings are expressed through a series of opposing Gnostic metaphors: drunkenness and sobriety, waking and sleeping, being healed and being sick, emptiness and fullness.

These metaphors belong to the common heritage of late antiquity, yet, taken together, they express themes typical of Gnostic teaching. The Savior utters teachings consisting of sayings, parables, and prophecies organized into a dialogue in which James asks questions of the Savior. As for Peter, he plays a small role in this dialogue, and he limits himself to a polemical statement showing his lack of comprehension.

The literary genre of the Secret Book of James is heterogeneous: the tractate is a letter reporting on a revelation shaped into the form of a dialogue. Although the classical rules of epistolary style are known by the author, the treatise is marked by themes belonging to the genre of esoteric teaching. The letter may even be a frame added later to the original content by a redactor. As for the body of the text, it is an example of a revelatory dialogue, in which an inquirer asks questions about hidden matters and a revealer provides answers. Well attested in Jewish and Christian tradition, the revelatory dialogue has evolved from a real to an imaginary dialogue.

Two capstone themes are present in the Secret Book of James: that of fullness and pain and that of prophecy. This part of the tractate is guided by the polemical intention of the author against Peter and the official church, but the polemical character of the Secret Book of James is veiled, and the author maintains a prudent attitude when dealing with these matters. The polemical features of the text may suggest that the Secret Book of James speaks to a situation in which authoritative structures are being established and the text is reacting against them. Other Nag Hammadi texts (Second Discourse of Great Seth, Revelation of Peter, and Testimony of Truth) show similar concerns.

Some of the sayings attributed to Jesus in the Secret Book of James can be compared with logia in the canonical gospels, but others have no parallels in New Testament tradition (e.g., The saying about the palm shoot).

Jewish apocalyptic and esoteric themes are combined in the treatise: the theme of the "chariot of spirit" that bears the Savior aloft recalls Jewish Merkavah speculations on the divine chariot of God; the vision James and Peter experience are paralleled in the Jewish pseudepigrapha, for example, in Enoch literature. After seeing and hearing angelic trumpets and a great deal of turmoil, the two disciples ascended to a higher place. They heard angels praising and rejoicing, as well as the celestial majesties (the highest classes of angels) singing hymns. Going further up in spirit, James and Peter approach the Majesty—the highest God—but they are allowed to hear and see no more.

The research on the Secret Book of James is rich. According to both Henri-Charles Puech and Gilles Quispel, followed by Jan Zandee and S. Kent Brown, this letter is a Gnostic composition belonging most likely to a Valentinian school of thought. This interpretation is strengthened by the fact that the Secret Book of James is part of a codex with Valentinian features. Some expressions referring to the Savior have a Gnostic flavor. For example, the Savior says, "I shall return to the place from which I came" and, in a similar vein, "I shall ascend to the place from which I have come". For W. C. Van Unnik, however, the present tractate is not Gnostic, and its provenance could well be situated in a small Egyptian community sometime after the Jewish rebellion of 135 CE.10 The Christology of the treatise shows no docetic tendencies, which are common in Gnostic texts, and the passion and suffering of the Savior are understood as having been real. Nevertheless, the Savior is said to be a preexisting entity.

The place and date of composition for the Secret Book of James can be fixed at the end of the second century or the beginning of the third, in Egypt, probably in Alexandria, in a milieu moving toward a break with the official church.

Section 3.4

Apocalypse of Peter

The Apocalypse of Peter, page 1:

When in the winter of 1886-87 a French archaeological team opened a grave near Akhmim in Upper Egypt, they struck gold. In the grave, they found a parchment codex with fragments of the Book of Enoch, the Gospel of Peter and the Apocalypse of Peter. The texts immediately drew the attention of the foremost patristic and classical scholars of the time.

The text can hardly be earlier than the end of the second century. The many references to texts that later became part of the New Testament preclude this. Brasher and Havelaar also point to the polemics directed at emerging mainstream Christians, notably the rejection of claim that 'mystery of truth' belonged to them alone. In the third century, the exclusive claims of the great Church were increasingly pressed upon minority groups that did not accept orthodox teaching and practice.

The dating of the Greek original to the end of the second century or the beginning of the third century. This means that the original version of the Greek-Eithiopic Apocalypse was written 50 to 100 years earlier.

The Apocalypse of Peter, page 183:

The Stichometry of Nicephorus is a list of canonical books. It probably dates from the middle of the ninth century. The catalogue divides the writings in three groups: recognised, disputed (antilegomena) and apocryphal. The disputed books of the New Testament are: the Apocalypse of John, the Apocalypse of Peter, the Epistle of Barnabas, and the Gospel of the

Hebrews. Apparently in ninth-century Palestine our writing was valued higher than the apocrypha. In the 5th century and beyond, the Apocalypse of Peter was known in Palestine and Egypt, around Constantinople, and probably in the West. We can say with certainty that it was read in a few local churches, but then it disappears before our eyes.

The Apocalypse of Peter, page 184:

It was only known in some parts of ancient Christianity, and its circulation was limited in time and space. Only in second-century Rome and in some local churches of fifth-century Palestine was this writing read in congregations.

As far as its geographical circulation is concerned, it was known in Rome (2nd-3rd centuries), Syria (2nd century), Palestine and Egypt (3rd-5th centuries), Edessa (3rd century), North Africa (3rd-4th centuries), and Asia Minor (probably by Methodius of Olympus at the beginning of the 4th century).

The history of the reception of the Apocalyse of Peter shows that canonicity is not an intrinsic value of a text. In this respect, Enrico Norelli is right when he claims that canonicity is the result of a historical process rather than being a condition of that process. It is necessary, in my view, to establish periods and contexts in the examination of early Christian literature. If we want to gain an appropriate picture of the development and evolution of Christianity in its first centuries, we should study not only the reception of the canonical writings but also of other texts, such as the apocrypha and the authors before the Council of Nicea. In this way, we can better understand how Christianity developed its institutions and doctrine, until it became the Religion of the Roman Empire at the end of the fourth century.

According Richard Bauckham, the Apocalypse of Peter 'deserved to be studied for the following reasons':

1) It is probably the most neglected of all Christian works written before the middle of the second century.

2) It derives from Palestinian Jewish Christianity during the Bar Kokhba war of 132-135 C.E. It deserves an important place in any attempt to consider the very obscure matter of what happened to Jewish Christianity

in Palestine in the period after 70 C.E. The date and provenance suggested by Bauckham are generally accepted by scholars (Dennis D. Buchholtz, Paolo Marrassini and Enrico Norelli).

3) Outside Palestinian Jewish Christianity, the Apocalypse of Peter evidently became a very popular work in the church as a whole, from the second to the forth centuries.

4) And finally, this work should be studied because it preserves Jewish apocalyptic traditions.

Section 3.5

Father of Their Error

The Apocalypse of Peter, Page 197-198:

Christ had predicted that some of his followers would not follow His teaching and accusing their leaders (the messengers of error) of siding his enemies. The "children of this age" would do what "the father of their error" wanted them to do.

Gospel of the Nazirenes, page 107:

Chapter 44, verse 12

12 Woe is the time when the spirit of the world shall enter into the Congregation, and my doctrines and precepts are made void through the corruptions of men and women. Woe is the world when the Light is hidden. Woe is the world when these things shall be.

The Revelation of Peter, page 494 of Nag Hammadi Scriptures:

Some Church Leaders Lack Knowledge and Lead People Astray

Others will wander from evil words and mysteries that lead people astray. Some who do not understand the mysteries and speak of what they do not understand will boast that the mystery of truth is theirs alone. In arrogance, they will embrace pride and will envy the immortal soul that has been used as down payment. For every authority, principality, and power of the ages wants to be with the immortal souls in the created world, in order that these powers, who do not come from what exists and have forgotten who they are, may be glorified by the immortal souls that do exist. The powers have not been saved or shown the way by them, though they always have wished to become imperishable. For if an immortal soul is empowered by a spirit of thought, at once it is joined by one of those were led astray.

Many others, who oppose truth and are messengers of error, will ordain their error and their law against my pure thoughts. Since they see from one perspective only, they think that good and evil come from the same source. They do business in my word. And they will establish harsh fate in which the generation of immortal souls will run in vain, until my return. For the immortal souls will surely remain among them. And I have forgiven the transgressions which they have fallen through their adversaries, and I have redeemed them their slavery, to give them freedom.

Some will create a mere imitation of the remnant in the name of a dead man who is Hermas, the firstborn of unrighteousness, in order that the little ones may not believe in the light that is. These are the workers who will be cast into the outer darkness, away from the children of light. For they who will not enter, nor do they allow those who are going to their destination, for their deliverance to enter.

The Revelation of Peter, page 495 of Nag Hammadi Scriptures

Still, others among them endure suffering and think they will perfect the wisdom of the brotherhood that exists, the spiritual fellowship with those united in communion, through which the wedding of incorruptibility will be revealed. Instead, what will appear is a mere imitation, the kindred generation of the sisterhood. These people oppress their brothers and say to them, "Through this fellowship our God has mercy, since salvation comes to us alone through this." They do not know the punishment of those who rejoice at what was done to the little ones, those who watched when the little ones were taken captive.

And there are others among those outside our number who call themselves bishops and deacons, as if they have received authority from God, but they bow before the judgment of the leaders [see Matthew 23:6]. These people are dry canals [see 2 Peter 3:17].

Matthew 23:6

6 And love the chief place at feasts, and to have the chief seats in the assemblies

2 Peter 3:17

17 These are wells without water, and clouds carried about with a tempest, to whom the black darkness is reserved forever.

The Testimony of Truth, page 620 of Nag Hammadi Scriptures:

Born Again by the Word

. . . word . . . upon the Jordan River when he came to John at the time he was baptized. The Holy Spirit came down upon him as a dove . . . accept for ourselves that he was born of a virgin and assumed flesh. He dwelt with us and received power.

Were we also born from a virginal union or conceived by the word? Rather, we have been born again by the word. So let us strengthen ourselves as virgins among male . . . . They dwell . . . the virgin . . . through . . . in the word . . . . But the word of . . . and spirit is the Father . . . for the man . . . .

Beyond Belief, page 178:

While Arius urged believers to emulate Christ, Athanasius declares this effort not only difficult but impossible, even blasphemous: on the contrary, he famously proclaims, "God became human so that humankind might become divine." All that a human being can do—must do—is believe and receive the salvation that God alone can offer. Thus, Athanasius extended what Irenaeus taught: whoever seeks access to God must first have recourse to the Word, whom the believer approaches initially through baptism, by confessing the orthodox faith as contained in the statements of the creed, and by receiving the sacraments—the "medicine of immortality" offered wherever orthodox Christians worship together in church.

Beyond Belief, page 177:

Although Athanasius intended the "canon of truth," now enshrined in the Nicene Creed, to safeguard "orthodox" interpretation of Scripture. He would allow the "heretics" that could still read the "canonical Scriptures" in an unorthodox way. To prevent such readings, he insists that anyone who reads the Scriptures must do so through dianoia—the capacity to discern the meaning or intention implicit in each text. Above all, he warns believers to shun epinoia.

What others revere as spiritual intuition Athanasius declares is a deceptive, all-too-human capacity to think subjectively, according to one's preconceptions. Epinoia leads only to error, a view that the "catholic church" endorsed then and today.

Author's note:

Christians are considered "born again" through the power of the Word (God's will). When we "knock on the door" in meditation, we are expressing our intention with a pure love to hear God's Love, God will respond with his Word.

Section 3.6

Female Spiritual Presence

Book of Revelation, 12: 1-18

1 And there appeared a great wonder in heaven: A woman clothed with the Sun, and the Moon was under her feet, and upon her head a crown of twelve Stars.

2 And she was with child, and cried travailing in birth, and was pained ready to be delivered.

3 And there appeared another wonder in heaven: for behold, a great red dragon having seven heads, and ten horns, and seven crowns upon his heads:

4 And his tail drew the third part of the stars of heaven, and cast them to the earth. And the dragon stood before the woman, which was ready to be delivered, to devour her child, when she had brought it forth.

5 So she brought forth a man child, which should rule all nations with a rod of iron: and that her child was taken up unto God and to his throne.

6 And the woman fled into the wilderness, where she hath a place prepared of God, that they should feed her there a thousand, two hundred and threescore days.

7 And there was a battle in heaven, Michael and his Angels, fought against the dragon, and the dragon fought and his angels.

8 But they prevailed not, neither was their place found anymore in heaven.

9 And the great dragon that old serpent, called the devil and Satan, was cast out, which deceiveth all the world: he was even cast into the earth, and his angels were cast out with him.

10 Then I heard a loud voice in heaven, saying, Now is salvation, and strength, and the kingdom of our God, and the power of his Christ: for the accuser of our brethren is cast down, which accused them before our God day and night.

11 But they overcame him by that blood of that Lamb, and by that word of their testimony, and they loved not their lives unto the death.

12 Therefore rejoice, ye heavens, and ye that dwell in them. Woe to the inhabitants of the earth, and of the sea: for the devil is come down unto you, which hath great wrath, knowing that he hath but a short time.

13 And when the dragon saw that he was cast unto the earth, he persecuted the woman which had brought forth the man child.

14 But to the woman were given two wings of a great Eagle, that she might fly into the wilderness, into her place where she is nourished for a time, and times, and half a time, from the presence of the serpent.

15 And the serpent cast out of his mouth water after the woman, like a flood, that he might cause her to be carried away of the flood,

16 But the earth helped the woman, and the earth opened her mouth, and swallowed up the flood, which the dragon had cast out of his mouth.

17 Then the dragon was wroth with the woman, and went and made war with the remnant of her seed, which keep the commandments of God, and have the testimony of Jesus Christ.

18 And I stood on the sea sand.

Author's note:

The woman in the verses of Revelation 12 is luminous epinoia (female spiritual presence-inner light). Reading verse 17, this is where the dragon (Satan) was trying to suppress the Jesus teaching of The Way.

Complete Books of Enoch, page 144:

2 Enoch, Chapter 30

I appointed it a name, from the four component parts, from east, from west, from south, from north. I appointed four special stars for it. I called gave it the name "Adam" and showed it the two ways, the light and the darkness. I told it, "This is good, and that is bad," so that I would learn whether it had love or hatred towards me, so that it would be clear which in the human race loved me.

For I have seen its nature, but it has not seen its own nature, so through not seeing it will do more wrong, and I said, 'After wrongdoing what is there but death?' I put sleep into it and it fell asleep. I subtracted a portion from it, and created woman, so that death should come to it by woman. I took his last word and gave her the name 'Mother,' that is to say, 'Eve.'

The Nature of the Rulers, page 193-194 of Nag Hammadi Scriptures:

Adam and Eve in the Garden

The authorities approached their Adam. When they saw his female partner speaking with him, they became aroused and lusted after her. They said to each other, "Come, let's ejaculate our semen in her," and they chased her. But she laughed at them because of their foolishness and blindness. In their grasp she turned into a tree, and when she left for them a shadow of herself that looked like her, they defiled it sexually. They defiled the seal of her voice, and so they convicted themselves through the form they had shaped in their own image.

Then the female spiritual presence came in the shape of the serpent, the instructor. The serpent taught Adam and Eve and said, "What did Samael [say to] you? Did he say, 'You may eat from every tree in the garden, but do not eat from [the tree] of knowledge of good and evil'?"

The woman of flesh said, "Not only did he say 'Do not eat,' but also 'Do not touch it. For the day, you eat from it, you will surely die.'"

The serpent, the instructor, said, "You will not surely die, for he said this to you out of jealousy. Rather, your eyes will open, and you will be like gods, knowing good and evil." And the female instructor was taken away from the serpent, and she abandoned it as something of the earth.

The Nature of the Rulers, page 193 of Nag Hammadi Scriptures:

They Eat from the Tree

The woman of flesh took from the tree and ate, and she gave to her husband as well, and thus these beings, who had only a soul, ate. Their imperfection became apparent in their ignorance. They recognized that they were stripped of the spiritual, and they took fig leaves and tied them around their naked bodies.

The leader of the archons came and said, "Where are you, Adam?" For he did not know what had happened. Adam said, "I heard your voice and was afraid because I was naked, and so I hid." The ruler said, "Why did you hide, unless it is because you ate from the only tree from which I commanded you not to eat? You did eat!"

Adam said, "The woman you gave me offered me the fruit, and I ate." And the arrogant ruler cursed the woman. The woman said, "The serpent deceived me, and I ate." The rulers turned to the serpent and cursed its shadow, so that it was powerless, and they did not know it was a form they had shaped. From then on, the serpent was under the curse of the authorities. The curse was on the serpent until the perfect human was to come.

The rulers turned to their Adam. They took him and cast him and his wife out of the garden. They have no blessing, for they are also under the curse. The rulers threw humanity into great confusion and a life of toil, so that their people might be preoccupied with things of the world and not have time to be occupied with the Holy Spirit. [See Genesis 3:14-24]

Genesis 3:14-24

14 Then the Lord God said to the serpent, Because thou hast done this, thou art cursed above all cattle, and above every beast of the field: upon thy belly shalt thou go, and dust shalt thou eat all the days of thy life.

15 I will also put enmity between thee and the woman, and between thy seed and her seed. He shall break thine head, and thou shalt bruise his heel.

16 Unto the woman he said, I will greatly increase thy sorrows, and thy conceptions. In sorrow shalt thou bring forth children, and thy desire shall be subject to thine husband, and he shall rule over thee.

17 Also to Adam he said, Because thou hast obeyed the voice of thy wife, and hast eaten of the tree, (whereof I commanded thee, saying, Thou shalt not eat of it) cursed is the earth for thy sake: in sorrow shalt thou eat of it all the days of thy life.

18 Thorns also and thistles shall it bring forth to thee, and thou shalt eat the herb of the field.

19 In the sweat of thy face shalt thou eat bread till thou return to the earth: for out of it wast thou taken, because thou art dust, and to dust shalt thou return.

20 (And the man called his wife's name Eve, because she was the mother of all living)

21 Unto Adam also and to his wife did the Lord God make coats of skins, and clothed them.

22 And the Lord God said, Behold, the man is become as one of us, to know good and evil. And now lest he put forth his hand, and take also of the tree of life, and eat, and live forever,

23 Therefore the Lord God sent him forth from the garden of Eden, to till the earth, whence he was taken.

24 Thus he cast out the man, and at the East side of the garden of Eden he set the Cherubims, and the blade of a sword shaken, to keep the way of the tree of life.

Complete Books of Enoch, page 163:

2 Enoch, Chapter 70 (partial)

Then the people turned from God and began to be jealous of one another, and people rebelled against each other, and they began to say nasty things about one another. They would say one thing but mean another. Then the diabolos began to reign for the third time, the first time before paradise, the second time in paradise, the third time outside of paradise, and continued until the deluge. A great dispute and confusion arose. When Nir the priest heard it, he was very upset, and said to himself, "I certainly understand that the time has drawn near, the end which the Lord spoke about to Methuselah, the father of my father Lamech.

Author's note:

Diablos are the cosmic rulers (fallen angels also "dragon") [see Rev. 12:7-12] and they ruled Earth for the third time up to the flood which is the year 1656 according to the Book of Jasher. That translates to 2104 BC.

2Peter 2:4-6

4 For if God spared not the Angels that had sinned, but cast them down into hell, and delivered them into chains of darkness, to be kept unto damnation:

5 Neither hath spared the old world, but saved Noah the eighth person a preacher of righteousness, and brought in the Flood upon the world of the ungodly,

6 And turned the cities of Sodom and Gomorrah into ashes, condemned them and overthrew them, and made them an ensample unto them that after should live ungodly,

Chapter 4

Unseen Forces

Unseen Forces is broken up into 5 sections. Section 4.1 talks about the nature of the rulers that began before the time of Adam and Eve. You'll see quotes and verses that described their nature and their intentions. Knowing that they were banished to eternal punishment, they wanted to stop humans from returning back to the Kingdom of God. Section 4.2 has details about "body prison". You will find out that your soul is placed inside an imperfect body that was designed by cosmic rulers. See section 1.5.2 for details about construction of human flesh. Your body is conductive to temptations because of the way it was designed. The soul was designed by the creator (see section 1.5.1). When you are a "born again", this is when you will appreciate the assistance of the Holy Spirit. This Holy Spirit will help you know "what is right and what is wrong". If you participate in your church affiliation, then, this spirit will help you acknowledge and get "wisdom" also you'll be able to enhance your love outside your family to help fellow human.

When Jesus was born, he did not remember or understand his holiness in his childhood. However, when he grew in understanding, with the help of the guiding angels, he recognized his potential and with the use of "epinioa", he realized the truth and remembered his divine origin.

Section 4.3 provided verses to discuss our struggles when we feel as Christians. Then section 4.4 shows verses and quotes from selected books to discuss the issue of the "armies of the devil" at the end of time.

Lastly, section 4.5 provides details about the angels and their roles shaping our lives. Also, definition of the "seven churches" from the Book of

Revelation is explained here. In addition, a Lord's Prayer is given in this section.

Section 4.1

Cosmic Rulers / Archon

The Apocalypse of Peter, page 191:

An essential feature of this vision account is the distinction made between the suffering Jesus and the impassable Saviour. What is more, the two figures are related to conflicting powers. The Saviour is an agent of the incorruptible Father, whereas the human body of Jesus is supposedly being a product the son of the cosmic powers. Such an interpretation implies that the wrongdoers who arrested and crucified Jesus, did not torture the Saviour but a human body. Thereupon, Peter reports, he perceived another figure:

And I saw someone about to approach us who looked like him and like the one who was laughing above the cross. He was woven in the Holy Spirit. He was the Saviour. And there was a great, ineffable light, surrounding them, and the multitude of ineffable and invisible angels, blessing them. And I saw that the one who glorifies was revealed.

After the vision of what seems to be a higher dimension of the Saviour, Christ resumed his explanations to Peter:

And he said to me, "Be strong! For you are the one to whom these mysteries have been given through revelation in order that you will know that the one they crucified is the first-born, the home of the demons, the clay vessel in which they dwell; it belongs to Elohim and to the cross that is under the law.

But he who stands near him, is the living Saviour, he who was him before, in the one who was seized. And he was released. He stands joyfully, looking at those who treated him violently. They are divided among themselves. Therefore, he laughs at their inability to see.

- So, the one who suffers will stay behind, because the body is the substitute.

- But the one who was released is my incorporeal body.

- I am the intellectual spirit filled with radiant light.

- The one you saw coming to me is our intellectual Pleroma, who unites the perfect light with my holy spirit."

Peter's visions are characterized as 'mysteries' given exclusively to him. In his explanations, Christ paid special attention to the temporal dwelling of the Saviour in the physical Jesus: until the arrest of Jesus, the Saviour was in him (he was in him before); after his 'release' from Jesus, he witnessed how (the one staying behind) was seized and treated violently.

In this view of man and the world, the innermost centre of the human being (designated as the mind, nous, the spirit, pneuma, or also the soul, i.e. the rational part of the soul) is related to the supramundane realm of God. In contrast, the soul (or its irrational part) is, supposedly, of the same ethereal substance as the stars and the p and was seen as a special kind of body'. In Hellenistic and Roman times, it was thought that when the immaterial soul or spirit left the supramundane world, it was wrapped in ethereal 'clothes'. The function of this ethereal body' was to protect the spiritual principle, to bridge the distance between the spirit and the earthly body, and, more specifically, to serve as a vehicle (ochema) for the spirit. In this body', the spirit descended to the lower world and, after the death of the earthly individual, returned to the world above.

Peter feared that in this way many of living ones' would be led astray, but Christ reassured him:

For a period of time determined for them in proportion to their error, they will rule over the little ones. But, after the completion of the error, the ageless (race) of immortal understanding will be renewed, and they (the little ones) will rule over their rulers.

Christ insisted that the suffering Jesus should not mistaken for the divine Saviour. In Christ's explanation, the human body of Jesus was merely a temporary dwelling-place. His followers could attain this level of protection if they allowed themselves to be enlightened by Christ's teaching and, accordingly, were prepared to live in this world as 'strangers' and 'children of light'.

Edgar Cayce on Angels, page 115:

The Hebrew word for "Satan" translates to "adversary." In the Old Testament's Book of Numbers, "Satan" referred to a job or office rather than an evil being: "And God's anger was kindled because he [Balaam] went; and the angel of the Lord stood in the way for an adversary [Satan] against him." (22:22)

In the New Testament, Peter was called a "Satan' when he tried to dissuade Jesus from going to Jerusalem. "Get thee behind me, Satan," Jesus said. (Luke 4:8) Although Peter thought that he had Jesus' best interests at heart, he was interfering with the fulfilling of Jesus' mission of his death and resurrection. Peter was an adversary of Jesus in this instance. In much of Christian literature and dogma, however, Satan is an evil, fallen archangel who opposes the activities of goodness and the light and is the director of all things which oppose God.

1 Corinthians 2:8

8 Which none of the princes of this world hath known: for had they known it, they would not have crucified the Lord of glory.

The Gnostic Gospels, page 7:

After Jesus' execution his followers scattered, shaken with grief and terrified for their own lives. Most assumed that their enemies were right- the movement had died with their master. Suddenly, astonishing news electrified the group. Luke says that they heard that "the Lord has risen indeed, and has appeared to Simon [Peter]!

After forty days, having completed the transfer of power, the resurrected Lord Abruptly withdrew his bodily presence from them, and ascended into heaven as they watched in amazement. Luke, who tells the story, sees this as a momentous event. Henceforth, for the duration of the world, no one would ever experience Christ's actual presence as the twelve disciples had during his lifetime-and for forty days after his death.

Psalms 68:21-23

21 Surely God will wound the head of his enemies, and the hairy pate of him that walketh in his sins.

22 The Lord hath said, I will bring my people again from Bashan: I will bring them again from the depths of the Sea:

23 That thy foot may be dipped in blood, and the tongue of thy dogs in the blood of the enemies, even in it.

1 Corinthians 15:24-26

24 Then shall be the end, when he hath delivered up the kingdom to God, even the Father, when he hath put down all rule, and all authority and power.

25 For he must reign till he hath put all his enemies under his feet.

26 The last enemy that shall be destroyed, is death.

The Gospel of Philip, page 159 of Nag Hammadi Scriptures

The wedding chamber is for free men and virgins"—free, that is, from the archons' domination and the burden of sexuality. Freedom comes from the truth: "If you know the truth, the truth will make you free" (John 8:32; Gospel of Philip 84, 8-9).

Colossians 2:10, 14

10 And ye are complete in him, which is the head of all principality and power.

14 And putting out the, handwriting of ordinances that was against us, which was contrary to us, he even took it out of the way, and fastened it upon the cross,

The Nature of the Rulers, page 197 of Nag Hammadi Scriptures:

I said, "My Lord, am I also from their matter?" "You and your offspring are from the Father, who was from the beginning. The souls come from above, from incorruptible light." So the authorities cannot approach them because of the spirit of truth within them, and all who know this way of truth are deathless among dying humanity.

"But that offspring will not appear now. It will appear after three ages and free them from the bondage of the authorities' error."

I said, "My lord, how long will it be?" He said to me, "Until the time when the true human in human form reveals the spirit of truth that the Father has sent. Then he will teach them about everything and anoint them with the oil of eternal life, given from the generation without a king. Then they will be freed of blind thought. They will trample death, which is of the authorities. And they will ascend into the infinite light where this offspring is.

Then the authorities will surrender their years and ages. Their angels will weep over their destruction, and their demons will mourn over their death.

Ezekiel 11:1-4

1 Moreover, the Spirit lifted me up, and brought me unto the East gate of the Lord's house, which lieth Eastward, and behold, at the entry of the gate were five and twenty men: among whom I saw Jaazaniah the son of Azzur, and Pelatiah the son of Benaiah, the princes of the people.

2 Then said he unto me, Son of man, these are the men that imagine mischief, and devise wicked counsel in this city.

3 For they say, 1It is not near, let us build houses: this city is the caldron, and we be the flesh.

4 Therefore prophesy against them, Son of man, prophesy.

Author's note:

Princes of the people are considered harmful.

Edgar Cayce on Angels, page 123-125:

Many religious doctrines hold that the fallen angels who went astray are not necessarily earthly people, but have great influence in the lives of earthly souls. In this light, Satan and his followers are a perfect creation gone perfectly bad, inherently evil and never to be redeemed, nor can they return to God. Their sole purpose is to defy God and distract earthly souls from remembering their divine origins.

Edgar Cayce on Angels, page 136:

The length of time from the advent of the fallen angels to the eventual removal of their influence spanned eons-200,000 years, in fact. During this period, the Cayce readings gave great detail to the conflict of the "sons of Belial" (the fallen angels) with the "Children of the Law of One" (souls of humanity who came to earth to regain their original divine heritage). There are several references in the Bible which indicate that Belial, "the children of Belial" go off to seek other gods instead of God (13:13) in the Book of Judges the "sons of Belial" abuse and rape a woman. (19:22) In II

Samuel, a man accuses and curses King David of being a "man of Belial." (16:7) St. Paul makes reference to Belial in II Corinthians: " . . . and what communion hath light with darkness? And what concord hath Christ with Belial? Or what part hath he that believeth with an infidel?" (6:14-15)

The activities of the children of Belial were in opposition to the spiritual ideals of the Children of the Law of One.

2 Corinthians 6:14-15

14 Be not unequally yoked with the infidels: for what fellowship hath righteousness with unrighteousness? And what communion hath light with darkness?

15 And what concord hath Christ with Belial? Or what part hath the believer with the infidel?

Edgar Cayce on Angels, page 136:

At this point, the calamity going on within the earth's realm drew the attention of the archangels Michael, Uriel, and Gabriel. They eventually intervened and forcibly removed the rebellious fallen angels from the earth's influence and imprisoned them in the celestial. Enoch goes into extensive detail in his revelatory vision. To cleanse the earth of the evil doings of the fallen angels, God sent the Flood, which is detailed in Genesis.

The Secret Book of John, page 130 of Nag Hammadi Scriptures:

They have been bound with dimensions, times, and seasons, and fate is the master of all. The first ruler regretted everything that had happened through him. Once again he made a plan, to bring a flood upon the human creation. The enlightened majesty of Forethought, however, warned Noah. Noah announced this to all the offspring, the human children, but those who were strangers to him did not listen to him. It did not happen the way Moses said, "They hid in an ark."

Rather, they hid in a particular place, not only Noah, but also many other people from the unshakable generation. They entered that place and hid in a bright cloud. Noah knew about his supremacy. With him was the enlightened one who had enlightened them, since the first ruler had brought darkness upon the whole earth.

The Apocalypse of Peter, page 196:

When the text was written, the Petrine Gnostics were still in conflict with other Christian groups and they had reasons to believe that they lived in a world dominated by cosmic rulers. They could feel encouraged by the last words addressed to Peter's exemplary reaction:

'You, therefore, be brave and do not fear anything, for I will be with you so that none of your enemies will domineer over you. Peace be with you. Be strong!'

When he had said these things, he (Peter) came to his senses.

Christ made a great demands on Peter (and, through, him on the others whom he had called to knowledge). He frequently encouraged and reassured the apostle. But he also feared future oppression by the cosmic forces and the people 'in their power'. Only gradually did the apostle overcome his fears; and through Christ's revelations he was led, finally, to a full understanding. Of course, the inner transformation of Peter was meant to set an example to the Gnostic readers of this writing.

Revelation 17:8

8 The beast that thou hast seen, was and is not, and shall ascend out of the bottomless pit, and shall go into perdition, and they that dwell on the earth, shall wonder (whose names are not written in the book of life from the foundation of the world) when they behold the beast that was, and is not, and yet is.

Complete Books of Enoch, page 47:

1 Enoch 21:1-10

Then I went to a place where things were dreadful. There, I saw neither a high heaven nor an established earth, but a desolate appalling spot. There I saw seven stars of heaven bound together in it, like great mountains of blazing fire. I said, "For what type of crime have they been bound, and why have they been thrown into this place?" Then Uriel, one of the sacred angels who was with me, and who guided me, answered, "Enoch, why do you ask, why do you earnestly inquire? These are those of the stars which have disobeyed the Lord's commandment, and are bound here until ten thousand years, the time of their crimes, have come to pass." Afterwards I went on from there to another dreadful place, more ghastly than the former, where I saw a huge blazing and glittering fire, in the middle of which there was a split as far as the abyss. It was full of huge columns of fire, and their descent was deep. I could not discover its measurement or magnitude, nor could I perceive its source. Then I exclaimed, "How horrifying this place is, and how difficult to explore!" Then Uriel, one of the sacred angels who was with me, answered me, "Enoch, why are you alarmed and amazed at this appalling place, at the sight of this place of pain?" He told me, "This is the prison of the angels, and they are kept here forever."

Author's note:

The fallen angels are locked up forever in Tartarus.

The Apocalypse of Peter, page 168-169:

Psalm 24 and Apocalypse of Peter 17.2-6

The second explicit reference to the Old Testament occurs in the final chapter of the book (Apocalypse of Peter 17). It is the last of the five visions of the reward of the righteous. Visions which were granted to the disciples, once they went with Jesus to 'the holy mountain'. After the vision of the true Temple, and the accompanying audition of the true Messiah (Apocalypse of Peter16.9-17.1), Apocalypse of Peter 17.2-6 describes the Ascension. The disciples witness the ascension of Jesus, with Moses and Elijah, first to the first heaven, where they meet people 'who were in the flesh'. Jesus took with him these people and entered the second heaven. I quote Apocalypse of Peter 17.2-6:

2a   And a cloud large in size came over head

b   and (it was) very white

c   and it lifted up our Lord and Moses and Elijah,

d   and I trembled e and was astonished.

3a   And we watched

b   and this heaven opened

c   and we saw men who were in flesh

d   and they came

e   and went to meet our Lord and Moses and Elijah

f   and they went into second heaven.

4a   And the word of scripture was fulfilled:

b   'This generation seeks him

c   and seeks the face of the God of Jacob'.

5a   And there was great fear and great amazement in heaven.

b   The angels flocked together that the word of scripture might be fulfilled which said:

c   'Open the gates, princes'.

6a   And then this heaven which had been opened was closed.

After the ascension, the disciples descended down from the mountain, glorifying God, who has written the names of the righteous in the book of life in heaven. The description of the ascension is connected with the Transfiguration scene in the Gospel of Matthew. In Apocalypse of Peter 17.1, which describes the audition of the true Messiah, Matthew 17:5 is quoted literally;

Matthew 17:5

5 While he yet spake, behold, a bright cloud shadowed them: and behold, there came a voice out of the cloud, saying, This is that my beloved Son, in whom I am well pleased: hear him.

The Apocalypse of Peter, page 169:

Also, the cloud in Apocalypse of Peter 17.2 ('And a cloud large in size came over head and (it was) very white') could be connected with the same verse. However, in Matthew the cloud overshadows the disciples who were with Jesus on the mountain, whereas in the Apocalypse of Peter the cloud became the instrument of an ascension, which is not described in chapter 17 of Matthew. This might be due to the influence of the ascension scene in Acts 1.1-11, where the cloud functions as a means to deprive the sight of the disciples, but seems to be at the same time the instrument of the ascension: 'He was lifted up, and a cloud took him out of their sight'.

It is not completely impossible that the princes of the quoted text from Psalms 24.7a, 9a are the same as angels mentioned in Apocalypse of Peter 17.5. In that case, the flocking together of the angels is the same action as the opening of the gates. However, it is more probable that they refer to another group, adversaries of the angels, servants of Belair, Satan. The quotation makes clear that it is the princes, the servants of Satan, who kept closed the gates. Most probably these are the gates that give entrance from the second into the third heaven.

The Apocalypse of Peter contains three explicit quotations, all from the Old Testament. All three have an introduction formula, a phenomenon that is exceptional in the Apocalypse of Peter. The form and function of the quotation differs in these places. In the first one, reference to Ezekiel 37 is fragmentary. It may be called a summarizing quotation. We did not exclude the possibility that Apocalypse of Peter did not make direct use from the biblical text, but from an intermediary text, although we did not accept this text as 4Q385, as others have done. It is, therefore, safer to say that the Apocalypse of Peter depends on a tradition of interpretation of Ezekiel 37. The second and third references are both to Psalms 24. The whole Psalm, in the version of the Septuagint is presupposed, although only very few phrases are actually taken over. It is an eschatological and cosmological interpretation of the Psalm. The Psalm is taken as a prophecy to the Ascension of the Lord during which adversary powers should be conquered.

Revelation 21:8

8 But the fearful and unbelieving, and the abominable and murderers, and whoremongers, and sorcerers, and idolaters, and all liars shall have their part in the lake which burneth with fire and brimstone, which is the second death.

2 Corinthian 4:4

In whom the god of this world hath blinded the minds, that is, of the infidels, that the light of the glorious Gospel of Christ, which is the image of God, should not shine unto them.

2 Corinthians 6:14-15

14 Be not unequally yoked with the infidels: for what fellowship hath righteousness with unrighteousness? and what communion hath light with darkness?

15 And what concord hath Christ with Belial? Or what part hath the believer with the infidel?

Complete Books of Enoch, page 15:

Then their leader Semjaza said to them, "I'm concerned as I fear that perhaps you won't agree to carry out this venture, and that I alone will have to pay the penalty for such a serious crime."

But they answered, "Let's all swear an oath, and bind ourselves by mutual curses, that we will not change our minds but carry through this venture."

So they swore all together and bound themselves by mutual curses. They were two hundred in number, they descended in the time of Jared, on the top of Mount Hermon. They called it Mount Hermon because they had sworn an oath on it and bound themselves by mutual curses.

Complete Books of Enoch, page 135:

2 Enoch, Chapter 18

"These are the Grigori, who with their chief Satanail rejected the Lord of light, and after them are those who are held in the great darkness on the second heaven, and three of them went down on earth to the place Hermon, and broke their vows on the shoulder of the Mount Hermon and saw the human women, and slept with them, and contaminated the earth with their deeds. In their times they caused lawless mixing, and Nephilim were born, amazing big people, and great hostility. So God judged them strongly, and they weep for their associates. They will be punished on the Lord's great day." (2 Enoch 18:3-4.)

Complete Books of Enoch, page 16-18:

Account in Psalm 82:1-8

1 Elohim presides over the assembly of El, he gives judgment in the midst of the elohim:

2 "How long will you defend the unjust and show favoritism to the wicked? Selah

3 Defend the cause of the poor and the fatherless, defend the rights of the oppressed and suffering.

4 Rescue the poor and needy, rescue them from the power of the wicked.

5 They know nothing, they understand nothing, they walk around in the dark, all the foundations of the earth are shaken.

6 I said, 'You are elohim, all of you are associates of Elyon.'

7 Yet you will die like mortals, you will fall like the other rulers."

8 Rise up, Elohim, and judge the earth, for you own all the nations.

Account in Isaiah 14:12-21

"How you are fallen from heaven, Lucifer, associate of dawn! How you are cut down to the ground, you who weakened the nations!"

"For you said to yourself, 'I will ascend to heaven and set my throne above El's stars. I will preside on the appointed mountain in the sides of the north. I will climb to above the height of the clouds, I will be like Elyon.'

"But instead, you will be brought down to Sheol, to the sides of the pit. Everyone there will stare at you and ask, 'Is this the one who shook the earth and the kingdoms of the world, that made the world a wilderness and demolished its cities and did not free the prisoners from Sheol?'

"The kings of the nations lie in splendid tombs, but you will be thrown out of your grave like a ritually abominable branch. You will be dumped like the remainder of those slain by the sword with those killed in battle like a corpse trampled underfoot, you will go down to the dungeon. You will not be given a proper burial, because you have destroyed your land and killed your people. The offspring of evildoers will never be proclaimed. Kill the children of this wrongdoer so they do not rise and conquer the land or rebuild the cities of the world."

Isaiah 14:12-21

12 How art thou fallen from heaven, O Lucifer, son of the morning? and cut down to the ground, which didst cast lots upon the nations?

13 Yet thou saidest in thine heart, I will ascend into heaven, and exalt my throne above beside the stars of God: I will sit also upon the mount of the congregation in the sides of the North.

14 I will ascend above the height of the clouds, and I will be like the most high.

15 But thou shalt be brought down to the grave, to the side of the pit.

16 They that see thee, shall look upon thee and consider thee, saying, Is this the man that made the earth to tremble, and that did shake the kingdoms?

17 He made the world as a wilderness, and destroyed the cities thereof, and opened not the house of his prisoners.

18 All the kings of the nations, even they all sleep in glory, everyone in his own house.

19 But thou art 1cast out of thy grave like an abominable branch: like the raiment of those that are slain, and thrust through with a sword, which go down to the stones of the pit, as a carcass trodden under feet.

20 Thou shalt not be joined with them in the grave, because thou hast destroyed thine own land, and slain thy people: the seed of the wicked shall not be renowned forever.

21 Prepare a slaughter for his children, for the iniquity of their fathers: let them not rise up nor possess the land, nor fill the face of the world with enemies.

Account in Ezekiel 28:11-19

"The word of Yahweh came to me, 'Human, weep for the king of Tyre and say to him, "Adonai Yahweh says, 'You were full of wisdom and beauty. You were in Eden, Elohim's garden. Your clothing had every precious stone: sardius, chrysolite, diamond, beryl, onyx, jasper, sapphire, and emerald, carbuncle, gold, and the making of the settings was crafted for you on the day you were created.

'You are the anointed cherub that defends. You had access to Elohim's sacred mountain and walked among the fiery stones. You were complete in everything you did from the day you were created until the day injustice was found in you.

'Your great wealth filled you with violence, and you sinned. So I banished you from Elohim's mountain. Mighty guardian, I expelled you from your place among the fiery stones. Your heart was filled with pride because of your beauty. You corrupted your wisdom because of your splendor. So I threw you to the earth and exposed you to the gaze of kings.

'You defiled your sanctuaries with your many wrongdoings and your dishonest trade. So I brought fire from within you, and it consumed you. I will burn you to ashes on the ground in the sight of all who are watching. All who knew you are appalled at your destruction. You have come to a terrible end, and you are no more."

Ezekiel 28:11-19

11 Moreover, the word of the Lord came unto me, saying,

12 Son of man, take up a lamentation upon the King of Tyre, and say unto him, Thus saith the

Lord God, Thou sealest up the sum, and art full of wisdom, and perfect in beauty.

13 Thou hast been in Eden the garden of God: every precious stone was in thy garment, the ruby, the topaz, and the 1diamond, the chrysolite, the onyx, and the jasper, the sapphire, emerald, and the carbuncle and gold: the workmanship of thy timbrels, and of thy pipes was prepared in thee in the day that thou wast created.

14 Thou art 1the anointed Cherub, that covereth, and I have set thee in honor: thou wast upon the holy mountain of God: thou hast walked in the midst of the stones of fire.

15 Thou wast perfect in thy ways from the day that thou wast created, till iniquity was found in thee.

16 By the multitude of thy merchandise, they have filled the midst of thee with cruelty, and thou hast sinned: therefore I will cast thee as profane out of the 1mountain of God: and I will destroy thee, O covering Cherub, from the midst of the stones of fire.

17 Thine heart was lifted up because of thy beauty, and thou hast corrupted thy wisdom by reason of thy brightness: I will cast thee to the ground. I will lay thee before kings that they may behold thee.

18 Thou hast defiled thy 1sanctification by the multitude of thine iniquities, and by the iniquity of thy merchandise: therefore will I bring forth a fire

from the midst of thee, which shall devour thee: and I will bring thee to ashes upon the earth, in the sight of all them that behold thee.

19 All they that know thee among the people, shall be astonished at thee: thou shalt be a terror, and never shalt thou be anymore.

Account in Luke 10:17-20

The seventy came back and were very happy. They said, "Lord, even the demons yield to us in your name!"

"Yes, I know," Jesus replied. "I was watching Adversary fall like a flash of lightning from the sky. I have given you the authority to trample on snakes and scorpions, and authority over all the enemy's power, and nothing will harm you. But all that aside, don't be happy just because the spirits yield to you, but instead be happy that your names have been written down in the heavenly places."

Luke 10:17-20

17 And the seventy turned again with joy, saying, Lord, even the devils are subdued to us through thy Name.

18 And he said unto them, I saw Satan, like lightning, fall down from heaven.

19 Behold, I give unto you power to tread on Serpents, and Scorpions, and over all the power of the enemy, and nothing shall hurt you.

20 Nevertheless, in this rejoice not, that the spirits are subdued unto you: but rather rejoice, because your names are written in heaven.

The Secret Book of John, page 129-130 of Nag Hammadi Scriptures:

He did not know that they surpassed him in thought and that he would be unable to grasp them. He devised a plan with his authorities, who are his powers. Together they fornicated with Sophia, and through them was produced bitter fate, the final, fickle bondage. Fate is like this because the powers are fickle. To the present day fate is tougher and stronger than what gods, angels, demons, and all the generations have encountered. For from fate have come all iniquity and injustice and blasphemy, the bondage of forgetfulness, and ignorance, and all burdensome orders, weighty sins, and great fears.

Thus, all of creation has been blinded so that none might know the God that is over them all. Because of the bondage of forgetfulness, their sins have been hidden.

Complete Books of Enoch, page 22:

Azazel is mistranslated "scapegoat" by several Bible versions, a mistranslation started by Tyndale's 16th century English translation and followed by such versions as the King James Version, and the New International Version. It is translated correctly as "Azazel" in the Revised Standard Version and the English Standard Version. Tyndale misread the Hebrew word to mean "escaped goat" and coined the word "scapegoat."

The name Azazel occurs 3 times in the Old Testament /Hebrew Bible, in Leviticus 16: 8, 10, 26. The context is that on Yom Kippur, the Day of Atonement, the high priest performed the set sacrifices for himself and his family then presented the victims for the sins of the people. These were a ram for the burnt offering, and two young goats for the sin-offering. The high priest brought the goats before Yahweh at the door of the tabernacle, and cast lots for them, one lot "for Yahweh" and the other lot "for Azazel." The goat that fell by lot to Yahweh was killed as a sin-offering for the people. The high priest laid his hands on the head of the goat that fell by lot to Azazel and confessed the sins of the people over it. The goat was then handed over to a man who led it to an isolated region and let it go in the wilderness.

Leviticus 16:6-10

6 Aaron will offer the bull as a sin offering for himself and shall make atonement for himself and for his family.

7 Then he will take the two goats and set them before the Lord at the entrance of the tent of meeting.

8 And Aaron will cast lots over the two goats, one lot for the Lord and the other lot for Azazel.

9 And Aaron will present the goat on which the lot fell for the Lord and use it as a sin offering,

10 but the goat on which the lot fell for Azazel will be presented alive before the Lord to make atonement over it, and it will be sent away into the wilderness to Azazel. And he who lets the goat go to Azazel will wash his clothes and bathe his body in water, and then afterwards he may come back into the camp."

Author's note:

It is intriguing to note that verses from Micah 6:6-8 and Hebrews 10:4-6 are saying that the blood of goats and bulls do not wash away sins. This is confirmed by Jesus in the Gospel of the Nazirenes, Chapter 7, and verse 10;

Chapter 7, verse 10

10 And to all he spoke, saying, "Keep yourselves from blood and things strangled and dead bodies of birds and beasts, and from all deeds of cruelty, and from all that is gotten of wrong; Do you think that the blood of beasts and birds will wash away sin? I tell you, no! Speak the Truth, be just, and merciful to one another and to all creatures, and walk humbly with your Creator." The verses in the Scripture are saying that the blood of goats and bulls do not wash away sin.

Complete Books of Enoch, page 22:

1 Enoch 8:1-4

Azazel taught humans to make swords, knives, shields, breastplates, and showed them metals of the earth and the art of alchemy, and bracelets and ornaments, the use of antimony and paint, the beautifying of the eyelids, the use of all types of precious stones, and all sorts of dyes. Then wickedness and immorality increased, and they disobeyed, and everything they did was corrupt.

Complete Books of Enoch, Page 20:

1 Enoch 7:1-6

"When humankind began to increase on the face of the earth, and daughters were born to them, those associated with God saw that the human women were beautiful and so they took wives for themselves from any they chose (Genesis 6:1-4). The Nephilim were on the earth in those times, and also afterwards, when those associated with God were having sex with the human women, who gave birth to their children. They were the mighty heroes of ancient times, the famous ones."

The Septnagint, Philo of Alexandria, Josephus, Justin Martyr, Irenaeus, Athenagoras, Clement of Alexandria, Tertullian, Lactantius, Eusebius, Ambrose of Milan, Jerome, Sulpicius Severus, and Augustine of Hippo all identified the "Sons of God" (correctly, "the associates of God") of Genesis 6:1-4 with the angels who came to earth and had sex with human women.

Edgar Cayce on Angels, page 75:

The "rebellion in heaven" is depicted in an interesting light in the Cayce readings. Long before our material universe came into being, all souls and archangels were companions of God, completely aware of their individuality, yet had communion with God.

Legions of angels and archangels who were maintaining their conscious relationship with the Creator became aware that great numbers of their own were beginning to "forget" that they were at some former time one with God. They became enamored with their own powers and creations. When the archangels tried to bring the wayward souls back to remembrance of the original plan of God's creation, there was great resistance and discord.

As Thomas Sugrue wrote in the biography, There is a River-The Story of Edgar Cayce: "Certain souls became bemused with their own power and began to experiment with it. They mingled with the dust of the stars and the winds of the spheres, feeling them, becoming part of them . . . This was the fall in spirit, or the revolt of the angels."

Halaliel is an archangel depicted as one of those who attempted to assist when this great dividing of the forces began.

Lucifer and Ariel, once great archangels in the realm of God, became leaders for the side of the angels and souls who desired to go their own way, irrespective of God's desires. Thus, the good and evil (remembrance and forgetfulness) became living states of consciousness, now represented by Light and Darkness. Today, eons of time later, this battle is waged in the earthly realm within the souls of humanity, as we daily confront the choice to be selfless or selfish.

"Halaliel is the one who from the beginning has been a leader of the heavenly host, who has defied Ariel, who has made the ways that have been heavy-but as the means for UNDERSTANDING."

Edgar Cayce on Angels, page 116:

In the beginning, God created Lucifer as an archangel, Lucifer-which means "light-bearer" or light-giver"-has since, however, become synonymous with Satan.

For purposes of chronology, the archangel whom God created before the fall will be referred to as Lucifer, and after the fall as Satan.

Lucifer was a ruler of the angelic realm of the Cherubim and had dominion over virtually all of the angel kingdoms. His role as a "supervisor" among the angels existed long before the earthly realm came into being. In that age, all beings were in spirit and consciously aware of being one with God.

" . . . Satan was God's second-in-command, chief among all His angels, the beautiful and beloved Lucifer. The service it performed in God's behalf was to enhance the spiritual growth of human beings through the use of testing and temptation-just as we test our own children in school so as to enhance their growth.

Problems arose when Lucifer fell in love with his own authority and power. The spiritual "fall" from grace was led by this great light-bearer. Lucifer led many of the archangels, angels, and souls deeper into creations which only glorified the individual entities, not God. The fallen souls had created their own identities through experimenting with various thought forms and energies. This was the beginning of a sort of self-absorbed "individuality," a state quite normal in our three-dimensional world.

Edgar Cayce on Angels, page 142:

During the great chaos of the early epoch of the creation of souls—the age of "giants in the earth," according to the Book of Genesis (6:4)-the earth was filled with all imaginable forms of inhabitants. During this pre-Genesis period, Satan and his legions had taken leave of the lighter realms of angels and made their abode in the unfinished earth and other areas. A promise, however, was born in the kingdoms of the angels that all those souls who had forgotten God and had become lost would eventually be led back by way of a divinely ingenious plan.

The Book of Genesis begins at this point, establishing it as the beginning of time: "And the earth was without form, and void; and darkness was upon the face of the deep."

The darkness represents the separation of souls from their awareness of their Creator—a darkness of consciousness. Satan and his legions were the embodiment of that darkness. Although eons had already passed since the souls had taken on identities fashioned by their own creations, this point in Genesis is the beginning of a divine plan, the start of a long process through time and space in which the sleeping souls would be awakened.

Genesis 6:4

4 There were giants in the earth in those days: yea, and after that the sons of God came unto the daughters of men, and they had borne them children, these were mighty men, which in old time were men of renown.

2 Peter 2:4-6

4 For if God spared not the Angels that had sinned, but cast them down into hell, and delivered them into chains of darkness, to be kept unto damnation:

5 Neither hath spared the old world, but saved Noah the eighth person a preacher of righteousness, and brought in the Flood upon the world of the ungodly,

6 And turned the cities of Sodom and Gomorrah into ashes, condemned them and overthrew them, and made them an ensample unto them that after should live ungodly,

Author's note:

This is the "old world" with sins brought forward by fallen angels according to 2Peter 2:5. Following the verse from 2 Peter 2:20, the fallen angels attempt to withdraw men from God to their old filthiness;

2Peter 2:14-22

14 Having eyes full of adultery, and that cannot cease to sin, beguiling unstable souls, they have hearts exercised with covetousness, they are the children of curse:

15 Which forsaking the right way, have gone astray following the way of Balaam, the son of Beor, which loved the wages of unrighteousness.

16 But he was rebuked for his iniquity: for the dumb beast speaking with man's voice forbade the foolishness of the Prophet.

17 These are wells without water, and clouds carried about with a tempest, to whom the black darkness is reserved forever.

18 For in speaking swelling words of vanity, they beguile with wantonness through the lusts of the flesh them that were clean escaped from them which are wrapped in error,

19 Promising unto them liberty, and are themselves the servants of corruption: for of whomsoever a man is overcome, even unto the same is he in bondage.

20 For if they, after they have escaped from the filthiness of the world, through the acknowledging of the Lord, and of the Savior Jesus Christ,

are yet tangled again therein, and overcome, the latter end is worse with them than the beginning.

21 For it had been better for them not to have acknowledged the way of righteousness, than after they have acknowledged it, to turn from the holy commandment given unto them.

22 But it is come unto them according to the true proverb, the dog is returned to his own vomit: and the sow that was washed, to the wallowing in the mire.

Complete Books of Enoch, page 39:

1 Enoch 12:1-6

Before all these things, Enoch was hidden, and none of the humans knew where he was hidden, where he had been, and what had happened. His days were with the sacred ones, and his doings were to do with the Watchers.

I, Enoch, was blessing the great Lord and King of ages, when the Watchers called me—Enoch the scribe—and said to me, "Enoch, you just scribe of justice, go and tell the Watchers of heaven, who have deserted the high heaven, the sacred everlasting place, who have been defiled with women and have done as the humans do, by taking wives for themselves, 'You have greatly caused corruption on the earth. You will never have peace or forgiveness for your crimes. You will have no delight in your offspring, for you will see the slaughter of their loved ones, and you will lament for the destruction of your children. You can make petition forever, but you will not obtain compassion or peace!"

Genesis 5:24

24 And Enoch walked with God, and he was no more seen: for God took him away.

Complete Books of Enoch, page 39:

1 Enoch 13:1-10

Then Enoch went on and said to Azazel, "You will not find peace. A severe sentence has gone out against you, that you are to be bound. You will find no relief, compassion, or granting of requests, because of the injustice you have taught, because of every act of blasphemy, lawlessness, and wrongdoing, which you have shown to humankind."

And I, Enoch, alone saw the vision of the end of all things. No other human saw what I saw.

Complete Books of Enoch, page 46:

1 Enoch 20:1-8

These are the names of the sacred angels who watch. Uriel, one of the sacred angels, who presides over the world and Tartarus.

Tartarus

The Greeks considered Hades to be the underworld, full of ghosts or wraiths of people who had died. Homer's Odyssey speaks of Odysseus raising spirits from Hades and notes that these spirits could be strengthened when they drank blood. It also speaks of people continuing their earthly ways—for example, one person was professionally hunting. It was spoken of as a terrifying, eerie place, but not specifically a place of punishment like Tartarus. Hades is commonly translated as "Hell" in most Bible versions, as are "Gehenna" and "Tartarus," yet to the Greeks, they were separate places. Tartarus was the lowest region of the underworld, said to be as far below Hades as the earth is under the sky. Tartarus was the place where the very wicked were punished. The Greeks believed Hades to be midway between heaven and Tartarus. See Aeschylus, Prom. 152-6: "Would that he had hurled me underneath the earth and underneath the House of Hades, host to the dead—yes, down to limitless Tartarus, yes, though he bound me cruelly in chains breakable."

The Septuagint translated Sheol as "Hades."

Complete Books of Enoch, page 144:

Chapter 31

Human has life on earth, and I created a garden in Eden in the east, so that the Human that could observe the decree and keep the command. I made the heavens open to the Human, so that the Human would see the angels singing the victory song, and the gloomless light.

The Human was continuously in the Garden, and the diabolos understood that I wanted to create another world, because the Human was ruler on earth, to rule and control it. The diabolos is the evil spirit of the lower places. As a fugitive he made Sotona from the heavens as his name was Satanail. So he became different from the angels, but his nature did not change his intelligence as far as his understanding of just and wrongful things.

He understood his denunciation and the wrong which he had committed before; therefore he conceived an idea against the Human. In this form he entered and beguiled Eve, but did not touch Adam.

Section 4.2

Body Prison

Galatians 5:1

Stand fast therefore in the liberty where with Christ hath made us free, and not be entangled again with the yoke of bondage.

Isaiah 42:7

7 That thou mayest open the eyes of the blind, and bring out the prisoners from the prison: and them that sit in darkness, out of the prison house.

Revelation 3:12

12 Him that overcometh, will I make a pillar in the Temple of my God, and he shall go no more out: and I will write upon him the Name of my

God, and the name of the city of my God, which is the new Jerusalem, which cometh down out of heaven from my God, and I will write upon him my new Name.

Isaiah 42:22

22 But this people is robbed and spoiled, and shall be all snarled in dungeons, and they shall be hid in prison houses: they shall be for prey: and none shall deliver: a spoil, and none shall say, Restore.

2 Timothy 2:26

26 And came to amendment out of that snare of the devil, of whom they are taken prisoners, to do his will.

The Secret Book of James, page 25 of Nag Hammadi Scriptures:

Believe in My Cross

I answered and said to him; "Master, we can obey you if you wish, for we have forsaken our fathers and our mothers and our villages and have followed you. Give us the means not to be tempted by the evil devil."

The master answered and said, "What good is it to you if you do the Father's will, but you are not given your part of his bounty when you are tempted by Satan? But if you are oppressed by Satan and persecuted and do the Father's will, I say he will love you, make you my equal, and consider you beloved through his forethought, and by your own choice. Won't you stop loving the flesh and fearing suffering? Don't you know that you have not yet been abused; unjustly accused, locked up in prison, unlawfully condemned, crucified without reason, or buried in the sand as I myself was by the evil one? Do you dare to spare the flesh, you for whom the spirit is a wall surrounding you? If you consider how long the world has existed before you and how long it will exist after you, you will see that your life is but a day and your sufferings but an hour. The good will not enter the world. Disdain death, then, and care about life. Remember my cross and my death, and you will live."

Author's note:

Jesus mentioned "being beloved through his forethought". Forethought is epinioa, and, this is where you get the Light.

"So I say to you, be sober. Do not go astray. And often have I said to you all together, and also to you alone, James, be saved. I have commanded you to follow me, and I have taught you how to speak before the rulers."

"See that I have come down and have spoken and have exerted myself and have won my crown when I saved you. I came down to live with you that you might also live with me. And when I found that your houses had no roofs, I lived in houses that could receive me when I came down."

"Trust in me, my brothers. Understand what the great light is. The Father does not need me. A father does not need a son, but it is the son who needs the father. To him I am going, for the Father of the Son is not in need of you."

"Listen to the word, understand knowledge, love life, and no one will persecute you and no one will oppress you other than you yourselves."

The Secret Book of John, Page 126 of Nag Hammadi Scriptures:

The Imprisonment of Humanity

The human being Adam was revealed through the bright shadow within. And Adam's ability to think was greater than that of all the creators. When they looked up, they saw that Adam's ability to think was greater, and they devised a plan with the whole throng of archons and angels. They took fire, earth, and water, and combined them with the four fiery winds. They wrought them together and made a great commotion.

The rulers brought Adam into the shadow of death so that they might produce a figure again, from earth, water, fire, and the spirit that comes from matter—that is, from the ignorance of darkness, and desire, and their own phony spirit. This figure is the cave for remodeling the body that these criminals put on the human, the fetter of forgetfulness." Adam became a mortal person, the first to descend and the first to become estranged. Enlightened Insight within Adam, however, was rejuvenating Adam's mind.

The archons took Adam and put Adam in paradise. They said, "Eat," meaning, do so in a leisurely manner. But in fact their pleasure is bitter and their beauty is perverse. Their pleasure is a trap, their trees are a sacrilege, their fruit is deadly poison, and their promise is death.

They put their tree of life in the middle of paradise. I shall teach you what the secret of their life is—the plan they devised together, the nature of their spirit. The root of their tree is bitter, its branches are death, its shadow is hatred, a trap is in its leaves, its blossom is bad ointment, its fruit is death, desire is its seed, and it blossoms in darkness. The dwelling place of those who taste of it is the underworld, and darkness is their resting place.

But the archons lingered in front of what they call the tree of the knowledge of good and evil, which is enlightened Insight, so that Adam might not behold its fullness and recognize his shameful nakedness. But I was the one who induced them to eat. I said to the Savior, "Lord, was it not the serpent that instructed Adam to eat?"

The Savior laughed and said, The serpent instructed them to eat of the wickedness of sexual desire and destruction so that Adam might be of use to the serpent.

The first ruler knew Adam was disobedient to him because of enlightened Insight within Adam, which made Adam stronger of mind than he. He wanted to recover the power that he himself had passed on to Adam. So he brought deep sleep upon Adam.

I said to the Savior, "What is this deep sleep?" The Savior said, It is not as Moses wrote and you heard. He said in his first book, "He put Adam to sleep." [Genesis 2:21] Rather, this deep sleep was a loss of sense. Thus the first ruler said through the prophet, "I shall make their minds sluggish, that they may neither understand nor discern."

Genesis 2:21

21 Therefore the Lord God caused an heavy sleep to fall upon the man, and he slept: and he took one of his ribs, and closed up the flesh instead thereof.

Author's note:

The first ruler had wanted to get off the "epinoia" from Adam which was designed by God the Father (see section 1.5.1 for details of the human soul). This is a tool that the Prophets, Enoch, Noah, and Jesus have used for meditation.

The Secret Book of John, page 131 of Nag Hammadi Scriptures

Hymn of the Savior

Now I, the perfect Forethought of the All, transformed myself into my offspring. I existed first and went down every path.

I am the abundance of light,

I am the remembrance of Fullness.

I traveled in the realm of great darkness, and continued until I entered the midst of the prison. The foundations of chaos shook, and I hid from them because of their evil, and they did not recognize me.

Again I returned, a second time, and went on. I had come from the inhabitants of light—I, the remembrance of Forethought.

I entered the midst of darkness and the bowels of the underworld, turning to my task. The foundations of chaos shook as though to fall upon those who dwell in chaos and destroy them. Again I hurried back to the root of my light so they might not be destroyed before their time.

Again, a third time, I went forth—

I am the light dwelling in light,

I am the remembrance of Forethought—

So that, I might enter the midst of darkness and the bowels of the underworld. I brightened my face with light from the consummation of their realm and entered the midst of their prison, which is the prison of the body.

I said, Let whoever hears arise from deep sleep.

A person wept and shed tears. Bitter tears the person wiped away, and said, "Who is calling my name? From where has my hope come as I dwell in the bondage of prison?"

I am the Forethought of pure light,

I am the thought of the Virgin Spirit, who raises you to a place of honor.

Arise, remember that you have heard and trace your root, which is I, the compassionate.

Guard yourself against the angels of misery, the demons of chaos, and all who entrap you,

Look, now I shall ascend to the perfect realm. I have finished everything for you in your hearing. I have told you everything for you to record and communicate secretly to your spiritual friends. This is the mystery of the unshakable generation.

The Savior communicated this to John for him to record and safeguard. He said to him, "Cursed be anyone who will trade these things for a gift, for food, drink, clothes, or anything like this."

These things were communicated to him in a mystery, and at once the Savior disappeared. Then John went to the other disciples and reported what the Savior had told him.

Jesus Christ

Amen

The Secret Book According to John

The Revelation of Peter, page 491-495 of Nag Hammadi Scriptures:

At first many will accept our words, but they will turn away again according the will of the father of their error, because they have done his will, and the father of error will disclose them in his judgment as servants of the word. Those who have associated with people of error will become their prisoners, since they are without perception. But the good person, who is pure and upright, will be handed over to the dealer in death, in the kingdom of those who praise a Christ of a future restored world. And they also praise people who preach this falsehood, people who will come after you. They will hold on to the name of a dead man, thinking that in this way they will become pure, but instead they will become more and more defiled. They will fall into a name of error and the hand of an evil deceiver with complicated doctrines, and they will be dominated by heresy.

Some of them will blaspheme the truth and proclaim evil teachings, and they will speak evil against each other. Some of them will give themselves a name, for they stand in the power of the rulers: the name of a man and a naked woman of many forms and many sufferings. And those who say all this will inquire into dreams, and if they claim that a dream came from a demon, which is appropriate for their error, they shall be granted perdition instead of incorruption.

Ephesians 4:1-21

1 I therefore, being prisoner in the Lord, pray you that ye walk worthy of the vocation whereunto ye are called,

2 With all humbleness of mind, and meekness, with long suffering, supporting one another through love,

3 Endeavoring to keep the unity of the Spirit in the bond of peace.

4 There is one body, and one Spirit, even as ye are called in one hope of your vocation.

5 There is one Lord, one Faith, one Baptism.

6 One God and Father of all, which is above all, and through all, and in you all.

7 But unto every one of us is given grace according to the measure of the gift of Christ.

8 Wherefore he saith, When he ascended upon high, he led captivity captive, and gave gifts unto men

9 (Now, in that he ascended, what is it but that he had also descended first into the lowest parts of the earth?

10 He that descended, is even the same that ascended, far above all heavens, that he might fill all things.)

11 He therefore gave some to be Apostles, and some Prophets, and some Evangelists, and some Pastors, and Teachers

12 For the repairing of the Saints, for the work of the ministry, and for the edification of the body of Christ,

13 Till we all meet together (in the unity of faith and that acknowledging of the Son of God) unto a perfect man, and unto the measure of the age the fullness of Christ,

14 That we henceforth be no more children, wavering and carried about with every wind of doctrine, by the deceit of men, and with craftiness, whereby they lay in wait to deceive.

15 But let us follow the truth in love, and in all things, grow up into him, which is the head, that is, Christ.

16 By whom all the body being coupled and knit together by every joint, for the furniture thereof (according to the effectual power, which is in the measure of every part) receiveth increase of the body, unto the edifying of itself in love.

17 This I say therefore and testify in the Lord, that ye henceforth walk not as another Gentiles walk, in vanity of their mind.

18 Having their understanding darkened, and being strangers from the life of God through the ignorance that is in them, because of the hardness of their heart:

19 Which being past feeling, have given themselves unto wantonness, to work all uncleanness, even with greediness.

20 But ye have not so learned Christ,

21 If so be ye have heard him, and have been taught by him, as the truth is in Jesus,

Zechariah 9:11-17

11 Thou also shall be saved through the blood of thy covenant. I have loosed thy prisoners out of the pit wherein is no water.

12 Turn you to the stronghold, ye prisoners of hope: even today do I declare, that I will render the double unto thee.

13 For Judah have I bent as a bow for me: Ephraim's hand have I filled, and I have raised up thy sons, O Zion, against thy sons, O Greece, and have made thee as a giant's sword.

14 And the Lord shall be seen over them, and his arrow shall go forth as the lightning: and the Lord God shall blow the trumpet, and shall come forth with the whirlwinds of the South.

15 The Lord of hosts shall defend them, and they shall devour them, and subdue them with sling stones, and they shall drink, and make a noise as through wine, and they shall be filled like bowls, and as the horns of the Altar.

16 And the Lord their God shall deliver them in that day as the flock of his people: for they shall be as the stones of the crown lifted up upon his land.

17 For how great is his goodness! and how great is his beauty! corn shall make the young men cheerful, and new wine the maids.

Section 4.3

Fiery Trial

1 Peter 5:8

8 Be sober and watch: For your adversary the devil as a roaring lion walketh about, seeking whom he may devour.

1 Peter 4:12

12 Dearly beloved, think it not strange concerning the fiery trial, which is among you to prove you as though some strange things were come unto you.

Ephesians 6:10-12

10 Finally, my brethren, be strong in the Lord, and in the power of his might.

11 Put on the whole armor of God, that ye may be able to stand against the assaults of the devil.

12 For we wrestle not against flesh and blood, but against principalities, against powers, and against the worldly governors, the princes of the darkness of this world, against spiritual wickedness, which are in the high places.

2 Corinthians 12:7

7 And lest I should be exalted out of measure through the abundance of revelations, there was given unto me a prick in the flesh, the messenger of Satan to buffet me, because I should not be exalted out of measure.

Luke 21:33-36

33 Heaven and earth shall pass away, but my words shall not pass away.

34 Take heed to yourselves, lest at any time your hearts be oppressed with surfeiting and drunkenness, and cares of this life, and lest that day come on you at unawares,

35 For as a snare shall it come on all them that dwell on the face of the whole earth.

36 Watch therefore, and pray continually, that ye may be counted worthy to escape all these things that shall come to pass, and that ye may stand before the son of man.

Romans 8:38-39

38 For I am persuaded that neither death, nor life, nor Angels, nor principalities, nor powers, nor things present, nor things to come,

39 Nor height, nor depth, nor any other creature, shall be able to separate us from the love of God, which is in Christ Jesus our Lord.

Colossians 2:15

15 And hath spoiled the principalities, and powers, and hath made a show of them openly, and hath triumphed over them in the same cross.

Edgar Cayce on Angels, page 123-125:

Similarly, every devotee who wants to make of his life a heaven reaching tower of wisdom must reckon with the price to be paid in renunciation, self-discipline, and meditation. Every devotee who would retain the kingship of his soul must know how, with the help of God and the wisdom of a master, to develop his strength by meditation and spiritual company to fight and defeat his evil enemy habits and the powerful hordes of baneful tendencies invading his mind and body.

2 Timothy 2:26

26 And came to amendment out of that snare of the devil, of whom they are taken prisoners, to do his will.

Section 4.4

End of Time

Matthew 24:29-33

29 And immediately after the tribulations of those days shall the sun be darkened, and the moon shall not give her light, and the stars shall fall from heaven, and the powers of heaven shall be shaken.

30 And then shall appear the sign of the Son of man in heaven: and then shall all the kindreds of the earth mourn, and they shall see the Son of man come in the clouds of heaven with power and great glory.

31 And he shall send his Angels with a great sound of a trumpet, and they shall gather together his elect, from the four winds, and from the one end of the heavens unto the other.

32 Now learn the parable of the fig tree: when her bough is yet tender, and it putteth forth leaves, ye know that summer is near.

33 So likewise ye, when ye see all these things, know that the Kingdom of God is near, even at the doors.

1 Corinthians 15:20-26

20 But now is Christ risen from the dead, and was made the firstfruits of them that slept.

21 For since by man came death, by man came also the resurrection of the dead.

22 For as in Adam all die, even so in Christ shall all be made alive.

23 But every man in his own order: the firstfruits is Christ, afterward, they that are of Christ, at his coming shall rise again.

24 Then shall be the end, when he hath delivered up the kingdom to God, even the Father, when he hath put down all rule, and all authority and power.

25 For he must reign till he hath put all his enemies under his feet.

26 The last enemy that shall be destroyed, is death.

The Apocalypse of Peter, page 50:

It is not quite clear what it means that everybody who believes in Christ will be saved. Who are those that did not believe? The logical answer would be that they are non-Christians, but this does not seem to be the idea of our treatise. Those who do not believe in Christ are Satan, his demons, and probably those human beings who hosted demons in themselves, if we correctly understand the phrase concerning the dwelling-places of the demons.

The Apocalypse of Peter, page 46:

Only Satan and his demons will descend into Sheol, and those who did not believe in Christ. Those who believed in him will not see the judgement of fire. It is a mystery that those who partook of the body and blood of Jesus will not descend a second time into the underworld, into the faith of Satan and his demons.

Thus, the central question is settled, but Jesus continues to give some more indications concerning the final events. I translate the passage which seems the most important to me: 'The children of Adam who have been resuscitated into life will then receive the rank of the throne of the devil and all his (Adam's) children will become the armies of angels instead of the armies of the devil. But as to the demons, God will enclose them into the terrible Gehenna together with their lord, the devil, and with everybody who had become a host for them, each one according to his inhabitant will be enclosed with them into the depths of Sheol." The resuscitated human beings will become the army of angels instead of the armies of the devil. According to several Christian writers, the thrones of the devil and his demons remained empty in the heavens after their fall, and these seats will be occupied by the blessed after the resurrection (consequently there are to be as many blessed after there had been fallen angels). Those human beings will be condemned forever, along with the demons who gave a place in themselves to a demon, that is, who became the prey of a demon. These souls will descend into the underworld, according to the demon that acted in them—an illusion probably to the demons of the sins.

Revelation 20:14-15

14 And death, and hell were cast into the lake of fire: this is the second death.

15 And whosoever was not found written in the book of life, was cast into the lake of fire.

Revelation 20:5

5 But the rest of the dead men shall not live again, until the thousand years be finished: this is the first resurrection.

Revelation 20:6-13

6 Blessed and holy is he, that hath part in the first resurrection: for on such the second death hath no power: but they shall be the Priests of God and of Christ, and shall reign with him a thousand years.

7 And when the thousand years are expired, Satan shall be loosed out of his prison,

8 And shall go out to deceive the people, which are in the four quarters of the earth: even Gog and Magog, to gather them together to battle, whose number is as the sand of the Sea.

9 And they went up into the plain of the earth, and they compassed the tents of the Saints about, and the beloved city: but fire came down from God out of heaven, and devoured them.

10 And the devil that deceived them, was cast into a lake of fire and brimstone, where that beast and that false prophet are, and shall be tormented even day and night for evermore.

11 And I saw a great white throne, and one that sat on it, from whose face fled away both the earth and heaven, and their place was no more found.

12 And I saw the dead, both great and small stand before God: and the books were opened, and another book was opened, which is the book of life, and the dead were judged of those things, which were written in the books, according to their works.

13 And the sea gave up her dead, which were in her, and death and hell delivered up the dead, which were in them: and they were judged every man according to their works.

Section 4.5

Angels: Messengers of God

Edgar Cayce on Angels, page 91-92:

The wisdom of the angels is indescribable in words; it can only be illustrated by some general things. Angels can express in a single world what a man cannot express in a thousand words.

" . . . the societies of angels in heaven are distinguished by their activities and customs. There are some societies that take care of the little children; others teach them when they grow up; others foster the simple and good in the Christian world and lead them toward Heaven . . . All these functions are functions of the Lord performed by the angels, because the angels perform them not for themselves, but on the basis of the divine order."

The Cayce readings indicated that the hosts of angels are not only mindful of humanity's development through the material world, but it is their greater mission to quicken us to the awareness of God.

These realms remain greatly unnoticed by most of us, except when we sleep and enter the higher dimensions through dreaming or enter into deep states of meditation.

"Here on earth we say, 'wisdom,' and say it is a higher attribute of attained knowledge. Here it is an idea," Dr. Rodonaia said, "In the spiritual world Wisdom is a thousand worlds."

The souls of all people on earth are like the leaves of a large tree; the angels and archangels are the branches; the entire tree is God. Humanity is considered one of the highest branches of God's creation.

Author's note:

Jesus is higher than the Angels per Hebrews 1:5-6 because he was the first begotten Son. He showed us The Way, how to "overcome death" and realize the Kingdom of God.

Hebrews 1:1-7

1 At sundry times and in divers manners God spake in the old time to our fathers by the Prophets: in these last days he hath spoken unto us by his Son,

2 Whom he hath made heir of all things, by whom also he made the worlds,

3 Who being the brightness of the glory, and the engraved form of his person, and bearing up all things by his mighty word: hath by himself purged our sins: and sitteth at the right hand of the Majesty in the highest places,

4 And is made so much more excellent than the Angels, inasmuch as he hath obtained a more excellent Name than they.

5 For unto which of the Angels said he at any time, Thou art my Son, this day begat I thee? and again, I will be his Father, and he shall be my Son:

6 And again, when he bringeth in his first begotten Son into the world, he saith, And let all the Angels of God worship him.

7 And of the Angels he saith, He maketh the spirits his messengers, and his ministers a flame of fire.

Edgar Cayce on Angels, page 108:

The divine angelic hierarchy is more than a collection of celestial beings; they are both inner and outer states of consciousness, constantly presenting an opportunity to us for our divine awakening. For many eons, communication from these beings was not comprehensible to our materialistic consciousness. Now, however, the souls of the earth are being roused from a long spiritual sleep and are being readied for the revealing (at the level of the conscious mind) of a great mystery-that we are part and parcel of the great angels of light and love. This is the reality which is unfolding before us like a flower, right now in our world and in our lives.

Second Coming of Christ, page 934:

"Angels" here refers to the astral bodies or luminous forms of nineteen elements in which souls with their past karmic patterns remain encased after death. The "Father which is in heaven" signifies the presence of God in the transcendental realm behind the astral light and the finer causal light of wisdom. A person identified with his physical body and its material surroundings cannot see that the whole world is light and not matter, and thus cannot be conscious of the underlying presence of God. Saints who through meditation have awakened the superconsciousness can perceive the Heavenly Father hidden behind and transcendent within His dream vibrations of light and consciousness. Also blessed to glimpse the "face of my Father" are children with pure consciousness who die before becoming fully identified with the material body and the sensory consciousness with its ignorance-perpetuating karma.

Mark 12:25

25 For when they shall rise again from the dead, neither men marry, nor wives are married, but are as the Angels which are in heaven.

Edgar Cayce on Angels, page 197-198:

Upon our physical death, these angels become our guides to the dimensions we have created for ourselves. Every one of our thoughts and deeds, according to the readings, become guides, angels, intelligences which either move us to a higher realm of consciousness at death or hold us closer to the earth. What we hold to in spirit in the earth will ensoul the angel who guides us in the realms after death.

"And I saw a new heaven and a new earth; for the first heaven and the first earth were passed away; and there was no more sea. And I John saw the holy city, new Jerusalem, coming down from God out of heaven, prepared as a bride adorned for her husband . . . And God shall wipe away all tears from their eyes; and there shall be no more death, neither sorrow, nor crying, neither shall there be any more pain; for the former things are passed away." (Revelation 21:1-2, 4)

The new heaven and new earth is the state of consciousness of the soul after its divine awakening.

Even in the midst of the most terrible visions of the activities of the beasts in Revelation, there is always the presence of the angels, the guides, and the Christ.

Author's note:

According to page 104 of "Embraced By The Light", Betty Eadie mentioned that "we all have the ability to reach God with our prayers." When we pray from our heart, our prayer is often heard, and this puts in motion help from the Angels. This is unquestionably true! However, receiving the Light may come later depending on your personal relationship with God. It takes time but praying, for your need or someone else's, does the work.

Edgar Cayce on Angels, page 123:

"For he shall give his angels charge over thee, to keep thee in all they ways. They shall bear thee up in their hands, lest thou dash thy foot against a stone." (Psalm 91:11-12)

One of the most reassuring ideas offered to us in the Bible and repeated often in the Cayce readings is that we are always in the presence of God, no matter how distracted we become by the cares of the world. But we must, of our own free will, call upon God and His angels to help us.

The Cayce readings indicate that God is lonely for the souls who chose individual experience without respect to His consciousness. There is a waiting, a watching, and, when necessary, intervention in our lives from His angels who come to remind us of whom we belong. The issue at hand is whether or not we are listening to these signs; our faithful God is calling us, in love, to return to the domain of consciousness with Him.

Edgar Cayce on Angels, page 105:

Archangel Gabriel (whose name translates to "hero of God", the most well-known of the Archangels next to Michael, is the messenger who appears in order to reveal God's will-whether it be in the spiritual realms or in the earth. In the New Testament, Gabriel announces to Zacharias that he is to be the father of John the Baptist. Around this same time, Gabriel also announces to Mary that she is to be the mother of Jesus (Luke 1:26-38).

Gabriel is also believed to be one of the luminescent angels whom the apostles saw in the tomb after Jesus' crucifixion. In Christian religious thought, Gabriel is the Archangel of resurrection.

Gabriel is also called the "angel of paradise." It is significant here to note that while Jesus was dying upon the cross, He spoke to one of the two thieves He was crucified with, saying, "Today shalt though be with me in paradise." (Luke 23:43) The Cayce readings defined paradise as a divine state of consciousness which souls gravitate to immediately after death, a place where souls are aware of a great sense of peace, as well as knowing they have just passed from the earth life and yet are aware of being in a contented, expansive state of consciousness.

The angels had been readied from the beginning for the great redemption of humanity.

Edgar Cayce on Angels, page 51:

Michael is an archangel that stands before the throne of the Father . . . Michael is the lord or the guard of the change that comes in every soul that seeks the spiritual way, even as in those periods when His manifestations came in the earth.

Michael is the Lord of the Way-and in the ways of understanding, of conception, of bringing about those things that make for the changes in the attitudes in physical, mental or material relationships, is the guide through such spiritual relations. This archangel's role in our time is vitally important for Michael helps humankind to harken and listen to the higher spiritual calling.

His manifestation in this age is a sign of light in the midst of the darkness; it is a divine reassurance as well as a call for each of us. Rather than fear the great upheavals, we should spiritually prepare ourselves. Often when various religious groups speak of biblical prophecy being fulfilled in our time, there is a tendency to concentrate on the "labor" the world is enduring and not the eventual "birth."

That war represents the archetypal struggle between good and evil within us. The good is represented by Michael, the darkness represented by Satan. He believed that Michael is a harbinger, bringing humanity to an understanding of Christ or "God incarnated within us." The cosmic drama between the high forces of Michael and Satan (the Dragon) are reflected within the psyches and souls of every one incarnated in the earth; we each must choose between good and evil.

Michael stands cosmically behind man, he said, "While within man there is an etheric image of Michael that wages the real battle through which man can gradually become free."

The movement of Michael's influence in the affairs of humanity is like the sunlight that breaks across the face of the earth in the darkness. The readings define darkness as a symbol of spiritual ignorance, and the light is the spiritual realization of the soul and its connection with God.

"Angels act as messengers of God. They communicate with us through inspiration. When we fill our everyday lives with spiritual essence and ask the angels to join us, we create angel consciousness . . . Angel consciousness helps us keep heavenly qualities alive right here on earth. We not only see the beauty around us; we feel it in our soul . . . Angels, as messengers of heaven, help us make life a true and meaningful experience."

Edgar Cayce on Angels, page 61:

The vibrations of the archangels are so powerful. It is loud, yes; but it is more the power than the volume that is overwhelming. The former priest gave an interesting analogy; an archangel operates at 15,000 volts, like an electrical current. A human being is operating at 120 volts. When such a force of a power like an archangel manifests itself, as Michael did through Cayce, it affects not just the channel, but the people in the room as well as the physical surroundings. "I knew I was in the presence of the Divine."

As Archangel Michael is Lord of the Way which leads to Christ, Uriel is the archangel of salvation or one who awakens the sleeping mortals to higher spiritual knowledge, "saving" souls from the purely materialistic consciousness. Archangel Raphael presides over the forces of spiritual and physical healing in the earth. Archangel Gabriel, who announced to the Virgin Mary that she was to give birth to the Messiah, is the angel of annunciation, resurrection, mercy, and revelation.

For example, the laws of enlightenment, wisdom, transformation, cause and effect are divine consciousnesses. The question was posed to Cayce in a reading, "Are angels and archangels synonymous with that which we call the laws of the universe?" "They are as the laws of the universe; as is Michael the Lord of the Way, not the Way but the Lord of the Way . . ."

This means that when people are in complete harmony with their spiritual ideal-or their spiritual purpose in life-they are complying with the universal law of love. Then Michael makes the way open so that they can be awakened to even greater spiritual awareness.

Edgar Cayce on Angels, page 217:

Cayce outlined a simple technique for practicing meditation which is effective in awakening the soul's ability to commune with the angelic realms, open up psychic abilities, and—the most important aspect of meditation-enter a realm where we become aware of God as a personal and present Companion. The readings say that in prayer we present Companion. The readings say that in prayer we speak to God, but in meditation we listen to God. The readings went so far as to say that in meditation, we meet God face to face.

Meditation is a key to becoming aware of angelic influence. It is important to practice meditating at the same time every day. This trains the conscious mind to be still. At first, a period of silence of fifteen minutes is sufficient. Then, as the body and mind grow accustomed to meditation, lengthen the period to thirty minutes-then to an hour.

Keeping your spine straight, sit in a chair with your feet flat on the floor or cross-legged in the lotus position. Close your eyes and open with a prayer, asking for divine guidance and protection.

"His forces" refers to the angels and archangels which make, as Cayce put it, intercession for the souls in the earth to God. Opening with a prayer of protection also helps emphasize the purpose and ideal for meditation.

Repeating the Lord's Prayer also helps the attunement process and was recommended in the readings because each of the verses corresponds to one of the seven spiritual centers or chakras in the body. Visualizing the body being filled with light as this prayer is said aloud helps to center the body, mind, and spirit for meditation.

Lord's Prayer

Our Father which art in heaven, hallowed be Thy name. Thy kingdom come, Thy will be done in earth, as it is in heaven. Give us this day our daily bread. And forgive us our debts, as we forgive our debtors. And lead us not into temptation, but deliver us from evil: For Thine is the kingdom, and the power, and the glory, forever. Amen (Matthew 6:9-13).

Second Coming of Christ, page 499-502:

Jesus came on earth to remind man that the Lord is the Heavenly Father of all, and to show His children the way back to Him. The way of effective prayer, he taught, is to banish diffidence and speak to God with joyous expectancy as to a devoted father or mother. For every human being, the Lord feels a love unconditional and eternal, surpassing even the sweetest human parental solicitude. This is implicit in Jesus' instruction to pray to "Our Father"—a Father who cares personally for each of His children.

Jesus gave a model prayer for both worldly people and spiritual people: The highly devout individual wants nothing from God but His love, and spiritual development; the materially minded person seeks God's help for all-round success and well-being in earthly life, including a modicum of spiritual achievement. "The Lord's Prayer" embodies a universal understanding of how the needs of body, mind, and soul may be fulfilled through man's relationship with God. The simple eloquence and spiritual depth of Jesus' words inspired in me the following interpretive perception.

When you pray, address God from your heart with the full attention of your mind; and in the manner I have shown to you, say: "Our Father Cosmic Consciousness, Fountain of the consciousness of all, present in the vibrationless region of Heavenly Bliss and hidden in the depths of Heavenly Intuition, may Thy Name be glorified on earth. May Thy hallowed Name, the cosmic vibrations emanating from Thee in earthly manifestations, be consecrated for cultivating Thy consciousness and not material consciousness. Let Thine absolute royal consciousness come forth and appear in human consciousness. May Thy spiritual kingdom come and be substituted for the material kingdom of earthly consciousness. Let Thy wisdom-guided will be the guiding force of deluded human beings on earth, even as Thy will is followed by angels and liberated souls in the heavenly astral realms."

"Give us our daily bread, the physical, mental, and spiritual manna that nourishes our bodies, minds, and souls: food, health, and prosperity for the body; efficiency and power for the mind; love, wisdom, and bliss for the soul." Forgive, Thou, our faults, O Lord, and teach us likewise to forgive the faults of others. As we forgive a brother who is indebted to us and forget his obligation, forgive us, Thy children, for our sins of not remembering our indebtedness to Thee—that we owe our health, our life, our soul, everything to Thee.

"Lead us not into temptation, even by way of testing our limited spiritual power. And leave us not in the pit of temptation wherein we fell through the misuse of Thy given reason. But if it is Thy will to test us when we are stronger, then, Father, make Thyself more tempting than temptation. Help us that by our own effort, through Thy spiritual force within us, we may be free from all misery-making, physical, mental, and spiritual evils."

"Teach us to behold the earth as ruled not by material forces, but by Thy Kingdom's power and glory which abide forever. We bow to Thee through our contact with Thee as the Holy Cosmic Vibration of Aum, Amen."

In Jesus' words, "Hallowed be Thy name," is the recognition that though this earth came from God's divine vibration, it is yet to be consecrated by His name, or pure holy vibrations, because of the wickedness of the people who reject that sacred presence among them. As God's bliss and wisdom are the only kingly powers that exist in the transcendence of Cosmic Consciousness, so in the words

"Thy kingdom come" Jesus prays that those absolute powers of God may manifest in human consciousness, which is erstwhile steeped in delusion. Jesus also prays, "Thy will be done in earth, as it is in heaven": As the angels and divine souls in the heavenly realms are in tune with the wisdom of God's will, so also might earthly people willingly be guided by God's wisdom, rather than by the rationale of their delusion-encapsulated ego.

"Give us this day our daily bread": It might seem trifling to include a plea for bread when praying to the Almighty; yet in those days there was much poverty among the masses; they often had little to eat.

Jesus knew he could not very well expect the people to hearken to a spiritual message that did not address their mundane concerns as well

—a person with a hungry stomach has little incentive to strive for spiritual realization.

In any case, Jesus was referring to an all-inclusive sustenance for body, mind, and soul, not merely physical bread. He had said, "Man shall not live by bread alone, but by every word that proceedeth out of the mouth of God." Man cannot live solely by material means. Every moment of his existence he is dependent on the life force flowing from God's creative Cosmic Vibration, His "word," and on the inherent wisdom and bliss of the omnipresent Christ Consciousness that supports his own consciousness. The more attuned one is to this divine vitality and wisdom, the more he is able to draw unto himself the fulfillment of his physical, emotional, mental, and spiritual needs. So man's first prayer should be for the spiritual bread of contact with God's Bliss, Wisdom, and Love, which alone feeds the soul; then efficiency for the mind in order to accomplish one's worthwhile goals; and lastly, material prosperity adequate to meet one's physical needs.

"Lead us not into temptation, but deliver us from evil": In these words, Jesus almost seems to make God responsible when man finds himself in the throes of temptation, having been purposively led into that predicament by his Heavenly Father. In a way it is true. God is the maker of delusion, so in that sense He is a tempter. But it would be wrong to think that God, with His wisdom, would lead mortals, who are poorly equipped with wisdom, into temptation just to test their response. That would not be fair. God is not a friendly prankster tempting man with a world of relentless enticements that may harm him. Good and evil are the light and shadows that create the contrasts necessary to produce God's cosmic motion picture. The white purity of goodness demonstrates its virtue on the dark background of evil. God's children are tested by this duality of maya-delusion to develop the wisdom to distinguish between good and evil, and the will to overcome all tests and thereby be free from Satan's cat-and-mouse game of temptation.

The Lord could easily countermand the influence of satanic temptation, but to do so would negate man's free will and make him a puppet. The intrigue of God's drama of creation is to see if perchance His children will choose Him over the allurements of His cosmic show—not from any compulsion on His part, but solely of their own freely chosen response to His love. He wants His mortal reflections to enjoy the grand drama in this cosmic movie house with an unchanging remembrance of their innate divinity. To prove that divine nature is to pass successfully through trials and temptations that teach wayward man to bring out and manifest in every condition of his life the hidden God-identity of his soul. The Lord knows that His children will ultimately assert the power of Spirit within them to vanquish the power of temptation.

So when Jesus prayed "lead us not into temptation," he intended no indictment of the Lord as having any part in man's miseries. Rather, he expressed man's need to supplicate God for help in overcoming life's unavoidable delusions: "Leave us not in the pit of temptation wherein we fell through the misuse of Thy given reason." Man falls headlong into the abyss of evil when he does not use properly the faculties of God-given free choice. Satan snares the unwary with cosmic delusion, subverting reason and will with ignorance. That is how he so successfully obstructs God. Thus Jesus prayed that the Heavenly Father deliver every soul from the evil enthrallment of cosmic delusion.

Edgar Cayce on Angels, page 217:

A series of breathing exercises was also recommended to open the seven spiritual centers in a safe way and manner.

It is important to acknowledge the messenger, or the Christ, or whoever appears, and consider the experience as a sign that you're on the right track.

At the close of meditation it is important to send out the energy which has been raised through the spiritual centers in the body. The best way to send it out is in prayer. Prayer is particularly powerful after meditation, and this is a good opportunity to pray for loved ones and friends as well as those who are deceased.

Author's note:

According to page 84 of "Embraced By The Light", Betty Eadie quoted, "I also was told that our prayers can benefit both spiritual beings and persons on the earth." In addition, she explained, "it is important for us to acquire knowledge of the spirit while we are in the flesh."

Edgar Cayce on Angels, page 180-183:

Within us, at the soul level, are the infinite realms which are replicas of the archangels of heaven. These are our highest spiritual aspirations and ideals that have been with us from the beginning—a spiritual reservoir which can open us to great enlightenment. But, we also have within us the representations of the fallen angels. These are the angels of the anti-Christ, the thoughts, desires, feelings which separate us from feeling at-one with God. There is the choice within each soul to experience life in the spirit of acceptance (which is a force, an angelic presence) or the spirit of rebellion (which is, as we've seen, the spirit of Satan). These active beings are at work within us every day, with every decision, every desire, and every deed. The Angel of Acceptance and the Angel of Rebellion have their lesser "angels," which are the very actions of our thoughts upon spirit.

The Cayce readings have often said that each soul is "only meeting itself" in the earth realm of experience. We have been through so many experiences throughout our many lives in the earth that we are now only meeting what we have created for ourselves. These are reflected back to us by the people in our lives. Each experience in our lives, therefore, becomes an active lesson or truth that will return again and again to us until it is perfected in us.

"People don't realize the power of thought and desire," Irion said, during a twelve-week course he taught on the Book of Revelation in 1986. "They are calling upon the very creative forces which brought the worlds into being: thought and desire. These are personified forces within us which have a life that we have given them. In the unseen realms they have an identity, a personality."

Are these personified forces angels?

"Each thought and desire has a life essence which acts as a messenger to us," Irion replied. "In that sense, yes, these are angels within us." All situations in life are given to us by the higher soul-mind which is attuned to its own guardian angel. Each experience is given to us as a lesson.

"The light and darkness we manifest in life," Irion said, "determines whose side we're on as far as the Angels of Acceptance or the Angels of Rebellion goes. My judgment passed upon another is merely my judgment of my concepts of another. In that I have judged my own self. Through situations, people, lifetimes, I am always meeting myself. The questions we need to be asking ourselves are these: In what spirit or by what guiding angel do I operate from in life? Dissension? Strife? Joy? Blaming others? Forbearance?

"The spirit in which I act will either release me or bind me," Irion explained, "just as there are angels who guide us to greater freedom or bind us closer to the earth-earthy consciousness." If the spirit of acceptance is manifested in life—in whatever the circumstance—then we are freed. "And ye shall know the truth, and the truth shall make you free." (John 8:32) Using positive affirmations to accept the circumstances of our lives will enable us to fully reawaken spiritually.

If we work with positive affirmations of acceptance, then we call into play the higher spiritual governing angels of God. We bring them into being in our consciousness, and they become living companions and guardians within us. Repeating spiritual words and phrases in an affirmation before meditation, during prayer, and in daily life is a powerful tool to "reprogram" the conscious mind to be more in attunement with the mind of the soul. These affirmations eventually become living principles in the soul and spirit, and any barriers to spiritual understanding will be broken down, and the mind of the soul will eventually become the conscious mind. Through Jesus' many lives, this was the pattern He set forth: that through making the individual will at-one with God's, God becomes the conscious motivating activity in the life of the individual. In this light, we become God, and God's power becomes us.

In understanding The Revelation, Irion teaches that it is important to understand that our reactions build actions. Each soul in the earth reacts to all it has created by itself, for itself. All experiences promote soul growth and awakening if the circumstance is lived in the spirit of acceptance. If it is not accepted in this spirit, the circumstance will return again and again, giving the soul endless opportunities to transform rebellion into spiritual growth. This is how we draw and grow from spiritual experiences. Our very thoughts and deeds return to us over and over until we learn the lessons. "When a soul finally accepts its circumstances and lives them as a spiritual opportunity," Irion explained, "then it can move on through into a more sensitive perception of reality as that soul created it. There, at that point, The Revelation becomes a living reality and the soul is free indeed."

This is the key to living a spiritual life in the material world: understanding that we draw to us the influences that we need for our development. We draw the spirits (angels) of acceptance or rebellion through our state of mind, thoughts, and being. "The experiences through which man passes," Cayce said, "as God gave in other periods, to become aware of his purpose for entrance into what we know as materiality [earth]. Then, the awareness of the way comes through the thought of man, the faith of man, the desire of man such as ever held by that One [Jesus the Christ] who became righteousness itself; passing through all the phases of man's desire in materiality."

Again our very desire to come to a spiritual understanding in our lives goes out through the spiritual realms as a message to the divine intelligences, the angels; through them we are given the keys to unlocking the mysteries of the essence of life itself.

What follows is an examination, based on the Cayce readings, of Revelation's verses which are significant to our study of angels and the great spiritual consciousness which is being born in our time. Of particular interest are John's references to the "seven churches" in Asia. The topic is introduced in this way:

"John to the seven churches which are in Asia: Grace be unto you, and peace, from him which is, and which was, and which is to come; and from the seven Spirits which are before his throne . . ." (Revelation 1:4)

What did Asia and the seven churches signify? According to the readings, the reference to Asia in Revelation actually symbolizes the physical body. The seven spirits before the Throne of God and the seven churches correspond to the seven spiritual centers within the soul-body;

Spiritual Center	Endocrine Gland	Color	Element	Revelation Church
1	Gonads	Red	Earth	Ephesus
2	Cell of Leydig	Orange	Water	Smyrna
3	Adrenals	Yellow	Fire	Pergamos
4	Thymus	Green	Air	Thyatira
5	Thyroid	Blue	Ether	Sardis
6	Pineal	Indigo		Philadelphia
7	Pituitary	Voilet		Laodicea

This is based on Figure 3, page 184 of Edgar Cayce on Angels.

Spiritual Centers or Chakras

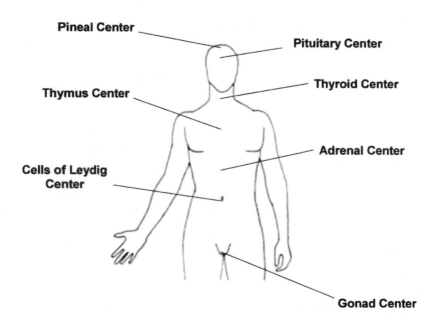

Pineal Center

Pituitary Center

Thyroid Center

Thymus Center

Adrenal Center

Cells of Leydig
Center

Gonad Center

There are physical glands within the body which correspond to these spiritual centers or chakras: the gonads, cells of Leydig or lyden, adrenals, thymus, thyroid, pineal, and pituitary. These ductless glands, which constitute the endocrine system, convey essential hormones to the physical body, but they are also the conduits through which spiritual energy flows into and through the body. These chakras are the same centers which were created in the beginning so that humans could journey through earth and yet maintain that all-important connection with the spiritual worlds.

"A study of the endocrine system is integral to the study of the Book of the Revelation," wrote Irion, "because the ductless glands play a great part in our awareness . . . These glands are the contact points for communication between the soul or psyche to the body and conscious mind." These chakras, which are referred to as churches throughout Revelation, contain all memories of the soul's experiences.

The remarkable aspect of these chakras is that they actually correspond to spiritual sources within the body as well as without—in the unseen realms. During a reading, the question was posed to Cayce:

"What is meant by the seven lamps of fire burning before the throne, described as the seven spirits of God—Revelation 4:5?"

Revelation 4:5

5 And out of the throne proceeded lightnings, and thunderings and voices, and there were seven lamps of fire burning before the throne, which are the seven spirits of God.

Cayce responded, "Those influences or forces which in their activity in the natures of man are without, that stand ever before the throne of grace—or God, to become the messengers, the aiders, the destructions of hindrances . . ."

Not only do we have the inner circuitry to attune to the inner realms of the soul, but those angels, those guides who have been in communion with God since the beginning are our intercessors. They actively provide us the needed strength, grace, and wisdom to move toward greater spiritual awakening, toward the reunion with God. In this light, we have the guidance and guardianship of the angels without and within. The chakras are the centers of these spiritual activities.

When spiritualized and awakened through meditation, the chakras become doorways to higher consciousness. Through them, we are able to experience the cosmic consciousness of Christ and a return to our awareness as co-creators with God.

The "throne" in Revelation is the culmination of all of our spiritual memories, even from the beginning of time. The throne refers to the memories held in the higher chakras—the pineal and pituitary. Cayce often stated that the body is the temple of the living God, the dwelling place of the individuation of God, the divine spark which makes us a soul.

Through these centers we can experience the highest manifestation of God consciousness.

Douglas F. Grady

Edgar Cayce on Angels, page 188-194:

This promise of divine fulfillment is the reason for all angelic activity now infiltrating human consciousness.

The Correlation of the Seven Churches and the Chakras

"Unto the angel of the church of Ephesus write; These things saith he that holdeth the seven stars in his right hand, who walketh in the midst of the seven golden candlesticks . . ." (Revelation 2:1)

The church of Ephesus represents the first spiritual center in the body; it is associated with the gonads. From this center springs the beginning of all creative activity. This center is the procreative and sexual energy within, but it can become a transformative light to the rest of the spiritual centers in the body. The energy begins as sexual, but can-by the power of the will-be transformed into spiritual energy.

Evidence of the power of choice between earth and heaven at this level of consciousness can be found in verse Revelation 2:4, which reads: "Nevertheless I have somewhat against thee, because thou hast left thy first love." Our "first love" was the union of our consciousness with God, before the earth came into being.

"And unto the angel of the church in Smyrna write; These things saith the first and the last, which was dead, and is alive . . ." (Revelation 2:8)

Through meditation, the body is "regenerated" from the raw earthy energy within it and transformed for spiritual awakening, a process which rises step by step, through the rest of the spiritual centers.

"And to the angel of the church in Pergamos write; These things saith he which hath the sharp sword with two edges . . ." (Revelation 2:12)

This angel represents the third spiritual center, associated with the adrenal glands. The inner "fight or flight" activity related to this center is a double-edged sword. In the physiology of the body, the adrenal glands sit atop the kidneys and are ruled individually by the two hemispheres of the brain. The angelic message at this center could be stated as: "Be at peace. Do not fight the spiritual impulse. Let yourself fly to the higher levels of God's awareness." Again, we are faced with material and spiritual choices at this center.

"And unto the angel of the church in Thyatira write; These things saith the Son of God, who hath his eyes like unto a flame of fire, and his feet like fine brass; I know thy works, and charity, and service, and faith, and thy patience, and thy works; and the last to be more than the first." (Revelation 2:18-19)

The divine messenger at this level represents the fourth chakra, near the heart, associated with the thymus. This spiritual center is the seat of love. The thymus center is the merging point of spiritual energy; it is of the earth, yet it is the midpoint between the three lower centers, representing earthly energies, and the three higher centers which are more heavenly oriented.

"And unto the angel of the church in Sardis write; These things saith he that hath the seven Spirits of God, and the seven stars; I know thy works, that thou hast a name that thou livest, and art dead. Be watchful, and strengthen the things which remain . . ." (Revelation 3:1-2)

The angel of the church in Sardis represents the fifth spiritual center, associated with the thyroid. It is the seat of individual and divine will which separates us from the animals and lower creations: the will to chose. It is at this level that the soul can choose to defy God through the forces of will. Yet, when that will is made one with God, then the Christ mind is awakened; the individual will becomes the will of God.

This eventuality has the blessings of the Master Himself, as verse Revelation 3:5 indicates:

"He that overcometh, the same shall be clothed in white raiment; and I will not blot out his name out of the book of life, but I will confess his name before my Father, and before his angels."

"He that overcometh" is directed to those who make their will one with God's. The reference to "white raiment" refers to the perfected aura. Each spiritual chakra vibrates to a given color. The gonads, red; leydig, orange; adrenals; yellow; thymus, green; thyroid, blue; pineal, indigo; pituitary, violet When the will is in perfect harmony with God, then these centers operate as one consciousness; there is harmony throughout the body, mind, and spirit. This harmony of all colors together is described by "white raiment."

"And to the angel of the church in Philadelphia write; These things saith he that is holy, he that is true, he that hath the key of David, he that openeth, and no man shutteth; and shutteth, and no man openeth . . ." (Revelation 3:7)

The angel of the church in Philadelphia represents the sixth spiritual center, associated with the pineal gland.

All experiences we have passed through during our evolution in the earth are kept locked within the center of the pineal gland. In mediation, the energy rises through the seven spiritual centers and gradually awakens the memory of soul-mind through this chakra to universal love.

When David in his youth and purity daily communed with God, he closely reflected divine love . . ."

The new understanding is represented by the "new Jerusalem," a city (consciousness) of God.

"And unto the angel of the church of the Laodiceans write; These things saith the Amen, the faithful and true witness, the beginning of the creation of God . . ." (Revelation 3:14)

The angel of this church is the seventh and highest spiritual center, associated with the pituitary gland. Everett Irion wrote: " . . . in the body [the pituitary] is 'the beginning of the creation of God.' The pituitary acts as if it were the original Creative Force itself, for it does its job just as does the God Force which animates the body.

When this center is opened in meditation, the person experiences "the silence," a vast reservoir of consciousness which is not merely an absence of sound, but a divine presence at peace and harmony.

Edgar Cayce on Angels, page 225:

Angels—The Messengers of Hope

There is a central message in these biblical stories of the protective guardian angels, and it is always a message of hope. Earlier chapters described the angels who nourished Elijah; the angels who visited Daniel with visions of what was to come on earth; Enoch the prophet, who was shown the great and terrible visions of the angels of God and the angels of Satan, as well as the coming of its own destiny as the Messiah.

But we are being led to turn inside of ourselves, where there is a reservoir of spirit which goes beyond words; a silence that's filled with peace, harmony, light, and-above all-hope for the next step in this grand spiritual drama being played out upon the world's stage.

As we have seen, Satan is an actual force. But his influence is only through the material world and that by choice. If there are a handful of people who have lost neither hope nor faith, regardless of what hell the world appears to have fallen into, then the angels of light can assist those who hope and pray and expect the better outcome; the angels can then do their work in bringing about greater awakening and peace on earth.

For we need that divine reassurance, the comfort, and the message that God is forever mindful of us, loves us, and wants to speak with us. All we have to do is be quiet. And listen . . . listen . . . listen . . .

Further Reading

The Apocalypse of Peter, ISBN 90-429-1375-4, authors/editors Jan N. Bremmer and Istvan Czachesz

The Gospel of the Nazirenes, ISBN 0-9644584-1-1, authors/editors Alan Wauters and Rick Van Wyhe

The Isaiah Effect, ISBN 0-609-80796-X, author Gregg Braden

Ancient Book of Jasher, ISBN 9-781438-266756, author Ken Johnson

Beyond Belief, ISBN 0-375-70316-0, author Elaine Pagels

The Gnostic Gospels, ISBN 0-679-72453-2, author Elaine Pagels

Complete Books of Enoch, ISBN 9-781453890295, author Dr. A. Nyland

The Nag Hammadi Scriptures, ISBN 978-0-06-162600-5, editor Marvin Meyer

The Second Coming of Christ, ISBN 978-0-87612-557-1, Paramahansa Yogananda

Edgar Cayce on Angels—Archangels and the Unseen Forces, ISBN 978-0-87604-513-8, author Robert J. Grant

Edgar Cayce on the Akashic Records, ISBN 978-0-87604-401-8, author Kevin J. Todeschi

The 1599 Geneva Bible, ISBN 0-9754846-1-3